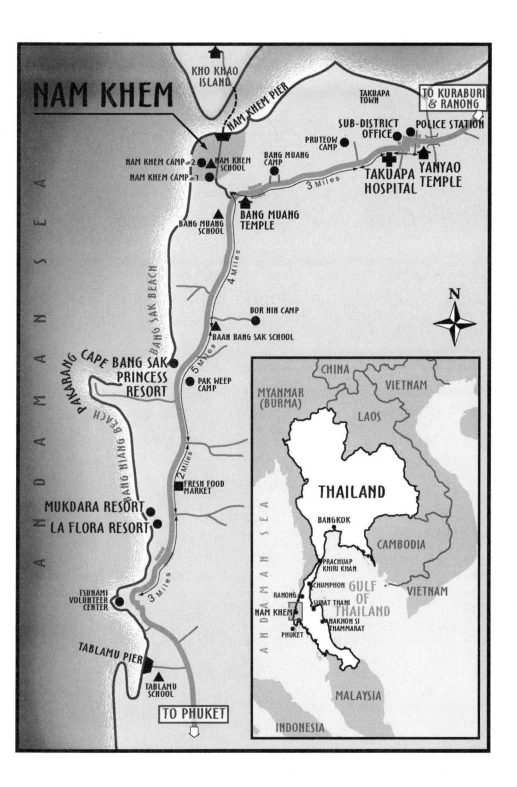

WAVE *of* DESTRUCTION

THE STORIES OF FOUR FAMILIES AND HISTORY'S DEADLIEST TSUNAMI

ERICH KRAUSS

RODALE

© 2006 by Erich Krauss

Illustrations by Erich Krauss
Photographs by Sudthida Somsakserm

Book design by Tara Long

Library of Congress Cataloging-in-Publication Data
Krauss, Erich, date.
    Wave of destruction : the stories of four families and history's deadliest tsunami / Erich Krauss.
        p.   cm.
    ISBN-13 978-1-59486-378-3 hardcover
    ISBN-10 1-59486-378-4 hardcover
    1. Indian Ocean Tsunami, 2004. 2. Tsunamis—Indian Ocean. 3. Tsunamis—Thailand—Nam Keam. 4. Survival after airplane accidents, shipwrecks, etc. I. Title.
GC222.I45K73 2006
959.304'4—dc22   2005024531

Distributed to the trade by Holtzbrinck Publishers

2   4   6   8   10   9   7   5   3   1 hardcover

LIVE YOUR WHOLE LIFE™

We inspire and enable people to improve their lives and the world around them
For more of our products visit **rodalestore.com** or call 800-848-4735

To the villagers of Nam Khem

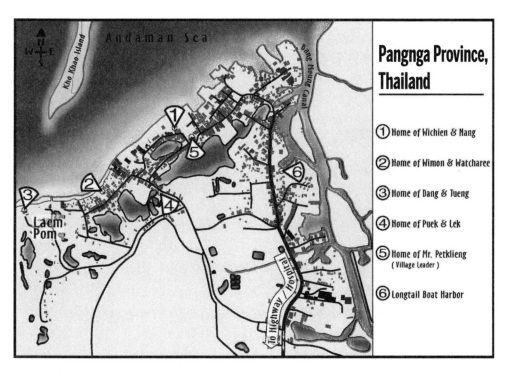

Pangnga Province, Thailand

1. Home of Wichien & Nang
2. Home of Wimon & Watcharee
3. Home of Dang & Tueng
4. Home of Puek & Lek
5. Home of Mr. Petklieng (Village Leader)
6. Longtail Boat Harbor

CONTENTS

ACKNOWLEDGMENTS viii

PROLOGUE ix

PART ONE: NAM KHEM

1. WICHIEN AND NANG 3
2. WIMON 16
3. PUEK AND LEK 23
4. DANG 29
5. WICHIEN AND NANG 38
6. WIMON AND WATCHAREE. 47
7. PUEK AND LEK 51
8. DANG 66

PART TWO: THE WAVE

9. WIMON AND WATCHAREE. 81
10. PUEK AND LEK 95
11. WICHIEN AND NANG 108
12. DANG 116
13. THE POLICEMAN AND THE DOCTOR . . . 123
14. WIMON AND WATCHAREE. 130
15. NANG 140
16. DANG. 143
17. PUEK AND LEK. 148
18. THE HOSPITAL 155

PART THREE: THE HUNT FOR THE MISSING

19. DANG 172

20. WICHIEN AND NANG 176

21. PUEK AND LEK 179

22. THE POLICEMAN AND THE DOCTOR . . . 184

23. WIMON 189

24. DANG 193

25. WIMON 196

26. DANG 199

PART FOUR: THE ROAD TO RECOVERY

27. PUEK AND LEK 206

28. DANG 210

29. WICHIEN AND NANG 213

30. DANG 220

31. WICHIEN AND NANG 224

32. DANG 228

EPILOGUE/AUTHOR'S NOTE 237

ACKNOWLEDGMENTS

A very special thanks to Sudthida "Nui" Somsakserm for devoting all her time and energy to helping survivors, and for contributing to this book in every way possible. For their editing, support, and selfless contributions to tsunami victims, I would like to thank Brooke Motta, Glen Cordoza, and Leland Ratcliff. I would also like to thank Frank Scatoni and Greg Dinkin, my two wonderful agents and friends, for helping me every step of the way. And finally, I cannot express enough gratitude to Pete Fornatale, my editor at Rodale, for steering me in the right direction at the beginning of my career, and now, many years later, for embracing this book, pulling it close to his heart, and offering exceptional guidance in the telling of this tragic event.

PROLOGUE

In the middle of the last century, a hundred men cleared a patch of jungle on the west coast of Thailand's Isthmus of Kra so that tin mines could be dug into the earth and huts could be built by their side for the laborers who would mine them. The village that sprung to life overnight had no original people, and as a consequence, it attracted two types—those who were desperate, and those filled with greed. The latter came in the form of hit men and ex-convicts and tin-mining bosses. The bosses used the hit men and ex-convicts to settle violent disputes with other mining bosses over the rights to the various mining areas. The bosses who triumphed made money hand over fist and built casinos and saloons and brothels that filled with prostitutes brought in by the truckload. Every morning, the bodies of men who'd been on the receiving end of the previous night's gunplay were placed into *sawngthaews* and carted up the long, windy road that connected the village of Nam Khem to the dirt highway and the rest of the country. Farmers and fishermen and even the police who lived and worked in the general vicinity ignored the village and closed their ears to the rumors of what went on there, but others didn't have such luxury. The desperate rolled in.

Sixteen-year-old Thana Phondaecha, a clean-living country boy who had eleven brothers and sisters to support, came in the summer of 1972. He planned to work a year and then leave the village in his past, but nine years later he married nineteen-year-old Suphee Namlakorn, who had come to live with her uncle and to discover if the sea was truly made from salt, as she'd heard. Wiroj Ruamwong arrived at seventeen to fish the waters of the Andaman Sea. During his second trip out, he got shot at by soldiers on a Burmese patrol boat and ran home to become a monk, before returning in 1983 with better street smarts and the intention of making a fortune. His wife, Loogin, followed him a year later, while lugging their baby on her back, to keep her husband out of the brothels and living straight. Wimon Thongtae had lived on the Gulf of Thailand side of the isthmus until he lost his home and all his possessions piece by piece to three massive floods. He arrived in 1977 and sold dried fruit to tin miners, eager to find a place where he could start life anew. Ratree Kongwatmai, born on the soft soil of a hut in the southern portion of the village in 1975, was the daughter of an out-of-work rubber tree tapper who had come to avoid starvation.

Each of these four families survived the ruthless years of the tin-mining boom while many others did not. They survived the five massive fires that swept through Nam Khem and claimed hundreds of homes and numerous lives. They survived when Southeast Asia fell into a massive recession, and years later they survived when the tin dried up altogether. The village to which they had come out of desperation to make their last stand had become their home. The wealth in the soil might have gone fallow, but the sea still held riches. They turned to fishing and diving for pearls and sailing into foreign waters to pilfer lobster. They opened small bistros and portable restaurants, which they carried up and down the village's muddy streets in sidecars attached to their motorbikes. They worked as day laborers and helped build massive hotel/resorts far south, on the island of Phuket; and when tourism spilled over to the mainland, they helped build the massive hotel/resorts all the way up to their backyard. Then a mining company claimed to own all the land on which they lived, and tried to sell it to money barons who wanted to build a hotel/resort in Nam Khem. They marched to the district hall in a mob that turned violent, and they survived that as well, and many walked away with deeds to their homes.

After thirty years of struggle and strife, each of these four families considered themselves original people from Nam Khem. They had made and lost fortunes on this patch of soil nestled between the jungle and the Andaman Sea. They had birthed and buried loved ones. They had put the violence behind them and looked ahead to nothing more than a simple life surrounded by family, palm trees, and a gentle breeze. Submersed in their daily routine, none of them saw the tsunami coming until it crashed down on their lives. It claimed more than they ever thought they had to give, and it thrust them headlong into the greatest battle they'd ever known. They weren't among the quarter of a million people who perished that day, but none of them truly made it out alive. Their lives tell the story of Nam Khem, one of a hundred coastal villages from Indonesia to India that got swept from the earth in the blink of an eye on the morning of December 26, 2004.

PART ONE

NAM KHEM

Nang and her daughter in front of their home in Nam Khem.

WICHIEN AND NANG

Two thousand five hundred and fifteen years after the birth of Buddha, in the Christian year of 1972, sixteen-year-old Thana Phondaecha bumped and jostled in the back of a bus making its way south along the dirt highway skirting the west coast of the Isthmus of Kra. The young man, whom everyone called Wichien, gazed out the window at the clear waters of the Andaman Sea. He had heard that huge deposits of tin were being dug from the earth in Nam Khem and that a young man with strong hands and a powerful back could become rich. If he could find a job that in one or two years' time would allow him to send a fortune back to his mother, who had eleven other sons and daughters to feed, he might still have a chance to return to school.

After six hours, the road veered inland and bustling downtown streets emerged. Wichien suspected that he'd just arrived at his new home, but the bus moved straight through the center of activity. It continued south on the highway, past a large district hall, past an equally large hospital, until civilization vanished and the jungle returned. After several miles, the bus pulled over at a small roadside market.

"Nam Khem," the driver called out.

Walking up the aisle, Wichien looked out the dust-caked windows on both sides, searching for any sign of the thriving village.

"This is Nam Khem?" he asked.

The driver smiled and pointed to a narrow road adjacent to the market that wound west through a tangle of brush, apparently down to the coast. "It's about three kilometers that way."

"Can you take me there?"

"I don't go to Nam Khem," the driver said. "Even the police won't go to Nam Khem."

Wichien reluctantly stepped out under the blaze of sun, and as the bus sped away, it spat up a reddish gray cloud of dust that coated his black hair and neatly pressed clothes. He bought some mango and sticky rice wrapped in a palm leaf at the market, and then he began the long hike down to the village. The surrounding walls of vegetation boomed with the *wee-wee* call of the mangwee bugs, which hovered around the rubber trees in the forest. He'd grown up in the country, where the combined racket of millions upon millions of insects had become as normal as the sound of his breath, but the strange noises of this unfamiliar jungle filled him with both fear and excitement.

He stepped out into the clearing thirty minutes later and froze, red rivulets of sweat running down his cheeks. The village clung to four miles of coastline, the center of which jutted out into the sea to give the village the shape of an arrowhead. The scene before him looked like one from the cowboy and Indian shoot-out movies they made in America. The gruff men sauntering around carried guns on their hips and had bleached red hair from spending months and years beneath the sea, diving for tin. Hundreds upon hundreds of young women, some no more than thirteen, lounged on benches in front of brothels and brushed the arms of men who passed by. They came from the poorest parts of the country, where a daughter's body became a means to support the family. They wore hot pants and tube tops or miniskirts, T-shirts, and boots. All of their faces were plastered with neon makeup.

Wichien began to walk. The majority of houses were small boxes constructed entirely out of sheets of aluminum. The few thatched homes he saw had holes in the walls and roofs. Nam Khem appeared to be the worst kind of slum, filled with the poorest of the poor, but at the same time, the village teemed with entertainment for the wealthy. He passed a shack filled with bench seats and a massive screen advertising the latest film starring Charles Bronson, an actor Wichien later learned had achieved legendary status in Nam Khem because his means of solving disputes was with a pistol. Then he passed another cinema, and another.

He peered inside half a dozen casinos, where men with red faces argued over dice and card games. He gazed inside smoky barrooms, where patrons dished coins into large machines that blared the latest hit songs. He passed thousands of men and women who wore rags strapped to their backs, yet they moved in and out of these places, obviously with money to burn.

Even in his small hometown, Wichien had heard that Nam Khem was the most dreadful village in all of Thailand, and now he knew why. This was no place for honest people who didn't drink, smoke, gamble, or have an itch for bar girls. He wasn't sure the town held anything for him. Then he caught site of the massive holes dug into the earth in the center of town. He walked to one and peered over the edge. At the bottom of the pit, fifty or sixty feet down, three men gripped a thick hose that ate away at the wall of the ditch with a powerful blast of water. As muck collected at their feet, a tube sucked it a hundred feet up and leaked it onto a shoot suspended by scaffolding that stretched over the ditch and then across the land for several hundred yards. As the water made its gentle downward journey, particles of tin, which were heavier than sand, clung to small ribs along the shoot, while everything else drained with the water into the sea. Those red and black particles were the reason he had come, the reason this entire village had been carved into the jungle decades before, and he promised himself that he would fight his urge to climb aboard the first bus out of here and would stay long enough to get his family out of the hole it had fallen into.

Having spent the last of his money on the bus ticket, that night Wichien headed into the jungle and hacked down bamboo poles and gathered leaves. He carried them toward shore in the southern reaches of town, which at the time supported a forest of towering pine trees. No one owned the land on the outskirts of the village, so no one told him he couldn't build a home there. In a matter of just a few days, he had constructed a small lean-to that would keep the rain off his head. Then he went back into the village to land a job.

The best he could find was a position as a laborer, which involved carrying heavy bags of dirt, cleaning pumps, digging with a shovel—whatever nasty job his tin-mining boss thought needed doing. He worked for twelve baht a day, roughly thirty cents, which worked out to be around two cents an hour. But

Wichien managed to live off less than two dollars a month. In one corner of a thatched hut his boss had built for his employees sat a pot of steamed rice from which Wichien had been told he could eat whenever he had the urge. He still needed to buy something to put on top of the rice, but he could get one small fish or a packet of curry in the market for half a baht. At the end of the month, he had plenty of money left over to send home to his mother.

Hauling bags of cement on his shoulder and digging ditches didn't bother Wichien, but the town of Nam Khem still did. As it turned out, Nam Khem was an even rougher town than he had first thought. When arguments arose, they were almost always settled with a gun. The village was extremely territorial, and the bosses who could hire the most hit men claimed the most land. And when the hit men weren't working for the big bosses, they were doing their own killing on the side. Many mornings, Wichien emerged from his hut to find a body that had been chucked to sea washed up on his shore. The hit men were easy to spot—they wore leather jackets, boots, and jeans, as if trying to copy the tough guys in America. They sold marijuana and heroin. They could kill and deal as much as they liked, because what the bus driver had told Wichien was true—the police had given up on Nam Khem long ago. When the drugs got out of hand years later, police started showing up in Nam Khem by the truckload, but they never came alone. A law officer alone on the streets of Nam Khem wouldn't have lasted five minutes.

After much thought, Wichien took a portion of his savings and invested in an unregistered pistol of his own. He had no intentions of shooting anyone with it, but on those nights when he heard men wandering around his home, threatening him, he could squeeze off a round to let them know he was not to be messed with. He still considered himself a country boy with good notions; as of yet, he hadn't taken a single drink of alcohol, laid a single bill on the betting table, or taken a single bar girl up to her room for a romp, but he had learned fast and hard that in this devil town, pushovers never lasted long.

As his skin darkened and toughened from the hard work under the sun, he began to realize that if he remained a laborer, he would be stuck in Nam Khem until he was an old man, or at least until his brothers and sisters reached an age when they could support themselves. By then his chances of returning to school would have drifted away. Every morning on the walk to work, he passed by men with red hair heading out on rafts to mine at sea. When he walked home at night, he passed those same men heading toward the whorehouses and casinos with pockets full of cash. He knew they had to be making a lot more than twelve baht a day. Wichien started looking for a new job.

Most tin-mining bosses told him to get lost, but when he agreed to work for ten baht a day rather than the customary twelve, he managed to land a position as a laborer on a raft boat. On his first day, he headed out to sea with six other men. Two of his co-workers strapped on masks and rubber shoes and climbed down a rope until they stood on the bottom of the sea. The divers remained sixty feet below the surface for two hours, using a hose to suck sand and little flakes of tin up to a trough on deck, which Wichien would then have to separate with a mining pan. Soon Wichien knew that he would become a diver. After the divers had given a cut of their find to the boat owner, they divvied up the rest of the tin among themselves, which fetched them a whopping 3,000 baht. Still, Wichien received only a petty ten baht for his services—there were no bonuses, no gratuities.

Wichien knew nothing about diving, so every chance he could, he gazed over the edge of the raft boat and watched the movements of the divers below. He watched how they held the hose, and how they descended and climbed back up. It didn't look all that hard, so when one of the divers on their team neglected to come to work one morning, Wichien quickly volunteered to replace him.

While climbing down the rope with a mask strapped to his face and oxygen shooting up his nose, he was terrified at first, but once he stepped foot on the soft sand down below, he felt just as at home under water as he ever had on land. He got a view of the fish, the lobsters, the stretches of colorful coral, and, most important, a rich deposit of tin. At the end of his first week, he had a sack that weighted thirty kilos. Knowing that tin sold for 170 baht a kilo, he quickly did the math and discovered that he was rich. He added to the pile each day, and at the end of the month he sold the whole lot for 15,000 baht, roughly $375, which was more money than he had ever held in his hand. Instead of digging a hole in his floor and burying the money, as nearly everyone else did in Nam Khem, he quickly sent the money home to his parents to avoid spending any of it.

The job carried occupational hazards. A few of the divers on his raft and many on other rafts came up too quickly and got sick. Some of them died. And everyone who dove in the sea ended up with bright red hair. But his vanity and the risk of death mattered little when Wichien stood on the raft boat at the end of the day with a pile of tin. If he kept this up, he would be back in school in no time.

But the money was hard to leave. Even if he went back to school and received an education, it would still be hard to find a job that would pay anywhere close to 15,000 baht a month. At the beginning of the month, he would tell himself that he would work thirty more days and then be done, gone from Nam Khem; and then, at the beginning of the next month, he would tell himself the same thing.

Years began to pass.

Wichien used some of his earnings to travel. He went to the north and west and southeast of Thailand, experienced the countryside, the cities, the towns, the villages, but he always went back to Nam Khem. He still didn't drink or smoke or gamble, but the village had worked down into his blood. The killings had become second nature, and when he stumbled across a body, he paused for a brief moment to see if it was someone he knew, and then he carried on. He found himself venturing into the heart of the village more and more to look at the young ladies who came from all over Thailand and Burma to work in the shops, the markets, the cinemas. He was twenty-five years old and had been living in Nam Khem for nine years, and never had he been with a woman.

Then, one afternoon while wandering the village, he saw the woman he would marry. She worked in a small restaurant by the shore. Her nickname was Nang, and she had arrived two months earlier. She was a small girl, no more than eighty pounds. Wichien didn't want a woman who wished to bear twelve children and could carry four sacks of cement on her shoulders, but at the same time he didn't want a woman who needed to be pampered day and night and was fearful at the thought of lugging a child in her belly. The first time Wichien mustered the courage to draw close to Nang, he saw that she was a happy medium. Her wrists and ankles were slim, yet her hands and feet bore thick calluses. From afar she looked dainty, but up close she looked determined. She had a smile and sparkling white teeth that could make even the most gruff miner drop to his knees. She was beautiful in a way that only a country girl could be, innocent and pure and so unlike the majority of women who came to Nam Khem to sell their bodies. She was perfect.

Soon Nang became all he could think about, and every afternoon when he got back from the sea, he would go and sit in her shop. He hadn't the slightest clue as to what to say to her, so he just sat there, staring at her.

She liked him—Wichien could sense it—but after two months passed, he began to notice that she had attracted the attention of other men in town. While he sat in a corner of the restaurant, gazing over at her as she washed dishes and cleaned the counters, other suitors confidently approached her. She would smile and bat her lashes at the men. Finally, Wichien couldn't take it anymore. He got up from his seat in the corner and headed over to her, ready to give her a piece of his mind. He would tell her that she wasn't a nice girl like he'd thought. He would tell this girl Nang that he never wanted to see her again.

Shortly after she was born, Suphee Namlakorn was given the nickname Nang, which means "woman." She grew up in a small village near the Laos border, and she studied until grade four, when she joined her mother, father, six sisters, and two brothers in the rice fields near their home. Despite the family's having so many hands out in the field, the weather had been so bad that the rice crop was nearly ruined. Her family wasn't earning enough to put food on the table, so when Nang was thirteen, and a man came to the village with a bus, looking for young girls to work in Bangkok, she got pushed aboard by her family, all of whom kept telling her how much they loved her and how sorry they were. Nang had never ventured farther than five miles from her home. She was on edge for the entire journey, and she began to cry as the bus entered the congested, smog-choked streets of Bangkok. She became certain the city would swallow her whole.

She was shuttled into a warehouse where twenty other young teenage girls waited with their small suitcases and worried looks. She sat in silence for several hours. Eventually a nice-looking man and woman came and picked her up. The company leader said that the family would pay her 300 baht per month and that she was to wash their clothes and clean their dishes. As she drove across town with the couple and saw the villa in which she would live, a smile actually crept across her face. Three hundred baht was more than her entire family made in the rice fields for a month of labor. The bright lights and tall buildings of Bangkok now began to intrigue her.

The enthusiasm didn't last long. The family she had been sold to was wealthy, yet they paid her only one hundred baht a month. They kept her working thirteen hours a day. She didn't mind cooking, cleaning, and taking care of the children, but the father of the home always wanted her to massage his legs, which wasn't proper for a young lady and made her feel strange. She did as she was told, but a couple of weeks in she made a mistake—she hadn't washed a dish or had forgotten to water a plant. She couldn't recall exactly what she had done wrong to cause what happened next. The father of the house threw her to the ground, kicked her in the stomach, and then beat her severely with a mop handle. A week later, he used a belt. The week after that, it was a metal clothes hanger. Nang tried to do everything perfectly, sat on the floor when they sat on the couch, kneeled when they stood, but the beatings kept coming. The few times she went out in public, she wore long-sleeved shirts and pants to hide the bruises. She thought about writing to her mother, but she didn't know what to say. She didn't even know anyone who could help her write such a letter. The beatings became her dark secret.

After working a year and a half in a constant state of fear, she met another housemaid, who worked in the villa next door. They hit it off and managed to spend a few hours together each week. They talked about where they were from, how much they missed their families, and what it would be like to one day have a husband and children of their own. A month after they had grown somewhat close, her friend asked her how she had gotten all the welts on her arms and legs. Nang told her friend that she had fallen down, but the lie kept her from sleeping that night. A few weeks later, she told her friend what had been going on.

"I can't do anything," Nang cried. "They are rich people, and I am so small. I have no mouth to argue with them."

"Why don't you escape from here?"

"Where will I go?"

"If you stay in that house, he will kill you," her friend said. "You must leave that house. I will meet you on the street."

Nang almost abandoned the plan, but at the last moment she silently gathered up her few possessions and sneaked out the back door. She met her friend in the darkness on the street, and together they walked out of the residential neighborhood, through an industrial district, and then into the downtown area. After nearly four hours of walking, they arrived at a noodle shop in Bangkok's Chinatown. A sweet little lady owned the shop, and once she learned Nang's story, she showered her with hugs and kisses and took her right in. It had been eighteen months since Nang had felt a human touch that wasn't violent, and she broke into sobs. She didn't stop crying until morning.

Nang lived and worked at the noodle shop for two years, until she was seventeen years old. She loved her boss like a mother, but there was no replacing her family and the countryside in which she had been raised. She had heard that the rice fields back home had returned to normal, so she caught a bus back there to once again work beside her family.

There was a celebration when she arrived, and it seemed to last for months and months. She told stories of her adventures in Bangkok to her sisters and roughhoused with her brothers after dinner. Every Sunday, the entire family lounged on the front porch, swatting mosquitoes and drinking green tea. They caught up on old times and had a lot of fun, but as much as she liked being home, Nang also wanted to see more of the world. In her village, people seldom traveled, and when they did, it was out of necessity. As a result, she had heard very little about the sea while growing up. But she'd heard all about the Gulf of Thailand and the Andaman Sea from the fishermen who had eaten in her boss's shop. They had made the ocean sound so romantic, saying that it was sparkling blue and stretched for as far as the eye could see. She longed to see it for herself.

"Mama," she said one day at breakfast, "I want to go to the south and work down there."

"Don't be silly," her mother shot back. "A fine-looking girl like you, they will kidnap you and sell you to a whorehouse."

"No they won't! I can take care of myself."

"No. I won't let you go. And that's final."

Nang held her tongue. She helped her mother work in the fields for a couple of years, but the urge to head to the south of Thailand grew only stronger. She thought about just leaving but decided against it. Then, when she was nineteen, an uncle who lived in the south came to their home to pay a visit, and Nang saw her chance.

The day her uncle left, the entire family went outside to see him off. Nang quickly said her good-byes and then headed into the house. When her mother had said her farewells and come back in, Nang slipped out the back door.

She followed her uncle to the bus station. As he stepped through the front doors and took a seat at the head of the bus, she climbed aboard through the rear doors and took a seat in the back, sinking down in the seat to avoid being discovered by her uncle. Unbeknownst to Nang, they needed to change buses in Bangkok. This time, her uncle spotted her as she attempted to sneak aboard.

"Nang, what are you doing?" he shouted.

"Please, please, don't send me home," she begged. "I have to see the south of Thailand."

"Nam Khem is not a place for a young country girl."

"But I really want to go with you."

A puzzled look came over her uncle's face. "Why?"

"I heard that the ocean is made from salt," Nang said sheepishly. "Is that true?"

Her uncle smiled. "Yes, Nang, it is true."

"Then you have to take me with you," she said. "I don't believe it. I have to see for myself."

Her uncle put up a few minutes of resistance, but when the bus driver made the last call, he gave in. They sat side by side during the eight-hour journey to Nam Khem. When they arrived, her uncle took her around, looking for a job. Her uncle obviously didn't want another mouth to feed, and she didn't expect to be one. She had been working thirteen hours a day since she was six. At the second food shop they walked into, the owner agreed to hire her for 300 baht a month. Nang was thrilled.

Later that night, Nang sneaked out of her uncle's home. She went down to the shore, dipped a finger in the water, and brought it to her mouth. When she tasted salt, a smile spread over her lips. She sat in the sand and gazed out over the shimmering water. She didn't move until the sun began to surface on the horizon.

In the months that followed, she washed dishes, cleaned the kitchen, and eventually learned how to cook. She felt good about herself, and she liked Nam Khem even though it was a rough place. There was always something going on, whether it was a fair or the cinema. And the boys—there were so many boys her age.

After about three months, one of those boys began frequenting her restaurant. He always took a seat in the corner and never said anything other than the occasional *sabai dii reu*, but she could tell that he liked her, because he was always staring at her. Every time he came in, she expected him to finally talk to her, but every day she was wrong. He'd come in, take a seat in the corner, and then just stare. Then came the other boys, all of them very handsome. She smiled and shifted her hips, partially because flirting was fun, but mostly because she could tell that it drove the shy boy in the corner crazy.

It went on like this for a week, but then one day, after she had spent an hour talking to a good-looking fisherman, the young man in the corner came over and introduced himself as Wichien. Then he ripped into her.

"So you want to have a husband to take you to bed," he said. "Is that why you're flirting with all these boys?"

This made Nang mad. She wanted to shout, *Who the hell are you? You're not my husband. You can't be jealous of me.*

"Yes, I want to have a husband," she said. She hadn't actually given the matter much thought, but she knew it would get to him.

"Be careful," he returned, pointing a finger at her. "I will kill you."

Nang experienced a brief flash of fear, but when Wichien stormed out the door, she felt a pang of regret. She figured that was it; he wouldn't come in and stare at her anymore. It bothered her for a couple of days, and then she put it out of her mind—she still had five or six suitors coming by on a regular basis.

About a week later, a young man named Kai, whom she had seen hanging around with Wichien in the past, stopped by the shop to invite her to a party. Nang felt overjoyed. She had never been to a party before, at least not one that her parents hadn't attended.

"What should I wear?" she asked.

"We're going to be taking pictures, so you have to dress really nice. White skirt and blouse will work. Do you have that?"

"Yes," Nang said, partially lying. She had what once had been a white skirt and blouse, but over the years of labor, they had turned an off-gray. Since photographs never turned out all that well anyhow, she figured it wouldn't matter much.

She had been told to arrive at the party at three o'clock in the afternoon on Saturday, but an hour before she planned to leave, some of Kai's girlfriends came by her shop. They were all nicely dressed, and they wanted to help her put on some makeup. Nang loved the attention, and she also loved how she looked when they were through.

They all headed off to Kai's house at three o'clock. The moment Nang walked through the door, she saw Wichien standing there in a suit. At first she thought he had put his friends up to this, but then she noticed that he was just as surprised to see her as she was to see him. She hesitantly walked over to him.

"Wichien, what's going on here?"

Wichien shook his head.

A few seconds later, Kai placed two chairs in the center of the room and told everyone that he needed their attention.

"Groom, this is your seat," he said to Wichien. Then he pointed to Nang. "And this seat is for the bride."

Nang had no idea what to think or say. She could feel her heart racing and her head began to spin, but she didn't know whether that was a good sign or a bad one. It was true that she had liked Wichien from the moment she saw him, but marriage was so serious and it lasted forever. She liked finally being able to act like a teenager. She still wanted to do so many things, but now it felt like she didn't have a choice in the matter. When she hesitated to say anything at all, Kai came forward. He took her hand and placed it in Wichien's.

"I don't know," Nang managed to say.

"Come on," Kai returned. "Every time Wichien comes back from the sea, all he can talk about is Nang. And you, I see the way you look at him. This is your wedding party, so you might as well enjoy it."

When Nang didn't issue any further protests, Kai tied a piece of twine around her wrist. Then he did the same for Wichien. From that moment on, they were husband and wife. For the rest of the night, they talked and laughed. Nang knew nothing about marriage, but it certainly had its perks. Everyone attending the party, mostly friends of Wichien's, had each placed 300 or 400 baht into a hat for them to begin their life together. A room in Kai's house had already been set up for the newlyweds, and they stayed in the house for fifteen days.

"Wichien," Nang said one day as they lay in bed. "We're going to need to buy a house."

"I agree," he said. "Tomorrow we look for a home."

The next afternoon, they bought a house for 2,000 baht. It sat less than fifty yards from the beach, had no deed, and was in need of serious repair. The mangrove support beams were rotten with bugs, and the aluminum walls kept the place blistering hot during the day and terribly cold at night. The concrete floors had cracked and fallen apart over the years, leaving big holes in which rats now lived. It wasn't a house suitable for raising children, but they didn't have much choice. A few months after they were married, Nang got pregnant.

She figured that Wichien would be able to make enough money in a couple of years to improve their home or buy another one somewhere else in the village, or perhaps in her hometown, but that wish never came true. A few months before they had their son, Nueng, the tin market started to dry up, and Wichien found himself out of a job. To support his family, Wichien, still a clean-living country boy at heart, strolled over to the dark side of Nam Khem.

2 WIMON

CHAPTER

Three decades prior, during the monsoon season of 1962, a storm swept over the Gulf of Thailand and across Talumphuk Cape at seven p.m., bringing with it hurricane-force winds and torrential rain. In a home perched on stilts six miles from shore, eight-year-old Wimon Thongtae dove under his mother's bed, joining his two sisters and four brothers. All of them had towels and blankets and shirts wrapped around their heads to protect from falling debris. Their confused cries soon turned to screams as the wind and rain tore away the walls of their one-room home board by board, ripped away the roof tile by tile, until only a skeleton of their house remained. They shivered and held hands beneath the bed, but eventually that too got ripped away into the night. Wimon clung to his mother, and his mother clung to her other children. If the storm wanted to take their family, it would have to take all of them.

In the six hours of violence that followed, Wimon opened his eyes only once. The countryside had drowned beneath a massive body of water. In the distance, he could see houses, pigs, and mattresses drifting in the darkness. Underneath him, he could see the powerful current bubbling up through the floorboards, which rested twelve feet off the ground. Then, beneath the surface of the water not far from his home, he saw a whiteness that he imagined to be spirits thrashing in the depths. He buried his face back in his mother's bosom and prayed that their lives would be spared.

The storm, which came to be known as the Talumphuk Storm and later have a movie made about it, lost its ferocity shortly after two a.m. In the morning, as hundreds along the coast hauled the bodies of loved ones who had drowned or been crushed beneath collapsed houses to the temple, Wimon crawled out from under a blanket. The wooden steps leading up to their home had vanished, so he dropped down into the mud and then slowly walked the perimeter of their property, which measured three rai, approximately 1.5 acres. Two years prior, just after his father walked out of their lives, Wimon had quit school to help his mother tend to their small rice field near their home. Now all his hard work and their only means of survival had washed away. They already teetered on the brink of starvation.

He headed into the village and saw that his neighbors were just as bad off. Everyone had lost their fields, and many had lost their homes. They gathered at the house of the village leader to await help from the government, but after they waited through the night and deep into the following afternoon, it dawned on them that the government had no intention of dropping so much as a single bag of food. If they were going to carry on, they would need to help themselves and each other.

One family had a few bags of rice that had survived, and they placed them on the floor so all could get a scoop. Another family had tools that hadn't drifted off, and they were passed around so fields could be salvaged. Day and night, they worked as a team, tilling the muddy earth, hammering scrap metal to roofs. Wimon's mother had kept a small stash of money tucked close to her bosom when the storm hit, and in the coming weeks she'd give Wimon a baht or two and send him to the market to buy rice. It was during these trips, at the age of eight, that Wimon first felt the sting of shame. His family had never had a radio or any other luxury items. They had never even had nice clothes to wear to temple. But every time he had gone to the market in years past, he had toted sacks of rice for sale. He couldn't think of anything more humiliating than a rice farmer having to purchase rice in order to survive.

Once they had replanted the field and put new walls and a roof on their home, Wimon decided against going back to school. The storm had taken something from his mother, drained her of happiness. Wimon loved her very much, and he couldn't stand to see her working out in the fields alone in such a miserable state. Over the next six years, while all his elder brothers and sisters trekked into town every morning to attend class, he remained behind to work by his mother's side. On occasion, when he'd see his siblings laughing with friends on their way home from school, he'd feel a bit envious, but in his heart he knew they were missing out on an even greater experience. He got to know the woman who had brought them into this world in a way that they never would.

Despite the inseparable bond he and his mother forged, the sadness brought on by the storm continued to grow inside her as the years skipped by. She would walk away from him in the rice field and hide her face from view, but he could tell she was crying. She silently wondered why her husband had left her with seven children to feed, why life had become so hard. Wimon grew angry that he wasn't yet old enough to support her. He promised himself that once he became a man, his mother would never have to work again. He would remain a loyal son and stand by her side always.

At the age of fourteen, Wimon decided it was time to fulfill his promise. The scrawny legs and arms, sunken face, and large forehead of his youth hadn't vanished, but despite his apparent frailty, he could work circles around boys twice his size. The hard labor in the rice fields had given him powerful hands, a stern back, and impressive determination. He decided to sell the family farm and move south with his mother to Cha-uat, a town in Nakhon Si Thammarat Province, where his elder sister, Thasanee, had moved several years prior. His other brothers had all trekked off to the rough village of Nam Khem, located on the opposite side of the isthmus, to strike it rich mining tin. His mother didn't mind much. She was happy as long as she had her little Wimon.

When they arrived in Cha-uat, Wimon told his mother that he would take care of everything and she wouldn't have to work anymore. It was a lot of responsibility for a fourteen-year-old, but Wimon had big plans. He began selling home-baked pastries at the market, and his sister joined him in the business a few weeks after he'd brought home his first empty tray. They made enough money to support themselves and their mother, but they still hovered around the poverty level. Although the cooking and selling kept Wimon occupied between dawn and dusk, he realized that there were still many more hours in the day that could be put to use. Instead of using that time to make friends and girlfriends, he decided to use it to follow a lifelong dream and scrape together a few extra bucks to boot.

One evening after work, he jogged to the outskirts of town where a traditional Muay Thai kickboxing camp had been erected in the jungle more than three decades before. For the next three hours, he watched boys between the ages of four and twenty-one jump rope, run circles around the gym, and then square off with an opponent to throw a barrage of knees to the sternum, elbows to the temple, and gloveless fists into each other's jaw. Their profession was a dangerous one. Wimon had seen what became of Thai boxers in their later years, their bodies so damaged they could hardly walk, but he also knew the benefits. Those versed in the ancient art of combat drew respect everywhere they went, and he'd heard that the champions who fought at Lumphini and Ratchadamnoen stadiums, in Bangkok, were watched on the television by ten million people each week. It would take a toll on his body—that he knew for certain—but he figured that after having spent ten years of his life in the field, his sinewy limbs could endure the abuse. If he got good and won a couple of fights, he could make some money for his mother. And if he made a name for himself, he would get invited to compete in small stadiums around the country. He would get to travel, a luxury he had never had, having grown up in a family so poor.

Six months after beginning his grueling days, he had his first fight. By the end of the first round, his forehead gushed blood from receiving a powerful elbow. He had a lump the size of an egg on his shin from kicking his opponent's knee, and his head had been knocked around so much by hammering fists that he had forgotten which corner was his. His trainers flagged him down after the bell, dumped cold water on his head, and then rubbed out the lumps in his shin. As Wimon stared across at his opponent, his body tattered and shell-shocked, he realized how important this moment was. He realized that while he might never fight before the big crowds at Lumphini or Ratchadamnoen stadiums, he wasn't a quitter. He would fight to the death if he had to. He headed back into battle, listening now to the oohs and aahs that burst out of the crowd every time he landed a knee, listening to the pace of the snake-charming rhythm of pipe and drum blaring through speakers around him increase with each round. He relished each second he had under the bright lights above him. At the end of the five rounds, after having dished out and received fifteen minutes of punishment, he walked away with a decision and 400 baht to give to his mother.

Wimon kept up the routine for the next six years: training in the morning, selling pastries during the day, training at night, and then fighting every other week. He was too busy to have fun, but his mother felt as if she had been reborn. No longer having to slave in the fields, she got out more and more and developed a group of friends. She even met a man who had a small food shop in the market. His name was Mr. Huan Lukkhanam, and Wimon didn't much care for him. He cared for him even less when Huan proposed to his mother and she accepted. Wimon eventually warmed up to him when, a year after the wedding ceremony, his mother gave him a baby brother. Seeing his mother laughing around the house filled him with warmth. She had finally lost her fear of the future, but having a stable life wasn't in the cards.

Huan had once been the captain of a large ship that ferried passengers from the mainland out to the islands. While making his way out one afternoon, a longtail boat darted into his path. The ship was too large to stop or maneuver around the smaller vessel, and Huan ran over it, killing the captain of the longtail. A police investigation ensued, and after a two-year trial, the courts decided that Huan wasn't at fault—there was nothing he could have done to avoid the collision.

The family of the longtail captain didn't find this satisfactory.

One evening there was a fair in Cha-uat, and Wimon had prepared a particularly large dish of pastries to sell. The whole family had gone with him—his sister, his mother, and his mother's husband. While Wimon stood behind his table, his family mingled in the crowd a few feet away. Screaming kids ran this way and that; bells and whistles sounded in the distance every time someone won a prize. There was so much commotion that no one noticed the hit man dressed in black, holding a gun. With specific instructions from the family of the longtail captain, the hit man walked right up to Huan and shot him at close range in the head. Wimon, now seventeen, watched his stepfather die at his feet. The truly terrible part was witnessing his mother's horror. Just as on the night of that awful storm, Wimon watched another piece of her die.

When he was twenty-one years old, Wimon's career as a pastry chef and a Thai boxer ended—like all young Thai men, he had to spend the next two years as a soldier. After his time in the service, he went back to Cha-uat for a short spell, but he found nothing left for him there. His sister had moved with his mother to Nam Khem to join his elder brothers, all of whom had made healthy sums of money mining tin. Wimon wasn't quite sure what Nam Khem held for him, but he packed his bags and headed to the rough village to be by his mother's side.

He stayed with his sister and worked as a laborer long enough to buy an old motorbike with a sidecar attached. Each morning, he filled the sidecar with fruit he purchased at the market at a discount price, and then he slowly patrolled the muddy streets, ringing a bell. As it turned out, he was just as good at picking fruit as he was at cooking desserts, and soon he had a group of loyal customers. In a year, he purchased his first home just around the corner from Yim-Yim, a popular Chinese food restaurant not far from the shore. His one-room plywood shack sat on a sliver of land between two much larger homes constructed from brick. His mother moved back in with him. A part of Wimon was thrilled about this, but he was also starting to think about getting married. Wimon was now twenty-five, and up until now, women had seldom crossed his mind. He'd made a promise to himself that he wouldn't get married and start a family until he owned his own home. Now he no longer had any excuses.

On his route around town, he met several interesting women with whom he could see building a life. He talked with them and flirted to the best of his ability, but everything changed again one night in 1981.

Pulled up from slumber by the smell of smoke, Wimon hefted his mother's small body into his arms and went running down to the beach. From a distance, he watched his home and a hundred others burn to the ground. Several of the residences around his had survived, because they were constructed from brick, but his little plywood house had gone up like a matchbox. So much for owning his own home. He put his desire to marry on hold.

Over the next decade, a series of fires continued to sweep through Nam Khem. Every time his home was destroyed, Wimon gave up on the idea of getting married. And when his home got reduced to cinder for the fifth time, Wimon gave up altogether. Throughout his tough life, he had harbored the belief that good things would eventually happen, that the only way to survive was to work for tomorrow. But each time he got back on his feet, it was gone with a fire. He sold his property for less than he had bought it for. He was thirty-seven years old, was single, and had no home. All he had was his mother, so he scooped her up, placed her in the sidecar attached to his motorbike, and left for the big island of Phuket, which now boomed with high-rise hotels and tourists from around the world. But Nam Khem soon drew them both back into its embrace. This time, the village would swallow them whole.

At the age of eighteen, Loogin Saikrasae, known by the nickname Lek, moved with her mother to a relative's house out in the country, where they worked washing clothes. The job required long hours, and she always had bloody knuckles, but by this point Lek had become accustomed to a hard life. When she was eight, her father had blown off his right hand dynamite fishing, and she and her six siblings had gone to work in the rice and bean fields. They sometimes went for days without eating a decent meal. It took its toll on all of them, but one day her younger brother Phiboon grew tremendously sick. After three days of shivering and wetting the bed, he died from a high fever. For the longest time, Lek thought she too would die—her skin had turned pale and she fainted all the time—but after she performed a ceremony at the temple for the dead monks when she was fifteen, her health improved. She had worked to support the family ever since.

A few weeks into her new job, she left her relative's house with an empty bucket. Down the street lived a wealthy fisherman who had a strong well from which he allowed the whole community to draw water. While at the well, Lek spotted a group of young boys employed by the wealthy fishermen lounging in the shade of a tree. She had been around many young boys when she had worked as a cook on a fishing boat, but she had never had any interest in getting to know them. But there was one among this group, a fifteen-year-old boy with light skin and broad shoulders, who drew her attention. She smiled at him and he smiled back. That was it. She went back home expecting to never see him again.

A few days later, her cousin, who spent a lot of time hanging out with the fishermen down the street, came around to talk with her.

"That guy you smiled at the other day is Puek, and I think he likes you. He won't shut up about you."

"What do you want me to do about it?" Lek asked, not sure how to respond.

"He wanted me to see if he could come over and talk to you."

"I guess it would be all right."

As her cousin raced down the street, nervousness filled Lek's stomach. She had never before talked to a boy who liked her, and despite the trouble that could come her way from flirting with a boy her mother hadn't formally met, she eagerly awaited his arrival. She hardly slept that night or the next, but when Puek still hadn't come to talk with her on the third day, she began to lose hope. She saw him around the village on occasion for the next couple of weeks, and they once again exchanged smiles, but then one day he just vanished from her life. After a month had passed, she tried putting him out of her mind for good.

The youngest of six siblings, Wiroj Ruamwong, who had been given the nickname Puek ("white") due to his fair skin, had become quite a hell-raiser. When his father died, three years prior, he had hit the road to support the family and learned the rough-and-tumble way of the fisherman. Because he had lived in six different port towns and worked beside gruff fishermen on a dozen large boats, his body already held an array of art. He had a tattoo of a tiger in the middle of his back. On his right shoulder, he had the head of Hunumaan, the ever-mighty monkey-god who had come to Prince Raam's rescue when the giant with ten faces came to steal his kingdom and wife. He had a turtle on his left shoulder to remind himself to be a patient person and hopefully live a stable life. Down his leg, he had a Chinese dragon, which he and the rest of his motley crew had each gotten to never forget their brotherhood. And on his right hand, he had a rooster, which he had simply woken up with one morning. It meant little other than that he had been too drunk the night before. His time in the ports had taught him a whole lot about the darker side of life. He'd slept with prostitutes and any other girl he could con into bed, but never before had he met a girl as beautiful or as intriguing as the one he'd seen fetching a bucket of water while he lounged in front of his boss's home.

He wanted to be with this girl, Lek, in a way that scared him. In all the places he'd gone in the past three years, never before had he fallen in love. He told himself that he couldn't fall in love, not while his mother was still alive. It would break her heart. The more he thought about this girl, Lek, the guiltier he felt. If he fell in love, he was sure his mother would die of loneliness.

Instead of going and talking with Lek, which he desperately wanted to do, he ran to his hometown of Prachuap Khiri Khan to see his mother. He showered her with attention for a couple of days and then headed back out to sea, where he remained for the next two years. There were many drunken nights and several drunken fights to go along with them. Standing five foot ten and broad shouldered, he dwarfed the average Thai, and seldom did he walk away from a scrap with so much as a bruise.

He grew up fast and always kept an eye out for adventure. During his journeys up and down the coastline of the gulf, he heard some tall tales about the small village of Nam Khem. He heard that a young man with good luck and street smarts could get rich from mining tin. He had avoided the village, because digging in the ground or under the sea held no appeal for him. He was a fisherman, and proud to be one. But he remained intrigued by Nam Khem's legendary nightlife. A few years after he had first heard about the village, a captain told him that a strong fishing industry had sparked up there overnight. The next day, Puek quit his job and caught a bus south. He wanted to see with his own eyes if Nam Khem was really as wild as everyone claimed.

He loved everything about Nam Khem right off the bat. He loved the casinos, the prostitutes, and the cinemas, which played an endless stream of films staring Charles Bronson, his favorite American actor. He met girls from Nakhon Si Thammarat, Chiang Mai, and every other province in Thailand. The village had every taste imaginable—bitter, sweet, sour. It was delicious. He'd pump coins into the jukebox in his favorite bars and flirt with young girls in the market. He'd sip from a bottle of whiskey while taking long walks down the beach. Sometimes he would just sit back and watch the hit men, robbers, ex-convicts, and wealthy mining bosses strutting down the street with their fancy shoes and chrome-plated pistols strapped to their side. He never got bored. Compared to his home-town, it was paradise.

Thinking he had found his new home, he talked with a captain who happened to hail from the same province as he did, and within fifteen minutes he climbed aboard a small ship and headed out to sea. Puek had never worried about storms or fierce winds, but while fishing off the coast of Nam Khem in the Andaman Sea, he learned that down here, there was a lot more to worry about than just Mother Nature. When the fish weren't biting just offshore, the captain sailed into Burmese waters. Fifteen minutes later, they were getting shot at by Burmese sol-diers on a patrol boat. The captain managed to cross back over the sea boundary before anyone got killed, but the whole ordeal made Puek realize that he was still a little too young for Nam Khem.

He returned home and found odd jobs to help support his mother. He gave her every baht that he earned, and when he needed a new pair of jeans or a new shirt, his mother would already have bought it for him before he had to ask. One time she even bought him a pair of Wrangler jeans, the hottest clothing item one could buy at the time. The tight fit had all the girls swooning. He also watched his mother have some fun for the first time in her life. She took a small portion of the money he gave her and got together with a group of friends to go shopping.

While walking around town one evening, Puek ran into an old friend whom he'd worked with at the age of fifteen. They started talking, and his friend casu-ally mentioned that Lek, the girl he'd fallen in love with years earlier, actually lived in Prachuap Khiri Khan. Puek couldn't believe it. He made some inquiries and got Lek's home address—she lived just a few miles away. After spending sev-eral days gathering up his nerve, he went over there and knocked on her front door. She came out onto the front stoop. They talked for several hours and learned a lot about each other. Just as he had thought, she was an honest girl. She had never dated a boy, let alone kissed one. It made him want her even more.

Before pursuing Lek, however, he felt he first had to do something nice for his mother. He went to the temple and lived the life of a monk for five months and ten days. It held much more significance than making a merit, which consoled those who had already died, because it honored his mother in life. It was his way of showing her what a wonderful mother she had been, and it would help her reach a good place after she died. So, for five months and ten days, Puek lived by the rules of a monk—no drinking, no smoking, no chasing girls. The rules forbade him to even think impure thoughts, but while tossing and turning on a hardwood floor, he couldn't help but imagine what Lek looked like beneath her clothes and where their future together would take them.

Shortly after he got released from the temple and had grown back some hair, he went to Lek's parents' house and asked her out on a date. He hoped that after he'd completed his time in the temple, his mother would understand. He had brought along one of his friends, and he asked Lek to bring along one of hers. He knew that Lek was a pure country girl, but hopefully her friend wouldn't be. His idea was that his friend and her friend would hit it off and then begin to make out. It would break Lek's defenses down, and perhaps at the end of the night, he might be able to steal a kiss. His plan, however, didn't pan out the way he had hoped. Lek's friend and his friend didn't exactly hit it off, and the whole date turned into a fiasco. The kiss never materialized.

Puek was not one to abandon a goal, but he had to take a break from pursuing Lek, because his mother had fallen ill. He pampered her day and night. When her condition worsened after a month had passed, he took her to the hospital. They put her through a string of tests. A week later, she was diagnosed with throat cancer.

Despite his mother's protests, Puek broke open the jar in which she kept all the money he had given her over the years. He gave a large portion of it to the doctors at the hospital in Prachuap Khiri Khan, but after several months of chemotherapy, they claimed the cancer had spread too far to save her. Unable to accept this bit of news, he took his mother to the hospital in Rachaburi Province and then the Siriraj hospital in Bangkok. He spent the rest of his money on doctors, but they all came to the same conclusion. His mother had only a short time to live. Her body shrunk away. Then one morning she didn't wake up.

Hundreds of people from his mother's hometown of Ao Noi turned up at the funeral. Puek fell off the deep end. He stayed out later, drank more alcohol, acquired more girlfriends, and got into more fights. But the pain inside him refused to disappear. Then he started thinking more and more about Lek. He had known her now for years, yet they had gone on only one date and he still hadn't so much as kissed her.

One afternoon, he knocked on her front door to talk with her parents. He said that there was a fair at the temple downtown, which was true, and that he wanted to take Lek to this fair, which was a complete lie. He said that the fair boasted a Thai classical dance show and a music show. After a good half hour, in which he used his best manners in talking to both her father and her mother, they agreed to let him take their daughter to the fair, just so long as he had her back at a decent hour. The moment he walked out the door with the girl he had been admiring for nearly a decade, he knew that she would be his. He loved her and she loved him, but sometimes that just wasn't enough. In order to pull her away from her family, he would have to kidnap her. No matter what she did or said, he wouldn't bring her home. Not ever.

In 1981, six-year-old Ratree Kaewaied, nicknamed Dang ("red") after her father's favorite color, began lining up with her siblings on the front porch of their home in the evenings. Her mother would strap a kangaroo bucket around their waists, give them each a lantern and a pan, and then lead them all down to the shore like a mother goose. Their objective was to collect little bits of tin, which really wasn't that hard. The big pits carved into the earth in Nam Khem had shoots that ran down to the beach. Most of the tin stuck to rivets on the shoot, but not all of it. With the sand being white and the tin particles being either red or black, it was easy to distinguish the difference by lantern light. When they spotted a deposit of tin, they'd scoop it up in their pan. After a few good twirls, most of the sand would have fallen through the holes in the bottom of their pan, and they'd dump what remained into the kangaroo buckets strapped around their waists. Sometimes they made 3,000 baht after a month of labor, and sometimes they made only 300. Either way, the family still struggled.

Dang's father had come to Nam Khem five years before her birth, after losing his job in his hometown near the Malay border. He had built the family two makeshift shelters out of grass and cardboard boxes along the village's southern border, a formerly uninhabited section of jungle known as Laem Pom. A few years later, after earning a reputation around town as an honest, loyal, and tremendously hard worker, he got hired as a supervisor to control all the workers in a tin mine and saved enough money to replace the lean-tos with a hut. In 1974, his wife gave birth to Somkid Kaewaied, a healthy boy. They were so happy with him that they decided to have a fourth child. This time they didn't have enough money to go to the hospital, so they asked an elderly woman into their hut to help with the delivery. The first thing Dang's hands touched, her mother later told her, was the land of Laem Pom.

Dang's earliest memory was jumping over the baby coconut trees her father had planted along the beach to replace the pine trees that had been cut down to build homes in and around the market in Nam Khem. Her father, a tall, thin man with dark skin from a lifetime of outdoor labor, saw her mischievous game and shouted, "If you kill my coconut trees, you'll be in trouble!" Dang ran giggling to the hammock and climbed on top, joining her sister on her mother's lap. Her fun continued as she began running free with her brother Somkid through the jungle surrounding their home. On occasion their adventures would lead them close to the village, and they'd hunker down in the bushes and watch the gruff-looking men working down in big holes in the earth. Many nights she'd hear gunfire off in the distance. Some mornings she would find dead bodies washed up on shore. The dead people always frightened her, but every time she grew afraid, there was always someone nearby to comfort her. Laem Pom had filled up with twenty families, most of whom were relatives or friends of her father's. She could walk into any home in the area at any time of the day and be greeted with a hug and a kiss.

The good times didn't last long. Tin mining became extremely territorial, and Yew, her father's boss, finally got bumped out of business. Her father took odd jobs working as a laborer. He cleared patches of jungle for crops, cleaned a local fish farm, and worked in construction. It just wasn't enough, and they went hungry a lot of the time. At the end of the day, when just a small plate of rice sat on the table for all to share, each child would get two spoonfuls, which they would wash down with a glass of what her mother liked to call "milk." It wasn't until many years later that Dang learned that the white fluid she drank every night of her youth was actually the water the rice had been cooked in, mixed with a touch of sugar. When things got really bad, the family held a meeting. It was decided that the kids needed to start pulling their own weight, and soon thereafter every child began wandering the beach in the evening in search of tin.

But it still wasn't enough to keep the family afloat. Shortly after Dang turned eleven, her father picked her up at school one day with a glum face. Dang already knew what he would say. Tears started to roll down her cheeks, but her father had no choice other than to speak right through them. He told her that for the time being, they needed to save every baht they earned. He no longer could afford to keep her in school. She wanted to shout at her father to find another job, find some way to make more money, but instead she nodded and kissed her father on the cheek. She told him that she understood, even though she didn't. The following day, a few months into the sixth grade, she said good-bye to the few friends she had made and her teachers. It was the last day of schooling she would ever receive.

The following week, her mother took her around the village to find a job. It was hard to find an employer who wanted to hire an eleven-year-old girl, but eventually a small salon shop took her in. Dang would have to leave home and live in the back room of the shop. She had never spent a single night away from Laem Pom. The first month was rough, but when her boss handed her 600 baht, her feelings of loneliness were overpowered by the pride of being able to contribute to her family. Clutching the money in her hand, she ran straight home and gave all of it to her father. He scooped her up in his arms, ruffled her hair, and gave her a big kiss on the cheek. He told her that she had made her father very proud.

Things went downhill from there. For the first thirty days, Dang had only had to work ten hours a day, and she got fed on a regular basis, but now that her boss knew that her family depended on the additional income, the job made in heaven became a living hell. A week into the second month, Dang was shaken awake three hours before normal to start her day. The sun hadn't even come up, yet she was told to scrub the floors, wash her boss's clothes, and prepare breakfast for her boss's family. She worked through the morning, past lunch, and well into the afternoon without so much as a bite to eat. At dinnertime, after cleaning the shop once again, she was given a small plate of rice. The fish or curry or chicken that had sat on top of the rice in the month past had vanished. If she wanted meat, her boss told her, she had to buy it herself.

For two years, Dang endured the abuse, because she didn't want to let her father down. She worked upwards of sixteen hours a day, seven days a week. She had never taken a day off, not even the weeks she had been terribly sick, yet she still made the same monthly wage as when she had started. She had grown sick and tired of her boss's demands and the belittling comments made by the other women who worked in the shop, and one day she voiced her disdain. Her boss exploded in a rage. Dang told her that if she wanted to fight, she was ready. Her boss backed down. Dang gathered her things and walked out the door.

After a brief spell living back home, Dang took a waitress job in a restaurant along the highway almost fifty miles south of Nam Khem. Hitching a ride to work her first day, she passed the statues of two famous heroines. Dang vaguely knew their story. Hundreds of years before, back when the capital had been in the south of Thailand, the Prince had left to attend to business in the north and placed the safety of his kingdom in the hands of his two daughters, best known as Jan and Mook. A Burmese army lying in wait saw opportunity, and they marched on the capital to seize it by force. Jan and Mook quickly erected a fence along the perimeter of the city to keep the Burmese at bay, and then they snatched up swords and took control of the Prince's army. Through a fierce battle, they led the people to victory. Dang wasn't sure if that's exactly how the story had been told to her, but that was the way she remembered it. It brought goose bumps to her arms and kept her imagination occupied for the remainder of the drive.

When she arrived at the restaurant, she began waiting on tables. Her job description had been neatly laid out for her the previous afternoon—stand by the customers' tables, take their order for food, and fill their glasses when empty. Apparently her job description had changed sometime in the past twenty-four hours, because now the customers, most of whom were middle-aged men, wanted her to sit down at the tables and fraternize with them. Dang refused each request, but then one man decided to reach a hand between her legs and clamp on to her crotch. Instantly the two heroines Jan and Mook flashed into Dang's mind. Without thinking, she dumped the beer over the man's head. He still didn't let go, so she crashed the bottle she held into his temple. He got the point and let go. Less than a minute later, her boss literally threw her out into the street.

It got tough after that. She worked a series of backbreaking construction jobs. Eventually, she managed to land a low-paying job at a restaurant in Nam Khem. Each day became more dismal than the last, but then a pleasant surprise caught her off guard.

His name was Tueng Kongwatmai, a good-looking young man whose well-to-do parents owned a butcher shop in the market. He wore fancy clothes and attended school in Bangkok. Dang couldn't figure out why a boy with so much going for him would want to spend every afternoon in her shop.

A few weeks later, her boss saw what was going on and immediately tried to put a stop to anything before it could start. Dang was her best worker, and she couldn't afford to lose her to a smooth-talking young man who had money in the bank.

"I know who that is," she said to Dang. "That boy smokes marijuana and breaks beer bottles in the street. I'm telling you to stay away from him. Turn your back to him the next time he comes here to eat."

The next time he came in, Dang wasn't sure what to do. She had worked since she was six years old. Her hands and back and feet hurt all the time. She wanted to have some fun. She decided to smile at Tueng as he took a seat. He waved her over.

"I've heard about you," he said.

"What have you heard?"

"I've heard that you are very poor, but I can also see that you're a hard worker. I admire that."

"I've also heard about you," she said. "I heard that you smoke marijuana and drink alcohol. I'm not an easy girl. I don't go running around with boys."

"I know, and that's part of the reason why I like you."

"I probably shouldn't be talking with you. You're a troublemaker."

"You have to give me a chance. I will be a better man. I just want to be your friend. Can you do that for me?"

She nodded casually, but inside she radiated. She thought that no man would ever like her. She was sixteen years old; her hands were already calloused, and her skin was dark from her having spent long days under the sun. The light-skinned girls always received the attention, their pale complexions being viewed as a sign of class. She didn't wear dresses or skirts but rather tattered old pants and T-shirts that were given away free with packets of batteries. She still had only three bras and three pairs of underwear. If he was willing to give her a chance, then she could certainly give him one.

He came in every day for a month to eat and chat, and it drove Dang's boss crazy with jealousy. She began working Dang harder and harder, keeping her in the kitchen as long as possible so she couldn't see Tueng. But if Tueng didn't see Dang inside, he would wait for her outside when she got her break. After several months of making small talk and exchanging smiles and glances, Tueng approached her one afternoon after work to ask her if she would go with him to the fair at Yanyao Temple, located on the highway a few miles north of the village.

"There are so many things I want to show you," he said. "They're going to have a magic show, people walking on charcoal, things like that. You have to go with me."

Dang had never before been to a fair. Before she could accept, however, she first had to ask permission from her boss. She went to her with big eyes and pouting lips, but before Dang could even finish her sentence, her boss gave her a firm "No." Dang had to obey. Her boss fed her, housed her, and gave her a paycheck at the end of the month. As long as she worked at the shop, her boss had the final say in all matters of her life.

Dang went back and reluctantly told Tueng that she couldn't go and that they probably shouldn't see each other anymore. From the look on his face, it felt like she had just stabbed him in the back. He sped off on his motorbike, and Dang expected that was the last she would see of him. But he came to the shop the following afternoon to once again ask her to the fair. It was the final day. Now or never.

"But I already told you that I can't go," she said.

"I'm not going to give up that easily. I like you. I like everything about you. You said that you would give me a chance, so you have to go to the fair with me. Like I said, there are so many things I want to show you."

Images of men walking on hot coals, and magicians making rabbits disappear popped into Dang's mind. Without so much as going back into the shop to get her change purse, she jumped onto the back of Tueng's motorbike, and off they went.

As they walked from booth to booth, Dang stood well away from him, at least three feet at all times. She was convinced that if she held his hand, or even stood too close to him, she could get pregnant. But she still had a wonderful time. They laughed and played games. By the time Dang thought to check the time, it was already eleven p.m. She knew that if she went back to the shop now, her boss would be waiting for her, ready to dish out a beating. She figured it would be much safer to give her boss some time to cool off, so she decided to head back in the morning. She asked Tueng to take her to her auntie's house. He acted like a perfect gentleman, rushing her over there on his motorbike and then leaving her at the front door without so much as a good-night kiss.

When Dang crawled into bed, a full range of emotions ran through her. She feared the repercussions of her actions, but at the same time she felt alive for the first time in years. She fell asleep with the memory of Tueng's aftershave. A few hours later, she awoke to a living nightmare. Her boss had spread rumors that she had slept with Tueng out of wedlock. When Dang headed to work, her father was already on the hunt. He dragged her home and told her that she was no longer allowed out of the house. And Tueng's parents were furious that he wanted to be with a girl so poor. But none of that mattered to Tueng. He quit school in Bangkok and got a job on a local fishing boat. When he caught a big load, he always brought Dang at least a couple of fish. Despite all the forces trying to keep them apart, they fell in love. When Tueng came to her father with a pile of money, asking for his daughter's hand in marriage, her father smiled at him for the first time.

"I am a poor man, but I do not need to sell my daughter," he said. "But you are going to have to move into my house and show everyone that you two are now together. If you do that, I will accept you into the family."

Dang had never expected marriage to make life any easier, but she was surprised when it made things a whole lot more difficult. A few months after Tueng moved into her father's home, she got pregnant. Her husband's parents had cut him off financially, and his job as a fisherman didn't pay much. Dang ended up having to work at a host of construction sites until she was eight months pregnant. Most of the sites were located miles from Nam Khem, and she saw less and less of her family. She would have worked up until the day she went into labor, but she didn't want to have her baby on a construction site. She returned to her father's home for the last month and then gave birth to Arthorn Kongwatmai, a beautiful nine-pound boy.

Tueng refused to let her go back to work right away. As a result, Dang spent a few months cradling her baby in her arms while lying in a hammock strung between two of her father's coconut trees, now all grown to amazing heights. During this time, she gazed mindlessly out to sea. She had long talks with her father and dreamed of the day when her boy would be old enough to go exploring through the jungle around her father's home. She realized just how much of Laem Pom was inside of her. She wanted to remain here forever and raise her family between the jungle and the sea. But after her two months of leisure were up, it was back to hauling sacks of cement and digging ditches for forty baht a day. Her job required that she go from village to village, sleeping under trees and in makeshift shelters, so she was forced to leave her son with her father. Months often passed without her getting to see him, and she cried terribly every time she had to say good-bye. She felt as if Laem Pom and the life of her son were slipping away from her, but there wasn't much she could do. She knew now what her father had gone through for so many years. In the back of her mind, she could always see the mouth she had to feed. Six years floated away.

A sickness in the family drew her back for good. Her brother Somkid had dropped from 167 pounds to eighty-eight. He'd worked as a laborer on a fishing boat for a number of years and then gotten promoted to captain. With a pocket full of money at the end of every month, he had started visiting brothels on a regular basis. He fell in love with a prostitute and they moved in together. Dang had discovered this upon one of her visits home, and she had begged him to drop her and find an honest woman. But there had never been any use in trying to talk sense into Somkid. He stayed with her for three years, and then he began to lose weight. Pretty soon he looked skeletal. When the family discovered that he had HIV, their father brought him home, but there was nothing they could do to ease the pain. He grew so weak that he could no longer walk. He wanted to see the sunrise and sunset every day, but when they tried to pick him up, he cringed in pain. They eventually had to place him on a piece of carpet so they could drag him into and out of the house. Dang would sit by his side and search for something to say. She cried a river of tears. Somkid eventually gave up eating. Twenty days later, he was dead.

It shook the family. Dang wanted to move back in to help comfort her father, but with two of her sisters having already moved in with their husbands and children, the house was too full as it was. Dang gave up on construction and got a job selling illegal lottery tickets around town. On a bad day, she earned ten times what she had made working in construction, so she decided it was worth the risk of arrest. After using her money to improve her father's home, she invested in materials for a home of her own and stacked them next to her father's house. When she had everything she needed, Dang spent every evening for the next six months laying the foundation and erecting the support beams. She had little time for sleep, but building a home was more important. She wanted to be able to watch her child run free around Laem Pom, just as she had done with Somkid when they were kids. She finally got pregnant again, after six years of trying, just a few months before her house was complete. She prayed that this one would be a girl, and her prayers were answered. She named her Phunnipha "Kwan" Kongwatmai. She wished that her daughter would find the happiness that came too infrequently in her own life.

5 WICHIEN AND NANG

CHAPTER

Wichien, who had come to Nam Khem at sixteen expecting to work for a year or two and then return to school, was now thirty-one years old, with a wife and a baby son to support. He'd made a lot of money diving for tin, but over the last couple of years, business hadn't been good. There were still rich deposits out at sea, and Wichien still had a knack for finding them. That, however, was part of the problem. When he'd first come, anyone who had a raft and a pump could paddle offshore, drop anchor, and pull up as much tin as they liked. Now every time he picked a spot, he would have only a few minutes on the seafloor before one of his partners on deck signaled that it was time to come up. While climbing the rope, he'd see that another boat had pulled up beside theirs. The moment he surfaced, he'd get confronted by a group of men holding M16s and flashing a piece of paper that stated they had purchased the rights to mine that particular area. Wichien and his crew would move on to another area. Ten minutes later, he'd get called back up to deal with another group of armed men. And when the men on the invading boat didn't have papers to show, they still brandished M16s. Sometimes they would climb onto Wichien's raft, load all the tin he and his co-workers had collected for the day onto their vessel, and then head back to shore.

Wichien had decided that tin mining had become too hazardous for his health. He hung up his mask and rubber shoes and went back to being a laborer. His wife, Nang, got pregnant again the following year. To prepare financially for the arrival of their second child, Nang started coming to work with him. They spent their days hauling heavy loads of cement up and down a hill on a small island not far from Nam Khem, but after Nang had a nasty fall and tumbled nearly a hundred yards down a slope, Wichien refused to let her work any longer. Their baby's life was too important. He would figure out something else.

The same year his daughter was born, Wichien joined forces with a few of his friends and the captain of a longtail boat. They set into the Andaman Sea, and by midday they had crossed into Burmese water. Lobsters had been picked dry in Thailand due to dynamite fishing and hundreds upon hundreds of traps set on the bottom of the sea, but Burma was still untapped. They cruised the foreign waters for an hour or more, searching for any sign of a buoy that dangled a horde of Burmese lobster traps. Eventually they found one. They pulled the traps to the surface, slid open the gates, and then snatched every lobster inside. With nervous smiles on their faces, they rushed back to Nam Khem to sell their stolen goods at the market.

They set out again the following week with a revised plan. Their first trip had been spontaneous, and they hadn't really considered the worst-case scenarios. If one of the dozen or so fiberglass Burmese patrol boats that cruised the sea border had spotted them, none of them would have made it back alive. The patrol boats were easily three times as fast as their longtail; the soldiers on board would have caught up with them and then put four or five bullets in each of their bodies.

To ensure that this didn't happen on any subsequent mission, they decided to pilfer only the traps located near Burmese islands. If a patrol boat spotted them, they'd start their motor and head directly for the closest one. Before abandoning the boat and their pilfered lobsters, one of them would grab the cooking pot they'd brought along, another the hefty bag of rice, and another a few jugs of water. They would grab as much as they could carry and then sprint off into the jungle and hide.

On the second trip, their contingency plan became a reality. The moment they saw a patrol boat off in the distance, they cranked up their motor and raced to the nearest island. They snatched up their supplies and then went running off into the jungle. They figured the soldiers would look for them for a little while and then get bored and give up. That's exactly what happened, but they hadn't considered what the soldiers would do to their boat before shoving off. Two hours after he had climbed a small hill and dove into a bush, Wichien walked down to shore to find that their longtail boat had been reduced to a pile of ash. There wasn't a Burmese soldier in sight, but Wichien could see them in his mind's eye. The soldiers had just stranded a group of their sworn enemies on an uninhabited Burmese island in the middle of the Andaman Sea. They were probably still laughing their heads off.

Luckily, they had to spend only one night on the island. When they hadn't returned, one of their friends who knew of their escape plan had come searching for them in his longtail. By chance, he happened to head to the right island. They headed back to Nam Khem to hug and kiss their wives and tell their story of adventure to their friends. The whole ordeal made it all too clear what could happen while burgling at sea, but after a couple of weeks, they began talking differently about their run-in with the Burmese patrol boat. They talked about their narrow escape as a victory. If on the off chance they were caught in the act again, they could simply run to the nearest island. The soldiers would undoubtedly burn their boat, but as long as they brought an old, dilapidated longtail, their ventures could still prove profitable. It seemed foolproof. They headed out again, only this time they brought a bigger pan and a larger sack of rice. It came in quite handy. At least once a month, Burmese soldiers spotted them pilfering lobsters and chased them down. The occasional bullet whistled over their heads, but because they never strayed far from an island, they always managed to reach solid ground before getting overtaken.

Despite the money he earned, Wichien's new profession bothered him morally. He seriously contemplated going back to mining tin. After all, it couldn't have been any more dangerous than his current line of work. But in addition to the territorial problems that had made him quit diving in the first place, the tin supply had finally started to dry up. Perhaps he could earn a few hundred baht a week, but that wouldn't be enough to feed his family. He had promised them that he would finish renovating the house in the next couple of years. Just six more months of pilfering lobsters and he would give up this nasty profession for good.

Those six months came and went, and still he continued to venture into Burmese waters with his crew. Their luck ran out in February 1997.

This time he had gone with six crew members instead of three, so they had brought a captain with a bigger boat into the picture. It was still considered a longtail, but it came equipped with a little control room in which the captain could sit under an awning and steer the boat. Because of the size of their vessel, they decided to go out under the cover of darkness. They made it across the border without a hitch and even found a Burmese trap teeming with fresh lobsters. But a 150-foot Burmese patrol boat was closing in on them in the pitch dark from the east. Wichien didn't notice anything out of the ordinary until he turned to place a lobster in a trough on deck. The lobster fell from his hands as his eyes turned upward. Directly above him, on the deck of the patrol boat, stood a dozen grinning Burmese soldiers holding semiautomatic rifles.

The night lit up with gunfire. Wichien dove into the captain's control room, curled into a ball in the corner, and stared out onto the deck. He saw bits of the boat get torn away and chunks of lobster spray across the deck. He hoped the soldiers were just giving them a warning, having a little fun, but then he saw one of his friends take a bullet to the head. They put a few bullets into his chest just to be sure he was dead. Then two more of his friends were riddled with bullets. Against all his instincts, Wichien reached a hand out from the corner he had burrowed himself into and hit the throttle. The longtail smacked into the patrol boat, bounced off, and then lurched forward into the night. The patrol boat crawled right alongside of them, matching their speed. The soldiers continued to put hundreds of rounds into the boat. Bullets tore through the walls and roof of the captain's room. One of the bullets entered a three-gallon canister of gas they stored in there. There was an explosion, and almost instantly Wichien could smell his flesh burning.

Knowing his life could end at any second, Wichien scrambled across the floor through the fire in the captain's room. He found a plastic water jug that he could use as a buoy. Then he scrambled to his feet, ran out across the deck of the longtail, and leapt into the sea. His body sunk deep, and he could hear bullets slicing through the water all around him. He tried desperately to swim away from the longtail. Eventually he could no longer hear bullets diving through the sea. He surfaced and found that he had traveled only twenty feet away from the boat.

The soldiers didn't see him; they were shooting at the longtail again, shouting. Wichien slipped quietly away into the darkness.

Twenty minutes later, he stopped his frantic dog paddle so he could turn back and look. The soldiers had stopped shooting some time ago. Their ship was gone, but Wichien could see the longtail ablaze in the distance, slowly sinking into the water. He had seen three of his friends die for certain. He didn't know if the other two, Ratt and Dum, had made it out alive. He couldn't think about that now. If he planned to survive, he needed to get to an island. It would be difficult. He was exhausted, and the waves were quite large. They kept pushing him closer and closer to mainland Burma.

He swam for half an hour and then stopped. He wasn't getting anywhere. The gallon jug tucked underneath his shirt kept his head above water, and he drifted for three hours. With each wave he went over, his left arm began to hurt more and more. He had seen some part of his body catch fire during the explosion, and he assumed now that his arm had gotten badly burned and the saltwater was stinging it. Soon the pain became intolerable, so he reluctantly lifted his left arm from the water. He had gotten burned indeed, but he had also been shot. A bullet had torn through one side of his biceps and then out the other. Another bullet had entered the top of his forearm. He turned his arm over to find an exit wound, but there wasn't one. The bullet was still inside him. He began to panic, so he submerged his arm. Assuming he would die if he didn't reach an island soon, he fought through his exhaustion and began to swim again.

Hours passed, but the sun never seemed to rise. Eventually he spotted what looked like an island ahead in the darkness and went for it. He reached the shore twenty minutes later. The sand was soft and inviting. His entire body screamed with thirst, his stomach grumbled in pain, and blood leaked from the three holes in his arm. He was exhausted. He let his face fall down on top of a wooden stump, and moments later he passed out.

The sun had just come up when he awoke. His head throbbed terribly and his arm ached. A few bugs had crawled into his wounds. He picked them out, tied his shirt around the bullet hole in his forearm to help stop the bleeding, and then went searching around the island for help. He found none. The island was totally uninhabited. To make matters worse, he could find no fresh water. He began combing the narrow beach in search of trash that had washed ashore. In minutes he found what he was looking for—another plastic water jug. He festooned both jugs to his cotton belt and set back into the water, destined for the small island he could see off in the distance.

At the halfway point between the two islands, he stopped swimming. He looked back at the island from which he had come, then at the island to which he headed. The new vantage point allowed him to get his bearings. Previously he had been on Ling Island, and in front of him stood Khang Island. He had never actually stepped foot on either one before, but just knowing where he was calmed him somewhat.

When he reached shore, he knew he needed water, any kind of water, so he crawled on all fours into the jungle. He found a stagnant puddle in the mud and tasted it to see if it contained any salt. It was pure. At that moment he didn't care how long it had been sitting there or how many mosquitoes had dropped their eggs on the surface. He drank with his face in the puddle until it was nearly gone.

He staggered to his feet and began to wander. He'd assumed that the island was uninhabited, but ten minutes into his wandering, he came across a group of Burmese hunkered down behind some trees. Wichien and the men jumped back at the sight of each other. They stared at each other for a few moments. Wichien wondered why they seemed as scared of him as he was of them; after all, this was their country. Then he caught sight of the chain saws scattered around and realized they were pirates just like him. They had come to the island to illegally cut trees. He stepped slowly forward with the intention of somehow showing them he was their friend, but he didn't even need to open his mouth. They caught sight of the bullet wounds in his arm and realized they all had the same enemy—Burmese soldiers.

They laid Wichien down on a patch of grass and poured fresh water into his mouth from a jug. Then they produced a bag that contained basic medical supplies. After feeding him antibiotics and aspirin, they went about cleaning his wound. One of them had a knife strapped to his belt, and Wichien pointed to it and then to the wound in his arm, which had swollen to twice its normal size. He wanted them to take out the remaining bullet, but none of them dared, for fear that they would kill him. They dressed his arm in strips of fabric instead.

Wichien needed to find his way back home. He drew a picture in the mud of a boat and asked if they had one. They did, but it wasn't here at the moment. It made sense; they were in the business of illegally cutting trees. If they kept their boat docked just offshore, it would surely be discovered by Burmese soldiers and burned to the ground.

From what Wichien gathered, their boat would return in five days. At that time, they would be more than happy to take him back to Thai waters for a small fee. Wichien thanked them and agreed, but that night he became certain that he wouldn't last for five days. He came down with a high fever. He assumed he had contracted malaria from drinking out of the stagnant pond. He tried to forget the pain in his arm and the even greater pain he felt because he would never see his wife or kids again.

In the night, several times he heard the sound of a longtail boat and went running to the shore. Each time, he saw nothing but an open expanse of sea. He thought his mind was playing tricks on him. He heard a similar sound the following afternoon and almost ignored it. He decided to head down just in case, and this time he did see a boat. He recognized it immediately. It belonged to a lady named Nui, a good friend of his. He figured she had rented it out for the day so his friends could come find him. He stripped off his shirt and waved it madly in the air. He shouted at the top of his voice. It appeared as though the captain of the boat saw him, but then the boat spun around and began heading back toward Thai waters. Wichien fell to his knees and began to cry. That was his last hope of survival. When he finally peeled his hands away from his face, he saw the boat again. It had come back. What the hell was going on?

As it crept upon the shore of the island, Wichien saw his good friend Pae standing on deck.

"You came to rescue me," Wichien shouted.

"No," his friend replied. "I had no idea you were out here. What the hell are you doing? And what the hell happened to your arm?"

"I got shot."

"By who?"

"By the Burmese soldiers."

"And the rest of the boys?"

"I saw three of them die. Ratt and Dum, I don't know where they are. Haven't seen them since after the shooting began."

"You know we almost left you?"

"I noticed. Why the hell would you do that?"

"The captain over there thought you were a soldier. We came to get lobster, and he's been scared ever since we left Nam Khem. I told him that even if you were a soldier, there was just one of you. I convinced him to come back and have a look."

"You saved my life," Wichien said, choked up with emotion. "I owe you my life."

Pae jumped off the deck and helped Wichien aboard. Before they headed out, Wichien grabbed a pile of magazines, cigarettes, and some food and handed it down to the Burmese wood pirates. He wished he could have given them more, but they seemed more than satisfied with his offering.

Despite the danger of running into another Burmese patrol boat, they made laps around all the nearby islands in search of Ratt and Dum. On their third lap around Ling Island, the one Wichien had been stranded on first, they saw a strange lump in the sand on the coast. They drew closer to investigate, and they found Ratt on the beach, where he had buried himself to be protected from mosquitoes.

They continued looking for Dum, and an hour after rescuing Ratt, they heard over the radio that another Thai boat had plucked a badly dehydrated man from the water. Clinging on to an empty water jug, Dum had drifted at sea for nearly forty hours. Wichien smiled, but it didn't last long. Now that the adrenaline was beginning to fade, images came leaping to the front of his mind. He had seen three of his friends die. Never again would he be the same.

By the time they reached the harbor in Nam Khem, Wichien no longer had the strength to walk. He was placed into the bed of a truck next to Ratt, and the two of them were taken to Takupa Hospital. Later that evening, shortly after getting the bullet dug from his arm, Wichien promised Buddha that he would be good from now on and never, ever again venture into Burmese waters to steal lobsters. The second part of the promise, he managed to keep, but the part about being good, he found harder to fulfill. The whole ordeal haunted him. While still lying in the hospital bed, he began sipping from a flask of whiskey and smoking a cigarette every couple of hours. His scrape with death had slaughtered any remaining innocence.

Wichien's wounds got infected, and he remained in the hospital for fifteen days. In order to pay the expensive bills, Nang had to find a job. Nam Khem wasn't exactly overflowing with opportunity. After a three-day search, she managed to get hired by a local coconut merchant. Instead of peddling the coconuts, however, she would be collecting them. Her job was to scale the trees, using only her feet and hands, and then find some way to hold on so she could hack the coconuts down with a machete. Despite her fragile appearance, her hands and feet were short and wide and strong. She learned quickly and got one baht for every coconut she felled. When she came to Wichien with more than 1,000 baht one afternoon for the hospital bill, he couldn't imagine how many trees she must have scaled. It broke his heart and wounded his pride that she had to work at such an awful job.

The first night that Wichien returned home, he made love with his wife. The next morning, he packed his suitcase, caught a bus due east across the isthmus, and then got a job diving for natural pearls on the Gulf of Thailand. He found the job much more relaxing than pilfering lobsters or even diving for tin had been, and getting a nice cut from all the pearls that he found, he managed to save up enough to finally finish the renovations on his home. His life finally started to come together. He had a good job, a beautiful family, and a house near the beach. He had no idea what lurked around the corner.

Wimon's life was completely different now. He had given up dessert making, kickboxing, and even Nam Khem for good. Shortly after Wimon moved to Phuket, his elder sister Thasanee decided to join him on the big island. She rented an apartment in Phuket Town, located approximately ten miles from the endless stretch of bungalows and hotel/resorts that had sprung up along the beach over the past decade. Wimon had been living in a cramped, one-room hovel with his mother, and when Thasanee proposed the idea of having them both move into her spacious apartment, Wimon jumped at the chance. His mother, however, wasn't thrilled; she actually preferred the one-room hovel, because it meant she could be closer to Wimon. He eventually talked her into it by promising to purchase a home of their very own in the near future.

Business on the island had proved quite lucrative. Each morning, he packed the sidecar attached to his motorbike with fresh and pickled fruit and then drove slowly around town, ringing a bell. He did quite well selling to businessmen in the downtown area at lunchtime, but nothing compared to the business he drummed up at the pier. His best customer there was a pretty nineteen-year-old girl named Watcharee Ruengkaew, who worked thirteen hours a day cleaning fish. Without fail, she purchased a handful of his fruit and gave him a big smile every time she saw him. He collected her money, gave her change, and returned a smile of his own. He could tell that she liked him, but he smiled back only to be polite. He still didn't own a home, which meant, in his mind, that he could not yet get married. He would have avoided the pier altogether to avoid her, but he couldn't afford to lose her business.

Things continued to improve. Each week, he got a new loyal customer, and he was saving a considerable sum of money on rent by living with his sister. There was nothing exciting or extraordinary about his life. Everything had become very routine, and although it was a bit boring, it was better than having to run down to the beach on a moment's notice and watch his home burn to the ground. He enjoyed the conversations he had with his patrons along his route, and he steered far away from drama when he saw it unfolding. When he looked into the future, he saw nothing that he didn't see every day of the week. It was still somehow wonderful.

Then, one morning six months after he had come to the island, he went to the pier as usual and waited for Watcharee. Instead of seeing her slender figure off in the distance, however, he saw the figures of three overweight, middle-aged women scurrying toward him as fast as their short legs would allow. He figured that between the three of them, they would buy his entire stock for the day, but as it turned out, they wanted nothing to do with his fruit. They were relatives of Watcharee's, and they each broke off into simultaneous speech as to why Watcharee would be the perfect girl for him to marry. They were all adamant about not allowing him to leave until he gave them an answer.

Wimon couldn't understand what all the fuss was about. He didn't have much money, he didn't have smashing good looks, and he still lived with his mother. Apparently, none of that mattered to Watcharee and her relatives. They told him that she was a sweet girl and a hard worker. This he already knew. They told him that she would make a good wife, and this he knew as well. Then they told him that if he couldn't make up his mind, they would instruct her to move on with her life and find a man who was willing to accept the responsibility. Wimon gave it a few moments of thought, and then he told the ladies that he liked what he saw in Watcharee and that he would marry her. After all, she had purchased his fruit every day for the past six months. He figured that the least he could do in exchange was become her husband. He still didn't own his own home, but he had saved enough to buy one in the near future.

That evening, Wimon took his time going home. When he finally mustered the courage to go upstairs and break the news to his mother, he wished he never had agreed to marry Watcharee. His mother was devastated. She claimed that the girl wasn't right for him, even though she had never met her. She also refused to go with Wimon to ask Watcharee's parents for their daughter's hand in marriage, which was Thai tradition. Wimon ended up going on his own, but everything turned out just fine. He found both of Watcharee's parents to be honorable people, and he began to warm up to the idea of marrying their daughter. If she took after her folks, things would turn out just fine. Before he left, they had all agreed to hold the wedding in the countryside outside of Phatthalung, which was where Watcharee had spent her youth.

The wedding was a lovely traditional ceremony. The only thing Wimon would have changed about that day was his mother's state of mind. She fumed silently in the back row and refused to talk with anyone.

He hoped his mother would warm to Watcharee when she moved in with them, but that was not the case. She made no attempt to hide her disdain for the new woman in his life. She refused to let them sit next to each other while she was in the room, and if she caught them holding hands, she'd throw a fit. For the first several months, she insisted that they sleep on opposite sides of the room. His wife wasn't happy about it, but she respected the bond he had with his mother and managed to hold her tongue.

With his mother ensuring that he didn't build a family anytime soon, Wimon concentrated on his small business, which generated more profits each month. As his money grew, he started looking into buying a small apartment somewhere near his sister's apartment in Phuket Town, but his mother quickly threw a monkey wrench into his plans. The city had too many people, she said, and she couldn't stand listening to the loud noises of the cars. Wimon asked her what she wanted to do.

"I want to go back to Nam Khem," she said.

In the beginning of 1996, after four years on the big island, Wimon packed his wife, mother, and the few possessions they had into his sidecar, and they all went back to the village perched between the jungle and sea. Three of his older brothers, Nikhom, Prakong, and Sukhon, had all used their savings from the old tin-mining days to each purchase a longtail boat and build homes side by side on a narrow plot of land near the beach. Wimon, now forty-one, thought it was about time that he started a family of his own. His brothers couldn't agree more. They sold him a sliver of their property on the beach for very little, and then they helped him build a home where he could live with his wife and their mother. Ten months after the home's completion, Watcharee gave birth to a beautiful baby girl. They wrote the name Rattikan Thongtae in the record book at the hospital, but she quickly became known as Frame.

Soon Wimon's younger brother, Supit, whose father had been murdered years before at the fair in Cha-uat, came to Nam Khem and built a home next to Wimon's. Neither knew how they would support their families in the long run. Their older brothers convinced them to join them in the fishing business, and a few days later, Wimon and Supit both bought longtails. The five brothers had officially become a family of fishermen.

Every morning at the crack of dawn, they all headed out to sea. They used rods and nets to catch their fish and looked down on those who used dynamite, because it seemed unnatural. The mornings that nothing bit, they told an array of jokes and headed home early. The days that they pulled vast amounts of fish from the water, they remained out until well past dark. On occasion, Wimon brought Watcharee. She worked hard, just as her relatives had claimed, but most of the time they would purposely drift away from Wimon's brothers in order to get some alone time, still a precious commodity, given his mother's watchful eye.

As time went on, they became successful. Wimon experienced a happiness he never thought possible. He lived close to the sea, next to his brothers. He had a beautiful wife and a lovely daughter, and he never strayed far from his mother's side. Feeling secure in life for the first time, Wimon and his wife decided to have another child. In October 2001, his wife gave birth to Sudarat Thongtae, who quickly became known as Film. Wimon fell in love with the little bundle of life the first moment he laid eyes on her. Every afternoon, still covered with grime after a hard day out at sea, he'd pick her up and cradle her in his arms, gazing into her little black eyes.

PUEK AND LEK

When Puek, the young tattooed fisherman, had gone to Lek's house and asked her parents if he could take her to the fair, Lek hadn't been certain that she wanted to go. Over the past few years, she had heard a lot about him. He supposedly had many other girlfriends, always got into fights, and drank heavily. She knew that he had loved his late mother dearly and that he fought so often because he was overly protective of his friends, but his large muscles and good looks frightened her as much as they appealed to her. As a fisherman, he had traveled all over the country, seen things she couldn't imagine, and experienced things she didn't know existed, and he might want to be with her in a way that she could not allow. She was twenty-five years old, and she still wanted nothing to do with men.

In the end, however, the idea of going to a fair had seemed too good to pass up. She had climbed onto the back of his Kawasaki motorcycle, but instead of taking her to the fair, he took her to a friend's house out in the country. When she escaped during the night and fled to a nearby market to catch a bus home, he tracked her down and took her to his sister's house in a foreign town. With every hour that passed, the chance of her parents accepting her back into their home diminished. Eventually, she made the decision to stay with him, and they were married shortly thereafter.

Now that months had passed, she began to regret her decision. They had run out of money. Before Puek would head off to faraway places to find work, he would promise to visit often. He kept that promise for a while, coming by once every two weeks, but now his visits had grown few and far between. Having no friends in the foreign village and uncertain about where to find a job, Lek spent the majority of her time gazing out the window for any sign of her husband. She felt she had become a terrible burden to Puek's sister, and she missed her family more than she could describe.

Four months into her new life, things got even more confusing. While taking a bath one morning, she noticed that her body had begun to change. She hadn't had her period since shortly after she had arrived but thought little of it. But now her belly had begun to swell. Her breasts had grown large and firm. The thought of bringing a baby into this world filled her with so much love, but it also terrified her.

She stood naked in the bathroom for the longest time, gazing at her stomach in the mirror. Puek hadn't contacted her in nearly a month. Would he expect her to raise this child alone in his sister's house? Her head began to spin, and nausea swept over her. She put on her clothes and began to pack her things. There were so many places Puek could have gone, but she suspected that he had probably returned to their hometown of Prachuap Khiri Khan to run wild with his friends. Lek didn't know whether Puek would have the courage to face the responsibility that lay inside of her, but the only way to find out was to give him the news. She took one last look at her belly in the mirror and then lugged her small suitcase down to the bus station.

The sights and smells of her hometown brought a flood of memories back to her, but she found them more depressing than comforting. She began the long walk across town. When she reached the house of Puek's elder sister, she hesitantly climbed the stairs to the front porch. A young girl with a belly even more swollen than hers answered the door. Before Lek could ask who she was, Puek's sister stepped between them. She took Lek by the arm and pulled her into the front yard to explain the situation.

"That's Puek's wife," she said, pointing to the other girl. "He accidentally got her pregnant, and now she has come to live with us. I assume you have also come here to stay with us, but as you can see, that wouldn't work out. My house would get torn apart if both of you tried living under my roof. I'm so sorry for all of this. Puek has been a very bad boy."

Lek looked into her eyes. "But I'm Puek's wife."

"That is something Puek has to work out. I'm sorry, but you have to go."

Lek left in a fit of tears, completely heartbroken. She wandered the streets of her hometown for several hours, trying to calm herself with familiar sights, but she soon realized that she no longer had a home. Her auntie was the only person who might help. Her parents had never forgiven her for running away with Puek, but perhaps her auntie would take her in. She walked across town and then stood in front of her auntie's house. She had always been poor, but it looked as if recent years had been particularly rough. Her thatched hut had huge holes in the walls and roof, and when Lek got invited inside, she found all the food cupboards bare. Lek promised that she would do what she could to pull her own weight, and her auntie said she would have to, because otherwise they would both starve. Lek slept that night on the floor and dreamt of the comfortable life she had lost as the result of a single decision.

The next day, she went down to the pier and got a job lifting heavy buckets of fish off the boat and carrying them over to the bin for washing. It was either work or starve. One afternoon, she felt sick, but she ignored the pain and continued to work. A few minutes later, warmth washed between her legs. Blood covered the lower half of her body. She cleaned herself up and went back to work. Four days later, she still felt sick and her skin had gone pale. She had also lost the firmness in her breasts. Fearing the worst, she took the little money she had saved and went to the hospital.

"Did you have an abortion?" the doctor asked sternly.

"Never," Lek said. "Abortions are illegal, and I would never kill my own baby."

"Well, this certainly looks like an abortion."

Lek instantly felt pain in her heart, in her whole body—she had lost her baby. The doctor cleaned her womb, scolded her for getting an abortion she had never had, and then sent her on her way. She limped home and then curled up on the floor. In the depth of her misery, Puek came by to see her.

She told him everything, expecting that he would run off and never return. Instead, he sunk down next to her and covered his face with his hands. He cried like a baby and begged for her forgiveness. Lek was still angry with him, but he seemed sincere. Maybe deep down, beneath his muscles and good looks, he was a soft, gentle man after all. She held him in her arms and they cried together.

"I can never make this right," he said. "But I promise you that I will be a good husband, and I will do what is right. I will go see your parents so you can finally go home. I have done so many bad things to you that I can never take back. I will try to make everything up to you. I will do my best, I promise."

She watched him ride away, carrying grief heavily on his shoulders. Lek honestly didn't know if she would ever see him again. Part of her loved him, but there was no way she could count on him to be there for her. He still might just be a wild boy grieving over the loss of his mother, and he would probably get shot or stabbed long before he ever mended his ways. But she had nowhere else to turn.

Puek pushed his motorcycle to tremendous speeds, but no matter how fast he went, the tears continued to flow. He had told Lek that he would make things right with her parents, and this time he planned to keep his promise. To do that, however, he first needed to be honest with everyone he had dragged into his life. The moment he walked into his sister's house, he confronted the girl he had gotten pregnant. He told her that she had to move out, that he planned to sell his motorcycle, his gold jewelry, and all his possessions. He would give that money to the parents of his real wife so that he would be accepted into her family and they could have a proper marriage. He told her that he didn't love her but that he would help support the child.

Puek had chosen the kitchen for this confrontation, and he shortly realized the error of that decision. The girl snatched a butcher knife from the counter and swung for his throat. He dodged back as the knife whirled by. She crumpled to the floor. The knife slid into a corner.

The girl left with hate in her eyes. Puek knew that she would never again be a part of his life. It was better that way, because he truly loved Lek. He would marry her, properly this time, and then they would get pregnant again and start a family. But before any of that could happen, he had to find some way to apologize to her father, who, according to rumor, was ready to kill him. Despite Lek's father's injury to his right hand years before, Puek felt that going over to see him on his own was too risky. He made some inquiries around town and learned that there was a local businessman who happened to be a good friend of Lek's father. He went to the man and told him about everything that had happened. The man went to talk with Lek's father, and then he got back to Puek to tell him how the meeting went.

"I've managed to cool him down a bit," he said. "I made an appointment for you two to talk. He promised not to kill you, but you better show up on time."

Three days later, Puek dressed up in his best clothes and stuffed down into his pocket the 10,000 baht he had earned from selling his motorbike and all his jewelry. Then he went to Lek's parents' house and knocked on the door. Her father answered with a scowl on his face. Puek quickly gave the one-handed man the 10,000 baht.

"You're lucky you sent my friend to talk with me first," he said. "I would have killed you."

Puek nodded. He talked softly, with the best manners he could muster. After an hour of discussing his plans for the future, making one promise after another, Puek was welcomed into the home. Instead of keeping the money, Lek's father gave the money to his daughter so they could get a proper start to their life. It went much easier than Puek had ever imagined. He kicked himself for not having done it sooner.

They used the money to purchase a piece of land near the market and build a small home. Lek got pregnant again, and Puek couldn't have been more thrilled. He tried to become a good, honest husband, but he couldn't do it. His gang of friends talked him into staying out later and later each night, and soon he stayed out with them all night at least four times a week. Everything quickly slid downhill. Within six months, he had gotten into a dozen fights, torn up five barrooms, and been arrested thirteen times. When Lek bailed him out of jail for the fourteenth time, it became quite obvious that she had reached her breaking point.

056

"I have a baby due any week now, and still you go out and get into trouble," she said. "If you want to be with me, if you want to have a family with me, then you need to start acting like a father and a good husband. I have always had a tough life, but now that I am married, my life has gotten only worse. I have to work so many hours—you don't want to lose another child, do you?"

Puek was not used to Lek talking to him this way. Her words resonated with him. He knew that if he was going to change for good, he had to get away from his old friends. He chose to return to Nam Khem. Supposedly, the fishing industry had grown even stronger there in his absence, and he figured it was as good a place as any to earn a few bucks.

When he arrived in the village, he discovered that the casinos and cinemas had mostly vanished, but the whorehouses still remained. He walked straight past them without so much as a second look. He landed a job as a chief on a fishing boat and found himself in charge of twenty-five laborers. He would work for twenty-two days straight and then receive an eight-day break. On his off weeks, once in a while he'd visit the brothels, but usually he rushed straight home with his hard-earned pay to see Lek and his baby girl, whom he had nicknamed Chomphu, after Thailand's sweetest fruit.

Three years passed. After Thailand was struck by Typhoon Gay, Puek's captain abruptly quit, having had enough of the sea after being trapped in the deadly storm. Puek applied for the job. His boss didn't want to give it to him at first, but he eventually came around and Puek got the job.

It was a risky position to accept, because he would work on commission rather than for a salary. If he caught a lot of fish, he got a lot of money. If he caught nothing, he got nothing. Puek wasn't concerned. He had been fishing since he was ten and had the utmost confidence in his skills. He even boasted to a few of his friends that he would shortly become the best fisherman in all of Nam Khem.

As it turned out, he was right. Early each morning, after gathering up all the men and the new chief of the boat, he would head out past the offshore tin-mining operations, which no longer consisted of raft boats but rather big ships that had strung massive pipes down to the seafloor, and then glide deep into open waters. Using sonar, radar, and satellite imagery, he would begin the hunt for a school of fish. The moment he found one, his crew would drop the nets and then spend the next eight or ten hours hauling them in. The captains of many other boats claimed that the waters had been bled dry, but Puek never had a problem finding the large schools. Every time he returned to the pier in Nam Khem, his boat would be filled to capacity, 33,000 pounds, grossing more than a million baht for his boss. Puek's boss rewarded him by taking him to fancy restaurants in his BMW convertible and buying him expensive bottles of whiskey.

In a few months, Puek became the talk of Nam Khem. In a year, he became the talk of the entire fishing industry in southern Thailand. Fishermen came from miles around just to meet him and hopefully learn his secret.

He sent money home to Lek on a weekly basis, but as his popularity grew in Nam Khem, he found it harder to leave during his days off. There was always a party to attend or someone who wanted to take him out for drinks. There was always some girl who looked too good to walk away from. These were his glory years, and he didn't want to miss a single moment.

Back in Prachuap Khiri Khan, Lek struggled to make ends meet. Her husband sent money, but not knowing how long the good times would last, she stashed every baht he sent under her mattress and lived off the money that she made. She sold pastries out of a small shop she had opened up in front of her home. The long hours didn't get to her, but the loneliness did. She spent all her free time cuddling Chomphu.

She gave Puek some slack, because she knew he was trying hard this time. When he came home on his days off, he always brought presents and took her to nice restaurants. Soon, though, the rumors about Puek's activities in Nam Khem began to reach her in Prachuap Khiri Khan. Despite everything she'd heard about how wild and dangerous Nam Khem was, in the end she decided that it would be much more damaging for Chomphu to be raised without a father. She was going to Nam Khem to save their marriage whether he liked it or not.

Puek was shocked to see Lek and Chomphu standing on his doorstep, but he rushed to embrace them. He asked her if something terrible had happened, and she told him that it had. She had heard about the mischief he had been making over the past couple of years. He didn't attempt to deny it. He encouraged her to stay in Nam Khem and assured her that he would put the other women aside and focus on the family. As always, he did well for a while. But soon he was involved in the nightlife once again. Now Lek realized that the only way he would ever truly be hers was if he learned a lesson.

One afternoon, Puek went to a neighboring village, where his boat was docked, to check in on his workers. Lek knew that this would take only an hour, and when he still hadn't come back in two hours, she hopped on her scooter and went looking for him. When there was no sign of him in or around the boat, she headed down the street to a bar where Puek liked to drink whiskey with his friends. Taking a deep breath, she tucked away her pride and walked through the front door. Twenty gruff-looking fishermen sat inside.

"I need to know where Puek is," she announced.

Everyone in the bar looked her over a couple of times, and then they all came back with the same answer. *"Haven't seen him."* Just before she stepped out the door, a young boy, a son of one of the waitresses, came up and took her hand. She wasn't quite sure what he wanted, but then he led her through the bar and up a flight of stairs. They stopped at a door to one of the bedrooms above the bar. The boy went back downstairs. Lek knocked on the door.

She heard a commotion inside. She knocked again, and when no one answered, she tried the knob. They hadn't even bothered to lock the door. When she opened it, the young girl didn't even look at her. She continued to run from one side of the room to the other, collecting her clothes. Lek stepped into the room, and the girl scurried out with her clothes in her arms.

With a small towel covering his bottom, Puek lay naked on the bed, pretending to be passed out. She kicked the bed and clawed at his back, but he refused to budge. She had come to teach him a lesson, and now it became clear what she had to do. Making no further attempts to rouse him from his pretend slumber, she went around the room and collected his pants, shirt, underwear, and even socks. Then she pulled the towels from the rack in the bathroom and picked up the sheet wadded up in one corner of the bed. She even removed the small towel covering his behind. Without another word, she left the room with the bundle in her hands and went back down to the bar.

"If I hear that any one of you gave Puek your clothes," she shouted in the most intimidating voice she could muster, "you are going to have serious problems."

Lek left the bar, dropped the bundle in a Dumpster down the street, and then hopped on her scooter and headed home. Puek called down for one of the fishermen in the bar to bring him up a pair of clothes, but everyone had headed straight out the front door. The only one left was the young boy who had escorted Lek up to the room. With no other option, Puek left the bar wearing the child's clothes. It was a ridiculous sight, a grown man with pants that came up to his knees and a shirt that barely covered his nipples. Worse yet for Puek, all his workers had seen him and had a good laugh at his expense. Lek had set out to teach Puek a lesson, and she felt she had most certainly done that.

After his little embarrassment down at the docks, Puek decided it was time to retire the late nights and girl chasing. He knew that Lek had stomached all she could. He put all of his energy into family and work, and then the money really started rolling in.

After having been the most successful captain in Nam Khem for more than five years, Puek decided to use his savings to purchase a fishing boat of his own. By 1992, he had thirty employees and could afford anything his heart desired. He bought seven properties around Nam Khem, including one on the beach, where he planned to build his dream home. He built a house in his hometown of Prachuap Khiri Khan where the family could take vacations. He gave money to his brother and sisters. He gave money to Lek's family. He bought a Nissan

Big M truck and five motorcycles. He bought Lek gold necklaces and rings and bracelets. He had hundreds of friends around the village, and each one was welcome in his home day or night. If any of his friends had no food, they could sit down at his table and fill their belly. Puek became known as not only the best fisherman in Nam Khem but also the most generous man.

In October of 1992, he became the proud father of Phongpat "Bang" Ruamwong, a healthy boy. As Puek's fortune continued to rise, he became convinced that the birth of his son had been a gift from the heavens that would supply him with 10,000 successful days to come. He threw parties and attended parties held in his honor. Women still beckoned him into bed, but he simply smiled at them and went on his way. Deep down, he'd always believed in the importance of family, but he had finally found the courage to live true to his beliefs. Wanting his children to steer far away from the path that he had led, he began regularly taking the family to temple.

For the New Year in 1997, he wanted to do something fun with his family, so he took them on a vacation to their hometown of Prachuap Khiri Khan. Puek took everyone to the temple to show their appreciation for all they had been given. Upon walking into the temple, Puek was approached by en elderly monk dressed in the typical bright orange gown. The monk looked into his eyes for several moments, and then a look of fear washed over the monk's face.

"You are going to die this year," the monk whispered.

"Excuse me?"

The monk studied his face for a few moments more. He nodded. "This year your life will go down to almost zero. You are going to lose much, perhaps even your life."

A chill crept over Puek. He believed that monks possessed a kind of sixth sense that gave them the ability to read the future.

"What can I do?" Puek asked.

The monk told Puek that he had to return to this temple before his birthday on May 6. At that time, they would perform a Bangsakul ceremony. Puek knew that the Bangsakul ceremony, usually performed on the dead, was a way to rid a person of bad luck, in either this life or the next. He vowed to return before his birthday to attempt to set things right.

The monk's words remained firmly etched in his mind, but he never managed to free himself long enough to travel to his hometown and have the ceremony performed. His business wasn't going well. He still found fish, but just enough to keep his business running in the black. And he spent every spare moment with his wife and kids. He figured that being with them was more important than visiting the monk. All his life he had been able to handle whatever came his way. If he kept his eyes open, he would see danger coming, just as he always did, and then he would make a plan on how to avoid it.

As his birthday approached without incident, he began to forget the old monk's warning. Then, on March 14, 1997, he dropped the first notch on the way to zero.

That day there had been a full moon. Puek spent the early morning stressing over how he could catch more fish in the days to come. When Lek saw how frustrated he was, she suggested that they take a drive to Pangnga to see a fortune-teller. Perhaps it would give them some fresh ideas on how to turn their luck around. Puek agreed that it might be a good idea, and he asked Lek if she could drive.

Once they turned right onto the highway above Nam Khem, Puek unlatched his seat belt so he could put his seat back and take a nap. He bolted upright thirty minutes later when he heard his wife scream. They were nearing the top of Khoa Lak Mountain, which rose sharply above the sea. A northbound car attempting to pass a bus lay directly in front of them. Puek's heart jumped, but he knew they were safe. His wife just had to move off to the shoulder of the road to let the car pass. But fearful of the cliff on their right, Lek froze. Before Puek could reach over and grab the wheel, it was too late.

Because he had taken off his seat belt, Puek's face was thrown violently into the windshield. A bright light flashed through his head, and then he crumpled back into his seat. Lek looked over at him. She began to scream again. Puek noticed that his vision started to grow blurry. He must have taken a harder knock on his head than he thought, but he would be fine. He could still breathe. He kept waiting to pass out, but he never did. He remained completely conscious, yet his vision continued to fade. Then it vanished altogether. Instinctively, he put his hands to his face to survey the damage. He had gone blind.

Puek spent eight days at the International Hospital on the big island of Phuket. He had two operations, which cost him 100,000 baht, but neither one restored his vision. He then transferred to the Ramathipbhadee Hospital, in Bangkok, hoping that they might help him. After he had spent a month lying in bed, the doctors gave him a chilling piece of news. Most of the nerves that connected his eyes to his brain had been severed, and they didn't have either the specialists or the equipment to tackle such an intricate operation. They suggested that he try a hospital in Malaysia that had all the latest technology. But to get the operation, he would need to sell everything, and then where would his family be? He still had to think about their future.

He instructed Lek to take him home. At first she refused. She wanted to sell the cars, the boats, the properties, the jewelry. She didn't want him to be blind. But even if they sold everything, there was no guarantee that the surgery would restore his sight. He put his foot down, and she took him home.

After putting Lek's brother Jui in charge of his boat, Puek retreated to his bedroom for several months. He tried to sleep as much as possible, but Jui kept interrupting him. As it turned out, he wasn't the most apt fisherman. Without Puek at the helm, the loads of fish grew smaller and smaller. Some trips out, they hardly caught any fish at all. To cover expenses, they needed to bring in 600,000 baht every thirty days. Lek's brother had trouble pulling in 400,000, and now debt was piling up. Puek's answer was to sleep it all away.

His daughter, Chomphu, who was eight at the time, and his son, Bang, who was five, had a hard time accepting that he was blind. Puek heard that a fair had come to Yanyao Temple up along the highway, and he suggested that Lek take the children so they could escape his misery for a little while. A few hours later, the telephone woke him. Puek eventually managed to crawl out of bed, feel his way across the room, and then pick up the phone. He could tell by the sound of the voice that it was Lek, but she was so hysterical that he couldn't understand a word she said. He told her to calm down, breathe. She managed to say three words that he recognized—"Bang," "hospital," and "serious."

Puek dropped the phone and made for the front door. Lost in darkness, he knew he would never find his way to the hospital on his own. He began screaming for someone to help him. Eventually, a neighbor put Puek in his truck, and they turned the fifteen-minute drive to the hospital into ten.

His wife was still screaming when he staggered into the emergency room. She came to him, and he held her tightly to get her to calm down. Through choking sobs, she gave him all the details that she could. They had gone to the fair as planned. Bang had seen some of his friends, and instead of going on the rides, they had chosen to run around on their own. They started to play near some Christmas tree lights that had been hung up for decoration. One of the lights had been blinking on and off, throwing out sparks. It was hot outside, and Bang had worked up a sweat. When he got too close to the malfunctioning light, there was a loud pop, and Bang fell to the ground. Lek ran over to him. She shook him, and a moment later he came around. She thought he would be fine, but then she noticed the piece of glass sticking out of his neck.

Puek pushed his wife away and began screaming his son's name. Lek tried to take his hand, but he was too upset. A nurse led him into the operating room.

"Bang!"

"I'm here, Papa," he said. "I'm going to be all right. Please don't blame Mama. It wasn't her fault. I'm going to be fine, Papa."

Puek started crying out of relief, but it didn't last long. In the commotion, the surgeon removed the piece of glass, which was lodged in Bang's jugular vein, without first inserting an IV. Puek noticed his son's voice getting fainter and fainter, and he called out his name but got no reply. He demanded the doctor tell him what was going on, but by then it was too late. His five-year-old son died from blood loss a few minutes before midnight.

Puek collapsed on the floor of the operating room. He wouldn't be able to remember how he got home or the few days that followed. Lost in a whirlwind of grief, engulfed by darkness, his mind ceased to function. He had failed himself and his family. There was no reason to go on.

He thought about suicide. Lek demanded that he pull himself together and continue to run the family. Had he given up on her and his daughter? Puek realized she was right. If he didn't figure things out, they were going to lose the boat, the house, everything. His wife and daughter would have nowhere to go, no one to support them. He needed to make decisions, but the only decisions he seemed to make were bad ones. A week after his son died, a captain who had seen his boat sitting vacant at the pier came to see him. He said he would pay Puek a considerable amount of money if he could take his boat to deliver a group of illegal Burmese workers to Ranong, 150 miles to the north, and then pick up another group there and bring them back to Nam Khem. Puek, who had never before used his boat for anything other than fishing, agreed without giving it a second thought. If this man could take his boat and bring some money to his family, he didn't have the strength or the pride to refuse him.

Puek got a call two days later from the Immigration Department. Apparently, a citizen in Ranong had seen illegal Burmese workers filing on and off his boat and tipped off the Immigration Department, with the hope of collecting a reward. The Immigration Department had stopped the boat just before it pulled back into the pier at Nam Khem. They found thirty illegal Burmese aboard. The captain was arrested and Puek's ship impounded. If he wanted to retrieve his boat, it would cost 300,000 baht.

Puek told Lek to go hawk three of his motorcycles, and she returned later that day with 35,000 baht. He placed the money in an envelope and then had Lek drop it off to the wife of the captain who had been arrested. If the captain had to spend six months in jail for a scheme they both had agreed upon, the least Puek could do was support his family during the time the man was away. The following morning, he had Lek take him down to the bank. Puek laid it out plain and simple—he owed the bank a lot of money, and the only way he could pay off that debt was to get his boat back. They lent him an additional 300,000 baht.

Eventually, Puek gave his boat, his homes, his properties, and all of his vehicles to the bank. Since business hadn't been good for some time, he had also borrowed money from various friends under high interest rates to get by. Now they came by the house to take his family's possessions as payback. Nearly everything—jewelry, their television, even their refrigerator—got taken. They were so defeated and ashamed, they just let it happen. His family was left with only the clothes on their backs. Puek was ready to ask Lek to find them a place out in the jungle to sleep, but luckily he still had a few true friends. Ko Sa and Sudjit

Rinphanit, two fishermen he'd known for more than ten years, pitched in to buy him a small home. His friends had hoped that having shelter would help him get back on his feet, but Puek hadn't the slightest idea where to begin.

Lek felt like she was losing her mind. After the car crash, she had begged Puek to sell the business. If he had listened, they might have had enough to fix his eyes, but he couldn't do it. Now they were bankrupt. She kept asking herself over and over, *Who will take care of my child? What will we do for the future?*

Then, a few months later, when they didn't have enough food to eat, Puek asked her to take him down to the pier to see if some of his old friends might be able to help them out. Not a year ago, he would have been greeted with a barrage of cheers, claps on the back, and invites to go have a beer. Now they only turned their backs, no one offering so much as a hello. She felt like shouting at them: *You, he gave you a motor for your boat three years ago and never asked for anything in return. And you, he gave you a fishing net worth 10,000 baht, and you never once tried to pay him back.* But she just gripped Puek's arm and led him home.

"Don't ever ask me to take you for handouts again," she whispered in his ear. "Don't ask me to take you to see anyone anymore. I can't handle these things that have happened to us. Your friends are no longer your friends. They have all changed. It is only us now."

She especially couldn't stand it when he sat out on the front porch and passersby gazed over at him with looks of pity. She built a fence around her property so no one could see in. She retreated to the bedroom with Puek and then watched helplessly as her husband tried to drown himself in the bottom of a bottle. She couldn't picture their lives getting any worse. She prayed that zero was as low as a family could get.

CHAPTER 8 DANG

In the early morning of December 7, 2002, a group of soldiers armed to the teeth invaded Laem Pom, the tract of jungle along the southern border of Nam Khem where Dang, her relatives, and fifty-two other families had lived for more than thirty years. The soldiers spilled from two massive trucks and began unloading cement poles and coils of barbed wire. As the soldiers received instructions from their group leader, a man named Siriphong Ninjan, head of a Special Forces unit, Dang and the other residents of Laem Pom emerged from their homes and gathered before the menacing force.

"I am here to inform you that this is not your land," Ninjan said to the crowd. He pulled a folder from his truck, opened it briefly to display a Nor Sor Sam, or pre-deed, and then quickly closed the folder and placed it back in his truck. "You have all been living here illegally."

"What are you talking about? This is our land," a man from the community shouted. "I've been living here for twenty-five years. You think we're just going to leave our homes? Leave everything behind and just walk away?"

"I'm not going to let you take my land," a woman shouted.

Ninjan produced a smile and patted the air in an attempt to calm everyone down.

"My employer has purchased this land, but our intentions are not to throw any of you out of your homes," he said. "We just need to see the boundary of your properties so that we know what land will belong to us and what land will belong to you. If you can help me with that, show me where your property begins and ends, I will put stakes in the ground to mark it. I've brought a camera to take pictures of you in front of your homes, and within six months we will send you a deed for your property. That way, we will both get what we want."

Ninjan's speech was quite convincing, and the people of Laem Pom had been struggling to obtain deeds for decades. If they got to keep their property and received a deed on top of it, they saw no reason why they shouldn't abide by the soldier's request. Dang, who remembered how not having the right documents had nearly gotten her kicked out of school years before, agreed that it sounded like a good deal for all involved. No problems arose until the soldiers reached the last home on the southern end of the community, which belonged to a man named Suwit "Baw" Kongsong. Unlike the rest of the residents, he hadn't bought a word Ninjan had said.

"If you want to come onto my land and put sticks in the ground, then you're going to have to show me your ID cards," he said. "I want to write down your names and see documents that prove this is official."

Ninjan approached him. "Why are you making trouble? Can't you see that everyone here wants to get a deed for their home? We don't have to give you anything. We own this land. But if you let us put stakes in the ground, we will send you a deed in six months' time."

"I don't believe you will send us anything," Baw said. "If this were official, you would have no problem showing me your ID card."

Ninjan took a step back and then called over a group of his soldiers. To show that defiance wouldn't be rewarded, he ordered the soldiers to build a fence around Baw's property. Materials were brought over and cement poles were laid in the ground. Instead of stringing barbed wire between the poles, the soldiers covered them with sheets of aluminum roofing. Baw was furious. They had left him just a small gap through which he could move in and out.

No one tried to speak with Mr. Baw, because they were all still confused about what was going on. Baw was also in no mood to talk. He spent all night cursing up a storm and trying to kick down the walls that had been built around his home. He confronted the soldiers the moment they arrived in Laem Pom the following morning.

"You are a terrible liar," he shouted at Ninjan. "You have not come here with official orders. You have been hired to come here and steal our land. You have come here to scare us with your guns, but I won't stand for it. I will get proof to show the government what you are doing here."

As Baw ran back into his home, the soldiers carried on with the business of mapping out property and constructing the fence on the edge of the community. Fifteen minutes after Baw had disappeared, one of the soldiers saw him holding a video camera. Ninjan approached Baw slowly and asked him to hand over the camera. Baw refused. He asked Baw a second time, and when he still refused, Ninjan pulled the handgun from its holster on his hip, pointed the barrel slightly above Baw's head, and squeezed off a round.

Instead of dropping the camera, Baw kept on filming. Realizing that his actions had just been captured on tape, Ninjan quickly reholstered his gun. He hesitated for a moment, trying to decide what to do. Then he called over a small group of his soldiers.

"Get rid of him," he ordered.

The residents of Laem Pom ran for cover as the early morning came to life with gunfire. Baw scrambled toward the beach, but despite the barrage of bullets flying in his direction, he didn't stop filming. When he reached the sand, he figured he had enough footage and focused all his attention on getting the hell out of there. With the soldiers still firing away and beginning to catch up, he saw a truck on a dirt road up in the distance and went straight for it. The man behind the wheel spotted Baw and the soldiers behind him. He started the engine and threw open the passenger door. Baw dove in, the man drove off, and in five minutes they reached the highway above Nam Khem. The driver took Baw to the local bus station, but when Baw saw that Ninjan had already sent three of his men to pick him up, they went to the bus station in the city of Ranong, 150 miles to the north. Baw thanked the man and climbed onto a bus. After that, he disappeared.

Three days after the shooting, Ninjan came to Dang's front door. She had just witnessed him trying to have Baw killed, and the mere sight of him flooded her with fear. She didn't want him in her home, but she feared that if she told him to get off her property, he might try to shoot her as well. She decided to open the door. Ninjan wore a smile on his face, but she could tell it wasn't genuine.

"I'm in a little bit of trouble," he said. "This bastard Baw. We had a meeting the other day and worked everything out. At least I thought we had. He sold me all the land that your community lives on for twenty-five million baht. He took the money, and now I can't find him. So I was wondering if you might be able to help me. Do you know what kind of car he drives? Also, I need a good description of him. I can't remember what he looks like."

The fear that Dang experienced just moments before became clouded with anger. She knew she should keep her mouth shut, but she had never been good at controlling her temper. She'd battled illness and fought hard her whole life just to live a quiet life in Laem Pom, and now this soldier, who'd just tried to kill one of her neighbors, wanted her help to find him?

"I want to ask you a question," Dang said. "Do you expect me to believe that you had a meeting with Baw a couple of days ago and you can't remember what he looks like? You are a liar, Mr. Ninjan. If you don't mind, I would like you out of my house."

Ninjan's face lost all expression, just as it had when he'd pulled out his pistol and fired at Baw, but Dang held her ground. Ninjan stared into her eyes a few moments and then turned and walked out. As Dang closed the door behind him, she felt quite certain that she had just made the biggest mistake of her life.

Matters intensified the following week. In addition to bringing a handful of soldiers, Mr. Ninjan also brought a backhoe. In 1998, a Thai woman married to an Australian man had purchased a plot of land in Laem Pom from Lei, a long-time resident. The Australian, John, had saved up a nice retirement fund, and he decided to use a portion of it to build three bungalows on the beach for tourists who wanted to escape the massive hotel/resorts just to the south. He had just finished laying the foundation and erecting the frames, and in the coming months he planned to attach the walls and roof. Apparently, whoever had employed Mr. Ninjan didn't want Aussie John to accomplish his goal. Without saying a single word, Ninjan had one of his soldiers hop in the backhoe and smash down the bungalows' frames and tear the foundation out of the ground. With their mission complete, they packed up their things and went away again.

The hostile act cast fear over the community. Everyone began to wonder whether one day Ninjan would arrive with a backhoe to smash down their homes. But the soldiers didn't return to their land for several months. And when someone did come to talk to them about the land issue, it wasn't Ninjan or one of his soldiers but a man they knew well, Mr. Sathaien Petklieng, the leader of Nam Khem. During the meeting with Petklieng, the residents of Laem Pom finally learned who was trying to take their land.

More than fifty years prior, Mr. Hok Jong Seng, a Chinese immigrant, had established the Hok Jong Seng Mining Company and been granted concessions by the government to mine huge tracts of land in Pangnga Province, including the patch of jungle where Nam Khem now stood. In the decades that followed, Mr. Hok Jong Seng became one of the wealthiest men in southern Thailand, and eventually he passed the business on to his children, and his children passed it on to their children, all of whom had taken on the Thai surname of Kullawanit. When their company had bled the ground of tin, instead of handing the land over to the government or to the people who had toiled for more than thirty years to make the Kullawanits their fortune, they pulled the right strings and were awarded a pre-deed for thousands upon thousands of acres, which included most of Nam Khem. The people couldn't figure out how the mining company could suddenly own the land on which they lived, so they had marched on the district office in 1996. Men like Wichien, who lived less than a half-mile from Laem Pom, in an area considered slumlike, got awarded a deed to his land after the second march. The families in Laem Pom got nothing, because their land was perched on the edge of the sea, several hundred yards south of the commotion of Nam Khem—the perfect place to build a resort.

To build a resort in Laem Pom, however, the mining company first had to get the residents off the land. Tu Kullawanit, grandson of Mr. Hok Jong Seng, had no way of achieving this. He was a miner, not an enforcer. So he combined his wealth with power by marrying Jintana Tancharoen, sister of Suchart Tancharoen, a powerful and reportedly corrupt politician. Kullawanit sold his company's holdings in Laem Pom to the Far East Company, which was run by Mr. Suchart Tancharoen. With backup in the government and military, Tancharoen had aggressive means of ridding plots of land of their residents.

Suddenly everything became clear to Dang. Instead of being up against the Hok Jong Seng Mining Company, the community of Laem Pom was up against Mr. Tancharoen, one of the most powerful men in the country, and anyone his company had paid off, which most likely included several local politicians and Mr. Ninjan. At first she wasn't quite sure why the village leader had shared so much information, but that too became apparent a few minutes later. Petklieng, the man they were supposed to turn to with their problems, told them he wanted them to leave Laem Pom. He told them they couldn't possibly fight such a large company as Far East, and they might as well not try. It became apparent that his whole intent for coming to them was to scare them off their land. Their supposed leader was on the take too. It made Dang angrier and more suspicious than ever. If the Hok Jong Seng Mining Company had acquired a deed for the land through legal means, the Far East Company would have had nothing to worry about. They wouldn't have needed to hire soldiers like Ninjan or local politicians like Petklieng. All they would have needed to do to get rid of the fifty-two families in Laem Pom was take the case to court.

"We will fight you," Dang spoke up. "You realize that, don't you?"

Petklieng shook his head and walked away. The whole encounter left Dang with a sick feeling in her stomach. The enemies were starting to pile up.

Dang expected repercussions from her outburst with the village leader, but nothing happened. The soldiers didn't return, and no one tried to convince them to leave. The residents dove back into their lives, all of them wanting to believe that the land issue had just gone away.

Then, on December 15, 2003, one year and eight days after the conflict with Baw, each of the fifty-two families in Laem Pom received a letter from the courts saying that they had to leave their land. Dang's hands trembled as she read the letter, but she knew that this wasn't the end. The courts couldn't just kick them off the land, at least not without first hearing their side of the story. She had told Petklieng that the residents intended to fight, and she planned to do her part in that battle. She hoped that someone would stand up to become their spokesperson, but everyone appeared to be too frightened to take on such a role. If the Far East Company planned to take the battle back outside the courtroom, the first person they would go after would be the chosen leader of Laem Pom.

Dang realized that the little power her community had came from their numbers, and if people started obeying the order of the court and moving away, all of them would lose. She organized a meeting. She had just wanted to get the ball rolling, get people talking, but when no one stood up and offered any bright ideas, she ended up just saying what she thought. She reminded them that the Far East Company had already bought off a powerful soldier and the leader of the village. They needed representation, but if they hired just one lawyer to plead all their cases, the chances were that he too would get bought off. They needed to hire many lawyers, perhaps one for every four or five families. They needed to collect all their documents, such as house registers, utility bills—anything that could prove that they had lived there for the past three decades.

A few weeks later, Dang began receiving phone calls in the middle of the night. The man who called never said a word; he just breathed heavily into the phone. She also noticed that she was being followed. She saw the same three men everywhere she went. She told no one about it but her husband, and continued to hold community meetings so they could prepare for their day in court. Dang had never wanted to be any kind of leader, but that's just what she had become.

When the fifty-two families from Laem Pom filed into the courtroom in March 2004, they had one lawyer per every five families. Dang had gone over what this day would be like a hundred times, but now that she found herself standing before a judge, her mouth went dry and her hands began to tremble. Everyone else was just as nervous. Dang's eighty-two-year-old grandmother, who had always associated courtrooms with murders and rapists, fainted from fright before she could make it halfway to her seat.

Dang told everything when it was her time on the stand. Speaking in her southern dialect, which drew sneers from the lawyers representing the Far East Company, she explained how she had witnessed the soldiers shooting at Baw, how they had come and torn down Aussie John's bungalows. She offered proof to show that she had been living in Laem Pom for thirty years, and then described how the Far East Company had come in overnight and tried to throw them off their land. After she said all she had come to say, nearly a hundred more residents from Laem Pom offered similar descriptions of the disturbing events that had started in December 2002. The Far East Company had only two witnesses—the leader of Nam Khem, and the Kamnun (the county chief). They were brought in to say that they had witnessed the transaction made between Hok Jong Seng Mining Company and the Far East Company, nothing more.

It became clear that the judge wanted to render a decision, but before he could do that, he needed more information from the Far East Company, which didn't even know the exact dimensions of the land they had supposedly purchased. Despite this, somehow the lawyers representing the Far East Company convinced the judge to put the case on hold. After months of preparation and meetings, the community of Laem Pom had accomplished nothing.

It was devastating news. Dang wanted to know what was going to happen, one way or another. If the courts ruled against the members of Laem Pom, Dang would leave her land without another word. If they ruled for them, they could all get on with their lives. Now they had to continue living in uncertainty. It surprised her that the company hadn't come better prepared. What did they possibly have to gain by dragging this case out?

A few weeks later, Dang got called back to the courthouse to testify against Siriphong Ninjan, the soldier who had caused so many problems in Laem Pom. Apparently Baw had managed to elude capture and get the incriminating videotape to the right people in the government. In the investigation that ensued, it was discovered that Ninjan had taken his vacation time to do a little freelancing work for the Far East Company, breaking more than a dozen military laws and regulations. He now faced serious charges.

The moment Dang entered the courthouse, Ninjan, who had been waiting for her in the lobby, grabbed her by the arm.

"Dang," he said with a smile. "Are you planning to be a witness in this case?"

"Probably."

"Dang, I beg you not to do that," he said. His grip tightened. "I beg you not to be a witness."

"I don't think I have much choice," she replied. "When you came and put sticks into our land, you said you would give us a deed in six months. You lied to us, and now we might lose our land because your boss took us to court. If you can't live up to your promise and let us keep our homes, then this case will have me as a witness too."

She pried her arm away from Ninjan's grasp and then walked into the courtroom.

Not long after giving her testimony, Dang was visited in Laem Pom by Nithat Siribenjakul, a member of the Pangnga Provincial Administration Organization Council. His job was basically city manager. He planned public parks, conducted research on various projects, and controlled the budget. Dang wasn't quite sure why he had wanted to meet, but that became evident after he spent half an hour trying to convince her to back down from her fight with the Far East Company. If she agreed, they were ready to offer each family fifty square meters of land. It was less than a quarter of the size of the property most families in Laem Pom currently owned, and it would be located along the road rather than on the beachfront, but she should seriously think about taking the offer. The Far East Company was a powerful organization, and they were just a handful of families. How could they possibly win?

The conversation was designed to scare her, but instead it filled her with confidence. First the lawyers representing the company had stalled in court, and now they were trying to make a deal. If everything was truly on the up-and-up, all they had to do was wait for the court to make a decision and then walk away with the land.

Dang had not tried to tell the story of Laem Pom to the soldiers or even the leader of the village, but she sensed that Siribenjakul was a sensible man who still had a heart. After he was through with his speech, she gave one of her own. She told him everything—how her father had come there thirty years before, how she had been born right there in Laem Pom, how most of the families in the area had nothing but their loved ones and their land. The more she talked, the more he began to sympathize with their plight. When she finished, Siribenjakul took a deep breath and apologized for having said such things. He promised to help them any way he could.

Finally, the community of Laem Pom had made a powerful friend.

This was not good news for the Far East Company. Dang wasn't sure if Siribenjakul had confronted the company after their little meeting, but something had made them even angrier. As a precaution, Dang had told all her friends outside of Laem Pom not to give any information out about her. That turned out to be a wise move. Having given up selling illegal lottery tickets a few years prior because the police were cracking down, she had added a sidecar to her motorbike and gone into business for herself. Each morning, she went down to the pier, bought fish straight off the boat, and then delivered it to several restaurants and hotels in and around Nam Khem. About a week after her meeting with Siribenjakul, a group of men stopped by the pier to interrogate Mrs. Ya Sakorn, a fish merchant Dang bought from regularly. They asked her all kinds of questions, but Mrs. Sakorn told them she didn't know anything and sent the men on their way.

Dang heard from other friends in other parts of the village that a group of men had come by, looking for her. She kept as low a profile as she could, but about a week after the strange men had first started snooping around, they discovered where she lived in Laem Pom. That night, one of her neighbors had to leave town, and Dang had agreed to watch her baby. At around midnight, the baby began to cry and refused to stop. Not wanting to wake her husband, she took the baby to the far end of the room and tried to cradle her back to sleep. Suddenly, both of her dogs began barking outside. Dang's mind hadn't slowed down since she had learned men were stalking her, and she crept across the room to look out the window. The moon wasn't out, and it was completely dark outside, but she swore she saw the silhouettes of two men. She woke her husband with tears in her eyes.

"Tueng, I think some people are outside," she said. "I think they might try to kill us. What will we do if they have guns?"

"Calm down," Tueng said. "I'm sure it's nothing."

Her husband slowly climbed out of bed, but before he could put his pants on to go outside and check, the barking stopped.

"See," he said, climbing back under the covers. "It wasn't anything."

Dang didn't sleep that night, and when she went outside at first light, she found both her dogs lying dead. It made her want to give up, but she knew that that was no longer a possibility. She had become the leader of the community's struggle. If she quit, everyone would quit. She remembered the story she'd heard as a child about Jan and Mook and how they'd bravely led their people to victory. She vowed to do the same.

In the days that followed, she tried to ignore the strange men lurking around the markets, pointing fingers at her. She tried to ignore the men who followed her from place to place. She tried to convince herself that the company would never go so far as to actually kill someone. But while taking a shower one evening, she got a call on her cell phone from a friend who was so lost in panic she could barely speak. Dang told her friend to calm down and take a deep breath, and finally she regained enough composure to speak.

"Dang, what are we going to do?" she said. "Mr. Siribenjakul, he just got murdered at the bus station."

Dang felt her heart drop down to her feet. Mr. Siribenjakul, who had first come to her on behalf of the Far East Company, had been working on their side for many months now. He kept Dang informed of developments in their case and gave pointers on how to take action. Dang had a strong idea what had happened—Siribenjakul had taken money from the Far East Company to help convince the people of Laem Pom to leave their land, and then he had switched sides. If Siribenjakul wouldn't help the company, he wouldn't help anyone. They had murdered him in cold blood.

Dang wrapped a towel around her body and went straight to her father's home. It had been so many years since he'd jokingly scolded her about jumping over his baby coconut trees, which had now grown sky-high. Bursting through the door in tears, she crumpled at his feet. Her father put an arm around her shoulders and stroked her hair. Eventually, she calmed down enough to tell him what had happened.

"Baby, give up," he said. "I will take you to stay in another place. Even though I love this land so much, I love you more. It's not worth dying over."

"Dad, I have to keep fighting. But just give me some time here. I just need to be with you for a while."

"If you still want to fight them after all of this," he said, "then I will help you fight. I'm an old man now, but I'll do whatever I can. I won't let you do this alone."

Her father lit a candle and some incense and placed them in front of the Buddha statue in the corner. Then he picked up his cell phone and called every family member who lived in Laem Pom. In fifteen minutes, Dang's sister, brother-in-law, and more than a dozen uncles and cousins had filled her father's home. Her father said a prayer for Dang and another for the safety of the entire family. They all slept that night together on the floor. While nodding off, Dang hoped to herself that even an entity as ruthless as the Far East Company had its limits.

PART TWO

THE WAVE

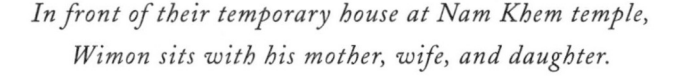

In front of their temporary house at Nam Khem temple,
Wimon sits with his mother, wife, and daughter.

On the morning of December 26, 2004, Wimon got up at four o'clock. He went to the wash bin in the kitchen, splashed some water on his face, and then returned to the bedroom to gather his clothes. He gazed at his slumbering family as he dressed. At fifty years old, he was married to a beautiful thirty-four-year-old woman who had given him two wonderful daughters. Frame, eight years old, and Film, his three-year-old, lay curled by their mother's side. Wimon was pleasantly surprised to see Frame sleeping well. She had broken her leg on a swing a few months back, and it hadn't healed right. The pain had kept her up many nights, but now either she had grown accustomed to the pain or it was beginning to fade. He kissed her on the cheek, hoping it was the latter.

He walked outside and saw his brother Prakong waiting for him down by the shore. They stood next to each other in groggy silence, and when Nikhom and his son joined them a few minutes later, they began gathering the necessities for the day—fishing poles, nets, buckets, ice, fruit for lunch, and two five-gallon gas tanks for the two boats they planned to take out. They probably wouldn't use more than three gallons of gas per boat, but they always brought a couple gallons extra just to be safe. The Andaman Sea was infamous for suddenly producing a train of decent-size waves that could make a longtail's return to shore rather perilous. If the waves were large, they would have to wait out at sea until the water calmed, and while they did so, the last thing they wanted was to run out of gas and drift into Burmese waters. More than a few of their friends had been shot and killed by Burmese soldiers over the years.

They packed their equipment into their motorcycle sidecars, and then they drove to the narrow inlet along the northern edge of the village that served as the longtail harbor for Nam Khem. Nikhom took his son in his fiberglass longtail, for which he had paid a hefty price a few years back. Wimon took Prakong in his wooden longtail, which was thirty feet long and five feet wide. It wasn't exactly considered a seaworthy vessel, but it was large enough for two apt fishermen to work side by side without butting heads. As Prakong took his customary position at the front of the boat, Wimon loaded his gear aboard and then shoved off to get a jump on Nikhom, who could glide through the water nearly twice as fast in his fiberglass boat.

There was a metal pole that ran from his shoulders down to the motor, and then eight feet back into the water. Gripping the pole, Wimon maneuvered out of the inlet. They were hard vessels to steer, and every morning, the inlet became a massive game of bumper boats as fishermen headed out to sea. Propellers were hoisted from the water, whirled through the air, and then dunked back in. In the commotion, it wasn't uncommon for a prop to come down on another longtail, producing a cloud of splinters. On occasion, the spinning blades came down on fishermen, which produced a much more horrifying sight. In the past three years, Wimon had nearly lost his life more than once on his hair-raising journeys out of the inlet, but thankfully this morning they were among the first to head out.

Working into the waters separating Nam Khem from Kho Khao Island, which was located approximately half a mile offshore, Wimon increased their speed. The sun began to rise as they headed south, skirting the coastline three miles out. During the hour-and-a-half journey to Pakarang Cape, located approximately nine miles as the crow flies from Nam Khem, Wimon looked out over the morning. The sky was a brilliant blue, the water calm, and the temperature blistering hot—a typical day for this time of year. By the time he arrived at the cape, Nikhom and his son had already caught up and pulled ahead.

Wimon chose a spot approximately three miles from shore. There were twenty-four other longtails in the area. A handful of fishermen had anchored farther out at sea, but the majority had chosen spots closer to the beach.

Prakong, who had napped on the ride out, rubbed sleep from his eyes and began dropping nets. Once Wimon killed the motor and stretched his arms, he did the same.

By ten o'clock, they had filled four buckets with fish suitable for sale in the market, as well as two buckets with smaller fish that later in the day would get dropped into the family's fish farm dangling from a buoy far out at sea. Neither Wimon nor Prakong had eaten breakfast, so they agreed to take an early lunch. Off in the distance, Wimon could see that Nikhom and his son had chosen to do the same.

Straddling the bench seat he had built near the rear of his boat, Wimon picked up the watermelon he had brought along and set it between his legs. He dug his knife in, cut out a slice, and then brought his head up to gaze mindlessly at shore. He squinted; there was something strange about the water. It had been clear all morning, but now it had gone murky. He scooted forward and looked overboard. He saw rocks below the surface. Even when the water was crystal clear, he couldn't see the bottom, not this far out. As he tried to figure out what was going on, he suddenly got the sensation of movement. He looked inland and saw that the beach had grown five times in size. The tide had gone out, way out.

"What do you make of this?" he asked Prakong.

Prakong, sitting at the front of the boat, spooned some rice into his mouth and then looked overboard. "It's funny, isn't it? I'm not sure. Could you pass me a slice of your watermelon?"

Wimon turned his eyes down to cut a slice. Before he could dig in his knife, his upper body got tossed violently back onto the bench and the watermelon rolled off his lap. Although Wimon heard no engine, he was sure another boat had just crashed into them. He tried to sit up but realized he couldn't. Something was lifting the boat at such a rapid rate he couldn't move. Then, in an instant, he felt weightlessness. His back lifted off the bench and his feet off the floor. He fell for what seemed like a great while, and then he landed painfully on the bottom of the boat. He tilted his head and saw Prakong, face flushed white, lying on his stomach at the front of the boat, clinging with both hands to one of the boat's protruding ribs.

"What was that?" Wimon shouted.

Prakong said nothing. He had shut his eyes.

Wimon sat up quickly. Off in the distance, he could see the mountains, which meant that he still faced the coast, but he could no longer see the beach or even the coconut trees that lined it. He pulled himself up onto the bench. From this slightly elevated position, things became a little clearer. He slowly realized that the wall of water they had just gone over was a wave. A very big wave. It also became apparent that the wave continued to grow in height as it neared shore. They were dealing with something Wimon couldn't have imagined in his wildest dreams.

Approximately two hours before, eighteen miles beneath the sea and a hundred miles off the west coast of Sumatra, the earth's crust had undergone a violent transformation at the western end of the Ring of Fire, an earthquake belt that produced the majority of the world's largest quakes. The India Plate dove dramatically under the Burma plate, producing an earthquake with a magnitude of 9.15, the second-largest earthquake ever recorded. The quake lasted ten minutes, and in that time nearly 800 miles of fault line slipped fifty feet along the subduction zone. The release of energy was so great that the earthquake was felt throughout Southeast Asia and even as far away as the United States. The earthquake itself caused extensive damage on land nearby, but with a portion of the seafloor having risen dramatically during the ten-minute siege, the true killer had just been born.

The massive displacement of water sent a tsunami radiating out across the Indian Ocean toward Indonesia, Sri Lanka, Thailand, India, and half a dozen other countries all the way to Africa. Traveling through the depths at nearly 500 miles per hour, it was an inconsequential bump hardly recognizable to the human eye. As the wave neared shallow water, however, its speed decreased dramatically, which in turn caused the height of the wave to increase. In less than an hour, waves sixty feet tall crashed down over the coastlines of Indonesia and Sumatra. The east coasts of India and Sri Lanka were struck in an hour and a half, and two hours after the earthquake, the tsunami approached the coastline of Thailand, first hitting Patong Beach on the island of Phuket, then Khao Lak, and then swooping in on Nam Khem.

Wimon stood, his eyes darting across the water in search of Nikhom and his son. He saw nothing but the back side of the wave and the misty foam that now sprayed off the top. The swell was easily twenty feet high, but that was looking at it from the rear. The front side would be twice as tall. No one would survive. Not Nikhom and his son, not any of the fishermen who had chosen spots closer to the beach. Wimon began to scream for the fishermen to head back to shore even though he couldn't see them. His shouting came to an abrupt end a moment later when he saw chunks of wood, buckets, and dozens of limp-bodied men get spat out the rear of the wave. He stopped screaming, because a sickening thought occurred to him—what if there was another wave?

Wimon spun around and gave a hard look out to sea. His body clinched tight and panic fluttered in his mind. Two miles out, perhaps two and a half, he saw an even bigger wave. The one he had just gone over hadn't developed a foaming lip until after it passed beneath him. The one out at sea spat water and mist five feet off its crown. It stretched north and south for as far as he could see, which meant there would be no getting around it. In this moment, Wimon had to make the most important decision of his life. Did he crank up the motor of his long-tail and head for shore, or did he charge headlong into the towering face?

"What do we do?" Wimon shouted to Prakong.

Nothing came back, not even a murmur. Wimon looked to the front of the boat to make sure his brother was still there, and he saw Prakong curled up in the same position as before. It made Wimon angry; both of their lives were at stake here, and he didn't want to make the decision alone. He shouted at his brother again, but when Prakong buried his head deeper into the bottom of the boat, Wimon looked inland. Strewn across the foamy black surface lay the scattered remains of what moments before had been twenty longtail boats. Some of the fishermen who had survived swam toward chunks of wood, and others simply treaded water in a single spot. If Wimon headed toward shore and the wave caught up with them, they would end up in a similar position. He didn't want to go out like that. Even if he did survive, Prakong most certainly wouldn't. In his current state, Prakong would most likely sink straight to the bottom. That made Wimon's decision for him. He would go against his instincts and head directly into the mouth of the monster, rather than away from it. He scurried to the rear of the boat and, with a quick jerk of the arm, cranked the motor to life.

"We're doing it, Prakong," he shouted, taking the tip of the boat's lengthy tail in both hands. "We're going into it, so just hold on."

Wimon forced the propeller to the right until the nose of the boat swung around and pointed out to sea. He figured there could be no easing into this, and he gave the motor a burst of gas. As they raced through the water, six other boats came into view. The captain of each had apparently come to a similar conclusion as Wimon, that the safest way to tackle this monster was to head straight into it. It bolstered Wimon's confidence, gave him hope that Nikhom and his son had survived. Three of the six boats were a quarter of a mile further out to sea, so they'd have to brave the unthinkable a few minutes before he would. This would give him some idea of what to expect.

The minutes that followed became the longest and shortest minutes of Wimon's life. As a child, he had hidden under his mother's bed as wind and rain stripped away the walls of their home and reduced their rice field to a pile of mud. As a teenager, he had stood on the roof of his home in Cha-uat as a torrent swallowed his home and all of his possessions. As an adult, he had stood on the beach in Nam Khem and watched fire claim his home on five separate occasions. He'd been certain that he'd left all that devastation behind. This wave appeared twice the size as the last, and even if he could ascend the nearly vertical face, the wave's breath, which sprayed in a hazy mist off the top, would consume him. Whatever spirits had been hunting him all these years had finally won. These were the last moments of his life. A part of him wanted to curl up at the bottom of the boat and close his eyes, just as he had wanted to do when he first stepped into the ring as a teenager. But his years as a kickboxer had taught him to stand tall. He didn't see any way out of his current predicament, but he would go down fighting.

Back in Nam Khem, Wimon's wife, Watcharee, sat on the front steps of their home with the girls. Frame had lost her appetite due to the constant pain in her leg, but Film had begged her all morning for some watermelon. Watcharee had just sat down to carve her a slice when she heard noise coming from down by the beach. She couldn't see what was going on, because of the cluster of trees in front of their home, but it sounded like two men were arguing with each other. She decided to just ignore them.

After she handed her younger daughter a slice of the watermelon, the voices down on the beach grew louder. Instead of just a few men shouting, now there were dozens. They screamed for people to run, that a massive wave was coming. Watcharee had lived in Nam Khem for fifteen years, and never before had there been a massive wave. She figured they were speaking figuratively, that the wave had to do with some injustice someone had done to them. Just to be sure, however, she left her kids sitting on the stairs and headed down to the beach.

She made it only halfway. Once she got past the trees in front of their home, she saw that the men hadn't been speaking figuratively. There was a massive wave coming straight at shore. It wasn't far off, perhaps 500 yards. Not sure what to do, she just stood there for a couple of seconds. Surely it couldn't be as big as it looked. Maybe it would break to pieces the moment it hit the shore, just like other waves. But this wave, instead of shrinking as it approached, *grew* in height. Soon it was as tall as a two-story building. Watcharee realized that the shore would not stop this wave. It would crash into the pier and then carry straight over the land.

Although she had walked less than thirty feet from her home, the run back to her children felt like miles. She screamed at them as she approached, but this only confused them. They stood up, sat down, and then got up again. They could see dozens of people now running away from the beach, and worried looks washed over their faces. When Watcharee reached them, she grabbed Film up with one arm and took Frame by the hand, expecting that she would run with her. Frame, however, resisted. She had grown so accustomed to using her crutch that it had become a kind of security blanket. She wanted to go back for it, but there was no time. Watcharee pulled her forcibly along.

Watcharee didn't look back to shore. She ran with her children through the alley on the south side of their home and then out onto the dirt street that ran parallel to the beach and cut through a long line of businesses and homes. She planned to run straight across the road and continue farther inland, but that wasn't a possibility. She had forgotten that on the other side of the road lay a pond that stretched a hundred yards across. Her only option was to run either north or south along the road, and with the wave coming at an angle from the south, she chose to run to the north. She tried to call forth in her mind a map of Nam Khem that would show her the quickest way to safety, but she could think of nothing but the massive wave, see nothing but hordes of people trying to escape, and hear nothing but the gruesome grating noise growing behind her and the screams of hundreds.

There was a family in a car up the road and she went for it. She planned to throw her children inside and dive in herself if there was time, but the family climbed out of the car a moment later and began to run as well. The noise behind her continued to grow louder and closer. Her eyes darted around the street as she moved forward on wobbly legs. Should she try to get into another car? She heard the twisting of metal behind her. Should she try to get her children up a tree? She heard the pop of wood snapping in two. Should she get her children inside a house? Buildings by the beach had begun to collapse.

If only she had just a few more moments to think.

A dark coldness grew on her back, and Watcharee clutched her children with all her strength. She told herself that she would hold on to them, that whatever happened, she would hold on to them. But it had been a hopeless thought. Her breath got knocked away and her face slammed into the road. Both of her children were gone in an instant as the wave was upon them.

Consumed by fear and her desire to survive, Watcharee thrashed her arms out before her as water shot deep into her lungs. Her sense of up and down vanished, and heavy things she could not see bashed into her arms and legs and back. It went on like this, tumbling and bouncing through a world of confusion. Having the sense of being in motion, but not knowing in which direction. Wanting to reach the surface, but not knowing where it was. Then she slammed against something solid, perhaps a wall, and her face came above the surface for a moment. She saw dozens of arms and feet and heads protruding from the water all around her. She saw a car tumbling down the street crash into a home and knock it down. But more important, she saw her elder daughter, Frame. She appeared to be suspended in the air, and it wasn't until Watcharee got violently swept back under that the image made sense to her. Frame had been caught on a clothesline tied between a pole and a building, but she hadn't been clinging to it with her hands. The clothesline had been wrapped around Frame's neck.

The horrifying image clung for a fraction of a second, and then it vanished in Watcharee's terror along with the thoughts of where her younger daughter had gone. Watcharee focused on her own life. She hadn't managed to take a breath when she came up, and now her head began to grow light. Her flailing had worn her out, but she could not stop. Her arms and legs cast mad circles despite the heavy objects they crashed into. Eventually, her feet struck something solid that didn't get pushed away. The sense of movement stopped. She tried to stand and realized that she could. She still had no idea where she was, but she knew it had to be on something very tall. The moment she found her balance and brought her head above water to get a quick breath, she got pulled back under. This time, however, she headed in the opposite direction. She had retained just enough sanity to know what that meant—she was getting carried out to sea. Her arms and legs thrashed faster now, and she screamed beneath the water until her lungs ran out of air.

Her body struck something solid again, something stable, and she managed to latch on to it with both hands. The current rushing past stripped the shirt, pants, and shoes off her body. She held on, and in a few moments the receding water slowed and her feet touched the earth. She still had water up to her neck, but she could breathe now and move by her own free will. She saw that the sturdy thing she had latched on to was the pole to a house. The first floor was gone, but the pole remained. Still clutching it, she looked around to get her bearings but recognized nothing. Where houses once stood, now there was nothing. She saw an eighty-foot fishing boat in the street, cars and trucks scattered around it. The clothesline strung between the house and tree was not there; neither was the house or the tree. There was no sign of either of her daughters, so as the water continued to recede, she let go of the pole with the intention of finding her way home. If her babies were still alive, that would be the first place they would go.

She pushed a few steps through the water and tried calling their names, but her throat had closed and she couldn't unclench her jaw. She took another few steps, and then the remaining water began to move back out to sea. It threatened to sweep her off her feet, so she waded back over to the pole. As the water continued to retreat, dozens of bodies sprung to the surface. Not far off, she saw an elderly woman whose body had been badly mangled.

"Help me!" the old lady cried. "Please help me."

"I can't help you," Watcharee whispered. "I have to help myself. I have to find my family."

With the water level having sunk below her knees, she prepared to head back home. Before she could take a step, someone grabbed her arm, startling her. It was a man she did not recognize telling her that another wave was coming and that she had to come into the house. No longer able to think for herself, terrified about having to brave another wave, she did as she was told.

Wading through the area where a kitchen had once been, she reached a flight of wood stairs that had somehow survived. The man helped her climb up the first part, and when she neared the top, two women already up on the second floor helped her the rest of the way. Immediately she went to the window that faced the street.

"Film, Mama's here," she called down. "Frame, answer me, baby."

Her eyes roamed across hundreds of dead men and women and children. She searched for her daughters' tiny bodies beneath the mud, around overturned cars and collapsed buildings. For another two minutes she searched, and then a second wave, twice the size of the last, came sweeping through Nam Khem. The water reached the second floor of the house in which she had taken refuge, and pieces of the walls were torn away. She fell over from fright and curled on the floor, listening to the wave tear down buildings and fling cars into trees. She sensed then that there was no way her husband could have survived out at sea and that both of her daughters were now dead. She couldn't cry or talk or move. None of this made any sense. What had just happened?

Out at sea, Wimon eased off the throttle and held his breath. The first longtail boat, which had pulled about half a mile ahead of him, was about to begin its ascent of the nearly vertical face of the second wave. The longtail's captain was a brave man indeed; he had his prop buried in the water and was charging full steam ahead.

At the bottom of the wave, the nose dug in, and then lifted up and up and up. When the tail of the boat reached the bottom of the wave, her nose still hadn't reached the top. She clung there like a slug on a wall. Fishermen at the front of the boat tumbled to the back and struck the captain, and then they all fell into the water. Despite the lack of a crew, the boat continued her climb. Her nose burst through the white spray at the top like a rocket ship. The body followed the nose, but before the stern could come up high enough to let the boat rock over the wave and come down the back side, she split in two, right down the center. The bottom half got pulled down on top of the fishermen, and within moments boards and nets and the bodies of men could be seen trapped and tumbling just behind the wave's cold black face.

Wimon looked over at Prakong, who still lay at the front of the boat, clinging on to one of the boat's ribs with both hands. He wanted to talk with his brother, but he didn't know what to say. Things didn't look good. The wave appeared to gather height and strength the closer it came to shore, which meant that it would hit them even harder than it had hit the first boat. He tried to convince himself that his boat was strong, that she would make it through, but he knew it wasn't true. Her wood was rotten and weak. She would break in half almost instantly.

Forcing these thoughts out of his mind, he turned his eyes back out to sea and watched the second boat, which was less than a quarter of a mile in front of him, make its attempt. He experienced a moment of hope when the nose and middle both went over the top without splitting in two. He became certain that the stern would shortly follow, but before it did, the whole boat suddenly stopped climbing. It was the strangest thing Wimon had ever seen. The longtail looked like a feather sticking out of the wave's head. It rode to shore in this manner for a few moments, but then the bow of the boat got tossed straight over its stern, flinging fishermen and gear in all directions. Before the fishermen had time to come up and take a breath, the wave scooped them up, adding their bodies to the chaos already locked in its midst.

When Wimon saw the third boat, less than 400 yards in front of him, snap in half just like the first, he lost any hope of survival. Turning back and heading for shore was no longer an option. Heading into the wave didn't appear to be an option either. He had made his decision, and now he would die by it. He looked over at Prakong.

"We're probably going into the water," he said. "I need you to do something for me. I need you to grab an empty water jug and hold on to it. Whatever happens, don't let go of it. When the wave passes, you should try to find something big, maybe a piece of the boat, to hold on to. Do you understand me?"

Without looking up, his brother nodded.

The only decision left for Wimon to make was whether or not to hit the wave with speed. All three of the boats that had been destroyed had attacked the wave with their props dug deep in the water, so he decided his best course of action would be to back off. He eased up on the throttle. The tide still retreated at a rapid pace, even way out here, and the moment Wimon let up on the gas, the nose of the boat began spinning to the left. He was about to give the motor a burst of gas to get the nose pointed forward again, but then a thought occurred to him. What if he didn't point his nose into the wave? What if he went at it sideways? His mind raced to discern the possible repercussions, and it came up with a few. Because longtails were built long and narrow, the stability of them was from front to back, not side to side. Wimon had learned this well during his first month as a fisherman, when three of his brothers had gone to one side of his boat at the same time and they nearly flipped over. So there was a big chance that the wave would overturn them before they had gotten halfway up the face. They also risked the chance of the leading edge digging into the wave and taking on water, in which case their boat would instantly become several thousand pounds heavier and sink right there at the bottom of the wave. But it was worth a shot, wasn't it? It was better than trying what hadn't worked three times in a row, right?

With the wave less than a hundred yards away now, he dropped the prop back into the water. Instead of correcting the slight turn the nose had made, he let it go. When he had gotten the boat parallel to the beach, and the wave was coming right at him, he cut the engine so that if they were flung into the water, they wouldn't get hacked to pieces. He looked one last time at Prakong, still curled in the fetal position at the front of the boat, and then he sat down himself. After bracing himself between two ribs at the rear of the boat, he contemplated whether or not to look at the wave. He decided that he had to. This monster had probably already taken the lives of Nikhom and his son, and now it would claim him and Prakong. Stuck on a boat three miles from shore, he knew there wasn't much he could do. All he had were his eyes; he could still curse this beast with them.

A forty-foot wall of blackness approached, grumbling so loud that it bled out all but the most horrendous of Prakong's screams. Wimon knew that the wave was a devil in disguise, because only the devil could make such a hideous sound. The wave rose higher than the telephone poles that surrounded his home. It rose higher than a three-story building. He began to scream as the longtail started its climb up the wave's face, but all the air was momentarily forced from his lungs and his chest was slammed down against one of the boat's ribs. He waited for the boat to flip over or for water to run aboard. He waited with his arms poised to swim like a madman—up, down, whichever way would carry him away from the blackness—but up and up they went. He entered a hazy mist and knew that he had reached the top. They had made it farther than any of the other boats had. There came a creak and then several audible cracks, wood splitting down the middle but hopefully not in half. He began to drop. For three stories, they dropped. Just as before, his hands and body and feet lifted off the floor of the boat, and he became certain that this time he would land in the water. He hit the deck headfirst. He looked down the length of the boat and saw Prakong, his mouth open in a silent scream.

Wimon sat up and examined the boat. He had heard another crack of wood when they landed, but he couldn't see anything broken. No water rushed aboard. Miraculously, everything appeared fine. He wiped dirty water off his face; he had survived. Thank Buddha for his burst of intuition—he would live to see another day. But none of the other fishermen had been so fortunate. Of the twenty-four boats that had been there twenty minutes earlier, his was the only one still intact. He could see dozens of men floundering in the water a half a mile or so closer to the shore. He looked at them for a moment, trying to decide what to do, and then something occurred to him. A terrible thought. Hesitantly, he looked back out to sea. A mile and a half out, he saw another dark line on the horizon. It was just as big as the last.

Earlier that morning in his home in Nam Khem, Puek sat down at the table to enjoy a cup of coffee and a cigarette he had rolled. Eight years had passed since he had lost his vision and his son. The depression that followed those traumatic events had nearly done him in. During the height of his misery, Lek had taken him to see half a dozen monks to help him out of his depression, but nothing had helped. Eventually, however, he had been brought back from the depths of depression by an unlikely source—a television show. It was titled *Waiting to Die*, and it focused on the handicapped and their struggle with thoughts of suicide. He heard a man who had lost both arms weep uncontrollably about how terrible his life had become. He listened to a woman who had lost one of her legs tell the audience how every morning she awoke with the intention of ending her life. They both sounded so confused and lost and utterly defeated, and Puek realized that he must sound the same to those he loved. He would never again be the able young man who stood tall and feared nothing, but he could still have pride and behave like a man. He realized what a fool he had been, trying to drink himself into the grave when he still had a wife and daughter to support.

That night, Puek put down the bottle for good. He sat in silence for many hours, trying to decide what a blind man could possibly do to support his family. The next morning, he went to the house of Ko Sa, the loyal friend who had kicked in a large sum of money to help build him a home. He told Ko Sa that he and Lek were thinking about learning traditional Thai massage. There was a school in Bangkok that would take them on as students for 20,000 baht. If Ko

Sa could lend him the money, Puek was pretty sure that he would be able to pay him back in a year or two. Ko Sa handed over the funds without a second thought. He gave Puek a hug and told him that he had been eagerly awaiting the day when Puek finally took the bull by the horns. They ended up talking about the old days fishing on the Andaman Sea; both of them grew quite emotional and had to choke back tears.

Puek graduated at the top of his class a few months later, and for the past six years, he and his wife had been giving massages to tourists vacationing at Kho Khao Resort on Kho Khao Island, located half a mile offshore from Nam Khem. They had slowly replaced all the household items that had been pilfered by their so-called friends seven years prior. They now had a stereo, a television, and a refrigerator.

A little past eight o'clock, as Puek sipped his cup of coffee and dragged on his smoke, Lek came out of the bedroom. She rattled around in the sink for a few moments, and then Puek heard her gasp.

"Puek, there is a giant crack in our house."

"A what?"

"A giant crack. It runs down one wall, across the floor, and then up the other wall. What on earth could have caused it?"

They talked about the mysterious crack for the next twenty minutes. Lek's father had been living with them for the past two months, ever since their daughter had left to attend Ratchamongkol University, in Bangkok. He joined in on the conversation. Then Puek and Lek had to rush off to the island to meet two German men who had made appointments the previous evening for massages. Lek mounted the small scooter they had purchased, and Puek climbed on the back. They drove the short distance down to the coast, and then over to the pier. The ferryboat arrived a few minutes later, and after paying their forty baht, they drove the scooter onto the ferry and began the twenty-minute trip out to the island.

Their conversation turned to business. Six months back, they had paid a group of Burmese workers a healthy sum of money to dig a deep hole in their backyard, into which Puek had placed thousands of baby pla-duk, a canal fish frequently served in Thai restaurants. Every morning for the past six months,

Puek had fed them, and they had finally grown to maturity. Just three days prior, a local merchant had offered them 50,000 baht for the whole lot. Lek had wanted to accept the offer, but Puek had turned the man down. He wanted to wait until the New Year, in the hopes of fetching a slightly higher price. On the ferry ride, they discussed how much they thought they would get and how much of the money they should reinvest in their farm.

When the ferryboat reached the shore of the island, they both hopped back onto the scooter and drove to Kho Khao Resort, on the east side of the island. A hundred yards past the front gate of the resort, they parked by the main lobby. Lek took Puek by the arm and guided him down a narrow walkway that led to the beach and the sala, the large gazebo where they worked alongside twelve other massage therapists. They climbed the few stairs and moved over to their customary mats. The German tourists hadn't yet arrived, so they used the time to organize their oils and herbs.

Both of them were glad that their new boss, Mr. Chalor, had decided to take the morning off. He was a local gangster who had acquired management rights for the sala by promising Mr. Sudjit Rinphanit, owner of the resort, that he would drum up new business. Puek had known Rinphanit for years. Many years ago, they both had been captains of successful fishing boats and helped each other whenever the other was in need. After Puek lost his sight, Rinphanit had been his only friend other than Ko Sa. He had offered to give Puek 300,000 baht for surgery to fix his eyes, and even offered to give Puek one of his own eyes if surgeons thought they could successfully make the transfer. Puek couldn't accept the offer—neither option would have necessarily restored his sight—but after graduating from massage school, he had asked his old friend if he could have a job giving massages at his resort. Rinphanit had instantly agreed, but instead of taking half the money from Puek's massages, as he did with all his other massage therapists, he told Puek that he could keep all the proceeds. Lek had to split her earnings, but it was still a good deal, considering that they charged 300 baht for a massage. But everything changed when the gangster came into the picture. Chalor tried taking 70 percent of all proceeds from both Puek and Lek. Rinphanit stepped in, telling Chalor that he wasn't allowed to charge Puek anything, but Lek had only two choices. Accept the deal or head elsewhere. It was all the more reason to get their fish farm off the ground.

When twenty minutes had passed and their clients still hadn't arrived, Lek lay down on the mat and Puek practiced his skills by giving her a massage. Once again, they talked about money. They might be able to use some of the proceeds from the sale of the fish to purchase a rubber tree farm or an orange grove. In the end, however, they both agreed that without the use of Puek's eyes, such investments would be too difficult to manage.

The Germans finally turned up just before ten a.m. Puek and Lek straightened out their mats and then laid the foreigners down on their stomachs. After applying a thin coat of oil to their backs, they dug in with their fingers and knuckles. Twenty minutes later, as Lek prepared to move on to her client's legs, she looked up and saw something strange out at sea. It looked as if a white line stretched from one side of the horizon to the other. She squinted at it for a few moments, and when it didn't become any clearer, she turned her attention back down and continued with the massage. A few minutes later, she looked up to see the same white line marching across the horizon.

"Puek, I wish you could see this," she said. "I want to know what kind of wave that is. It looks white like a cloud. It's so big."

"A wave?" he asked.

"It looks like a white wave far out at sea."

Puek shook his head. His wife was imagining things. He had been a fisherman since he was ten years old, and never had he seen a wave like the one she described.

"It's probably a low-lying cloud," he said.

"No, it's certainly not a cloud. I'm pretty sure it's a wave."

"Tell me exactly what you see."

"It is a big white wall in front of us, four or five kilometers away."

It suddenly made sense to Puek. It wasn't a big wave but rather a massive storm front. "Okay, I want you to keep an eye on it," he said. "If it's a storm, we have to prepare ourselves. You'll have to grab our things, and we'll head inside the hotel. Keep watching it, and let me know when it gets closer."

As Lek continued with the massage, she kept her eye on the horizon like Puek told her to do. She watched the wave grow and grow. It wasn't until the white wall swept over Kho Pah, a tiny island just a mile offshore, that she grew truly afraid. The island had completely vanished. She was about to tell Puek what she saw, but at that moment she heard someone shouting. It was Rinphanit, the owner. He was telling people to run.

Sudjit Rinphanit had been conducting a business meeting in the lobby of his resort all morning. Around ten a.m., his secretary approached with a cell phone. He figured it wasn't an important call, because she stood off to one side instead of interrupting the meeting. At all hours of the day, he received phone calls from the men and women of the island. Each of the five villages on the island had its own leader, but because he was the county chief, or Kamnun, people always came to him with their more serious problems. He talked for another ten minutes, and then his business partners stood, placed their palms together above their chins to show respect, and headed out of the lobby. His secretary, who had been waiting patiently, stepped forward at once.

"Before, we got a call from Phuket saying there has been a tidal wave on Patong Beach," she said. "Everything there has been destroyed."

"Are you sure?"

"That's what the man said."

"We'd better go down to the beach and check."

Rinphanit left the lobby, but instead of taking the path to the right, which led down to the sala, he took the path to the left, which spat him out on the beach a few hundred yards south of Puek and Lek. About three miles offshore, he saw a white line marching across the horizon. He had never before seen a tidal wave. The line looked harmless, but after what he'd heard about Patong Beach, he wasn't going to take any chances. He needed to evacuate his resort, but it wouldn't be easy. He currently had more than 200 employees on duty, as well as eighty rooms filled with guests. He had never imagined that anything like this could happen, so there was no contingency plan.

Concluding that the beach would be the best place to start, he looked to both his right and his left. There were more than fifty people tanning in the sun and wading in the water. Not wanting to cause panic, he began walking up and down the beach, trying to tell people they had to evacuate because of a massive wave, but all of his guests were foreigners and they didn't understand. They smiled and nodded and stayed right where they were. Rinphanit began raising his voice. Soon he was shouting. He managed to frighten several of his guests, but they still had no clue what he was trying to say.

Rinphanit was more than a little relieved when his secretary, who had gone back to the hotel, returned with several of his staff members who spoke English. After instructing them to round up all the guests and bring them to the front gate, Rinphanit ran up to the lobby. There he gathered more of his employees and led them out the back door to the dirt parking lot. He had two vans and two trucks that he normally used to shuttle people from the ferryboat to the hotel, and he told his staff members to take them to the front gate and load up the guests. Once they had a full load, they were to drive out the front gate, down the dirt road that ran parallel to the beach, and then up the slow hill. When they reached the intersection, which he suspected was at a high enough elevation that it wouldn't get hit, they were to unload the guests and come back for another batch.

Rinphanit ran back down to the beach. To his surprise, there were more than a dozen foreigners still lying on the sand, enjoying the sun. He began shouting at them, pointing to the wave out at sea. A couple of them got up, took a couple of steps inland, and then stopped. He could tell they wondered why they had to leave while he remained behind. It was as if they thought he would rush to their rooms and rob their valuables the moment they turned their backs.

Rinphanit stopped to examine the wave. It was still two miles out, but it had grown significantly in height. This worried him, because about $1^1/_2$ miles off-shore he could see a longtail shuttling guests from his resort to Kho Pah Island for snorkeling. He wasn't sure if a longtail boat could withstand the wave. A quarter of a mile in front of the longtail transporting his guests was another longtail, and it was only moments away from impact. Rinphanit expected that the captain would turn around and make for shore, but he didn't. He buried the nose of his boat directly into the wave. Rinphanit watched as the longtail slid up the vertical face, and then he watched as the wave snapped the boat in two and chucked the fishermen into the foaming surf.

Rinphanit pulled the walkie-talkie from his belt and tried to contact the captain hauling his guests, but he got no response. He saw the wall of water reach Kho Pah Island, which had pine trees in the center of it that towered forty feet. After the wave passed over the island, there was nothing left—no trees, no island. To attack the wave meant certain death, yet the boat filled with his guests still did not turn around. A few seconds later, he watched the boat get torn to pieces just like the first. People sprung to the surface with life vests strapped to their chests, but Rinphanit couldn't tell if any one of them was alive.

He slid his walkie-talkie back into his belt and plucked out his cell phone. He dialed the number of the sheriff at the district office, located on the highway several miles north of the turnoff to Nam Khem.

"This is Rinphanit. In a few minutes, a tidal wave will hit Kho Khao Island. We will have flooding here, so I will need your help."

"Really?" the sheriff asked.

"It just hit Kho Pah Island. There is nothing left. Please send as much help as you can!"

Rinphanit hung up his phone and looked around, trying to decide what to do next. To his dismay, he saw that half a dozen foreigners had still not left. It had become clear to him that anyone who remained on the beach would die. He physically pushed those who ignored his demands toward the front gate. Most of them started walking in that direction, shooting strange looks at him over their shoulders as they went, but one foreign man, who was in his late forties or early fifties, refused to move. Not wanting to leave him behind, Rinphanit called over one of his staff members who spoke English. He too tried to convince the man to leave, but the man still refused. He didn't believe that the wave would come over the shore.

"Okay, forget him," Rinphanit said to his staff member. "We have to run now."

While his remaining employees evacuated, Rinphanit headed to his home, which wasn't far from the main lobby. In all the commotion, he had forgotten to warn his wife and daughter. When he got inside, he bolted up the stairs, but the house was empty. He figured his family had heard all the shouting and had already left, so he went back outside and tossed a few remaining life vests to the foreigners who had just come out of their rooms, and then together they made for the main gate.

After seeing the wave sweep over Kho Pah Island and hearing her boss, Mr. Rinphanit, shout that everyone had to evacuate, Lek stopped massaging the German lying beneath her and jumped to her feet. Now that she looked properly out to sea, she could see that several boats had been overturned and several more had been broken in two. Nearly fifty heads bobbed in the water.

"Oh, Puek, many boats have sunk," she said. "It is a wave, Puek, it's a wave. It has white water spraying off the top. There are people drowning in the water, Puek. There are people dying out there."

He couldn't quite believe what his wife was saying. "We better run," he said. "First you must gather up our oils and massage license. Then you have to lead me out of here."

"Puek, we're going to die!"

"We're not going to die. But you do have to help me."

Puek lifted an arm for his wife to take, but he quickly pulled it back in. He remembered about the two Germans lying next to him. They couldn't see the wave, because they both had their faces down on the mats. And because they didn't understand Thai, they had no idea what everyone was shouting about. He grabbed his client's shoulder and shook it.

"Mister, you run. You run."

To make sure the Germans got the point, Puek slapped both of them hard on the back and then pointed into the breeze, which at this time of day usually came from the sea. Both men gasped, and then Puek heard them running with the rest of the massage therapists in the direction of the front gate.

Lek took Puek by the arm. They traveled slowly across the sala and down the steps, but once they reached the path, Lek pulled him forward at a pace faster than Puek had traveled since he'd lost his vision. As Puek ran, images of a storm he had seen while working as a technician on a boat at seventeen flashed in his mind. That day, chaos had started as a very small wind, but then it grew stronger and stronger. The captain of the boat, fearing for their safety, powered toward shore. Taking refuge at the front of the boat, Puek had peered over the lip. He saw a gust of wind pick up four houses along the coast and toss them out into the jungle. He saw trees and plants get torn from the ground. Not being able to imagine the massive wave his wife had described, Puek figured the same thing was happening here. A storm was coming, a very powerful storm.

"Stay away from the trees," he shouted at Lek. "They will blow over and fall on us. Just stay away from trees and poles."

"Okay, Puek, but you're not running fast enough," Lek cried. "You need to take off your shoes."

Puek forced his body to a stop and then kicked off his shoes. He expected that Lek would grab his arm and run again, but she didn't. He reached his hands forward, and they landed on his wife's shoulders. Her entire body had gone stiff. He knew what had happened without having to ask—Lek had looked back to shore. She had frozen, just as she had on the day of the car accident in which he had lost his sight.

"It's coming," she shouted.

"Then we have to keep running! You mustn't be scared!"

"I can't run anymore," she cried miserably. "I can't move."

Puek slid his right hand down to her wrist. Once he had a firm hold, he began to run in the direction they had previously been heading, pulling his wife along. He didn't know where he was. It was terrifying, because he realized that if he ran into a tree or a pole and got knocked unconscious, it would be the end of him. Lek would try to drag his body off, and that would be the end of her as well.

"Lek, I need your help," he continued to shout.

After about ten paces, Lek regained some of her composure and took control again. All around he could hear children screaming, "Mama! Papa!" He could hear what sounded like a jet engine growing behind him, chasing them. Then came the popping sound of wood splitting in half.

"The sala—it is gone!" Lek shouted.

"Go, go, go, go," he returned.

There was a truck up ahead; he could hear the motor. He could hear people climbing into the back. They too would get into the back and go speeding away. Everything would be fine. Then the motor revved and he heard tires spinning in gravel.

"It's leaving, Puek," Lek shouted.

"Don't stop running! Find another truck."

The breaking, bending, twisting noises and the scream of the jet engine crawled right up their backs. Puek could no longer hear any cars. The only people he could hear were far in the distance. He became certain that they were the last ones at the resort. Never had he experienced this type of fear, not even when he had gotten shot at while fishing in Burmese waters at seventeen. Then he ran into something solid and fell over forward. Someone grabbed his legs and threw them up, making him do a kind of somersault. When he landed, he lay on top of a dozen or more other people. He heard cameras clicking in his ears, and then the truck lurched forward and they were off.

Although Puek couldn't see the road, he knew it well. He drove it every morning on the back of Lek's scooter and could tell how many seconds lay between the bends. While running toward the front gate, they had headed away from the beach, but now that they had come out of the front gate, they traveled on a dirt road parallel to the beach. He could hear the water chasing them. He kept waiting for impact, but surprisingly it never came. (It wasn't until later that he learned that the wave had hit the coast at an angle rather than head-on, which was the reason it didn't sweep over the road all at once.) When they made it to the bend, which led to higher ground and the intersection, Puek thought a miracle had occurred. He called out for Lek, and when she took his hand, he began crying and laughing at the same time. He was certain they had left the terror behind.

When they reached the intersection, Lek saw otherwise. Survivors were placing the broken, tattered bodies of men, women, and children on the side of the road. She had no idea how so many people could have died. Most of the people at Kho Khao Resort had gotten out before the wave struck. The other side of the island, the side that faced Nam Khem, must have also gotten hit, but she couldn't for the life of her figure out how that could have happened, because the wave had come from the sea. She concluded that the tidal wave had somehow wrapped itself around the island.

Whatever had happened, hundreds of survivors had converged at the intersection. There were people crying, screaming, and running around in circles. Traffic had backed up at all three points of the intersection. Everyone was trying to decide which way to go in order to save their lives, but no one made any decisions. Survivors continued to drop, alongside the road, the bodies of men and women who had been injured or killed.

Sitting in the back of the truck, there was no way Lek could take it all in. She focused on one man lying beside the road. His belly was bloated to the point of bursting, his eyes had rolled back into his head, and he didn't appear to be breathing. Mud and sand and twigs covered his body, and she became certain that if she left him alone in his current state, he wouldn't last long; that was, if he wasn't dead already.

"Puek, I need you to stay in the truck," she said. "Don't move. Don't go anywhere. I have to go help one man."

Lek climbed out of the truck and walked the few paces over to the man. She stood looking down on him for a moment, at his massive belly and his rolled-back eyes, and she realized that she knew him. His name was Rong, and he made a living ferrying foreigners from Nam Khem to the island on a longtail boat. She bent down and tried pressing on his stomach in hopes some of the water would come out. As she did this, she discovered that she held a jar of balm in her hand. She must have instinctively grabbed it from the sala before running. She unscrewed the lid, scooped some balm with her fingers, and began rubbing it on the man's belly. A shadow crawled over her a moment later and she looked up. Puek had climbed out of the truck to help.

"Is he breathing?" he asked.

"I don't know. I'm trying to massage his belly. I think he's swallowed a lot of water. His stomach is so full."

Puek, knowing just as little about medicine but wanting desperately to help, began giving Lek instructions. "Rub him under his chest," he said. "Try rubbing under his ribs."

She did exactly as Puek said, and within a few moments she noticed that the man's eyes had rolled back down. He started blinking. It became clear that the massage was helping, and she wanted to continue, but then a young man came running up the road, shouting that another wave was coming. He said that it was even larger than the last. Lek tried to lift Rong's body, but she didn't have enough strength. The engine to the truck started, and if they didn't act quickly, they would be left behind. She took Puek by the arm and rushed back to the truck, praying that Rong would find the strength to get up and run.

Other than the middle-aged foreigner who refused to leave the beach, Rinphanit was the last person to exit the gates of his resort. He reached the madness at the intersection only moments after Puek and Lek and pushed his way through the crowd, searching for his wife and daughter. He found them a few minutes later and scooped them both into his arms. While inspecting their bodies to make sure they were unharmed, he got a call over his walkie-talkie and was informed that another, more powerful wave would strike the coast within five minutes.

Rinphanit kissed his wife and daughter and then pushed on. If another, bigger wave was indeed coming their way, he feared it might reach the intersection. In his mind, the only safe place on the island was Khao Phrapichai Mountain, which lay twelve miles to the north. He ran to the front of the traffic jam and then worked his way to the back, giving the driver of each vehicle instructions on where to head. He was the most important political figure on the island, and people listened to him. As the last of the vehicles began pulling out, Rinphanit put his wife and daughter in the bed of a truck and told them that he would join them shortly.

As he walked back to his three employees who had chosen to remain, a ten-wheel truck filled with sand pulled up to the intersection. How a ten-wheel truck had escaped devastation, Rinphanit didn't know, but it was just what he needed. He flagged the driver down and told him to dump the sand on the side of the road. The driver was confused but didn't argue. Then Rinphanit told his three employees to break into the mini-mart at the corner of the intersection.

"Take all the rice, dry food, gas—take everything from the store and load it into the back of the truck," he ordered. "I'll pay for everything later."

Another truck pulled up to the intersection, only this one was a water truck. Rinphanit couldn't imagine much better luck. As he walked over to commandeer the truck, the driver got out and went to the tank on the back. He unscrewed a valve and began draining the water, thinking he'd make better time out of the area without the weight.

"Stop that!" Rinphanit shouted. "We're going to need that water to survive. I'm headed with that ten-wheel truck up to Khao Phrapichai Mountain in just a few moments, and I need you to follow me. There are people there who need our help."

They now had nearly everything they needed for a large group of people to survive until help arrived—food, water, and gas to use for cooking. Before they headed off to reach the others, they had only one thing left to do—collect the wounded off the side of the road. At first, Rinphanit and his employees collected everyone they came across, even the dead, but they soon realized that this was taking too long. Rinphanit had no idea how many had been killed on the island, but he could see more than a hundred bodies in the vicinity. He instructed his employees to load up only the wounded. They would come back for the dead later that night when rescue teams arrived. At the time, he had no idea that help was more than forty-eight hours away.

11 | WICHIEN AND NANG

CHAPTER

Three days prior, Nang had walked Wichien to the bus station. Diving for tin had gone by the wayside, and diving for pearls had become highly competitive. Wichien had gone without work for quite a spell, but then he landed a job diving for sand used for ceramics. The only downside to his new occupation was that he had to spend a few weeks each month at the bottom of a river in Nakhon Si Thammarat, located on the gulf side of the isthmus, approximately 186 miles from Nam Khem. He never liked leaving, and this time it was especially hard, because Nang had come down with a high fever. With their daughter now eighteen and attending a university in Bangkok, and with their son, Nueng, spending most of his time running around with his friends, Wichien wanted to stay home and take care of her. Nang wouldn't have minded the pampering, but they needed money. Wichien had promised that this coming year he would finally finish renovating their home. That meant more to her than having company during her illness. She kissed him on the cheek and said good-bye.

Nang retreated to the loft of their house and spent the next two days curled in a ball on the mattress. On Sunday morning, she got tired of the loft, which grew tremendously hot during the day, and decided to go downstairs and lie on the cool tile floor. Despite the construction going on outside and the racket of Burmese laborers grinding ice for the fish coming off the boats, she slept soundly until approximately ten twenty a.m., when she was awoken by the voice of one of her neighbors saying something about a coming tidal wave. Her bones were sore from the fever and the hard tile, and it took her a moment to rise and walk to the door. When she got there, her neighbor was already gone.

A Burmese worker ran past in the direction of the road. Then another, and another. She stepped a little further outside, and she saw that hundreds were fleeing from the beach. She couldn't see the shore, because several houses blocked her view, but she could feel that something terrible was about to happen. Not wanting to leave the safety of her home, she ran across the tile and climbed the ladder to the loft. She went to the window, and peering out, she saw the wave not far from shore. It was tall, very tall, and it stretched in both directions as far as she could see. Instinctively she began calling out her son's name, but then she remembered that he had gone up to the market along the highway just before she had gone downstairs to sleep. She tried to decide what to do. She could stay in the loft and hang on to something, but then, out the window, she saw other people emerge from their homes, which were also two stories, and escape toward the road. She began worrying about her home collapsing and trapping her beneath the rubble. She decided to run.

She was back down the ladder and across the room in a matter of seconds, but she paused just outside her front door. An elderly woman who lived next door leaned up against the sidewall of Nang's house, clutching her hands to her chest and trembling with fright.

"Take me with you," she said to Nang. "Take me with you."

Nang took the old lady by the arm and pulled her down an alley. Instinct told her to head as far inland as possible, but when she reached the main road that ran parallel to the beach, she realized she had to rethink her plan. A massive pond made by tin miners decades before lay just on the other side of the road, preventing anyone in the general vicinity from heading farther east. Not sure what else she could do, Nang turned north on the road. Most of the vehicles were well ahead of her, heading for the bend that led up to the highway, but one truck remained, as if it had been waiting for her and the old woman. Nang joined the handful of other people in the back, most of whom were children, and then she reached down and helped the old lady in. A moment later, the driver hit the gas and the back tires spit up a cloud of dirt. They raced forward at a tremendous speed, but soon they slowed down again.

Nang closed her eyes, hoping that when she opened them, she would realize this had all just been a horrible dream brought on by her fever. Screams now

110

came from all around her, and she could hear a strange sound off in the distance. She began to pray. The faces of her parents, both of whom had died years prior, appeared in her mind. She could see the wrinkles on their skin and every other detail of their faces. Never before had she remembered them this clearly. She became convinced that their sprits had somehow joined her. She looked right into her daddy's eyes and begged him to save her.

The truck came to a sudden stop. Nang knew that they couldn't have traveled far, and she opened her eyes. They were still close to where she had climbed into the truck, stuck in a traffic jam. Up ahead, a Burmese worker had crashed his motorcycle, and the wreck was blocking the road. People were trying to move him and his bike off to the side so cars could pass, but the terrible sound in the distance was growing louder. They were all going to die unless they started moving again.

A hand landed on Nang's shoulder. Looking over the side of the truck, she saw a woman she knew holding her two children under one arm. One child couldn't have been older than eight months, and the other was around three years old. The woman let go of Nang's shoulder and snatched the eight-month-old up by the arm. She dangled the baby out before her.

"Auntie Nang, take this little one with you," she cried.

"No, I can't," Nang returned. "I don't even know if I can survive."

"Please, just take her."

"I can't," Nang repeated, but instinctively she reached her arms out, because it looked like the baby might fall. The woman released the child into her hands and began to run again. Nang, not knowing what else to do, pulled the baby close to her bosom and gazed down into her little black eyes. A fraction of a second later, Nang looked up to see a forty-foot longtail boat coming straight at her, riding on top of a jet-black wave as tall as the buildings around her. She took a deep breath and held the baby as tightly as she could.

The wave crashed down, pinning her to the bed of the truck. Completely submerged under water, Nang saw something dark, which she assumed was the longtail boat, pass over her. That was the last thing she saw before the world around her became too painful and confusing to watch. She shut her eyes. Her mind instructed her to fight, but she didn't know how, so she lay there, frozen. The metal beneath her began to shake and tremble as the truck got pushed across the road. It ran into something solid and stopped, but then whatever it had run into broke to pieces, and the truck started moving again. Her heart and mind raced.

In what seemed like an hour but was probably closer to a minute, she noticed the chaos begin to dwindle. The truck began to slow, as did the water rushing past her. She slowly opened her eyes. Water still engulfed her, but the surface had come considerably down. Pushing off with one hand, fighting the current for balance, she stood up in the truck's bed. Her head broke the surface.

After she took a massive breath, the first thing she noticed was that nearly all of the people who had been in the truck with her were now gone. There had been five or six children, as well as a number of old people. The only ones who remained were a young boy and girl, both around six years of age, and the elderly woman Nang had led up to the road. The children had a hard time keeping their heads above the water. Before Nang could reach out and help them, she felt something wriggling against her bosom. She remembered the baby she still held in her right arm.

She pulled the baby girl from the water and held her above her head. The girl's lips had turned blue, her breath gurgled, and her eyes had rolled back into her head. Nang began to scream for someone to help her, but when she looked around, she saw no one in a position to help. The entire village was submersed. Buildings had fallen down, boats had washed ashore, and dozens of motionless bodies floated everywhere. She knew that screaming would do no good, but she couldn't stop. Someone had to still be alive. There had to be someone who could help her and this little girl. Her eyes continued to dance from the left to the right for several minutes, but then she heard it again—that same noise began to grow in the distance. Another wave was coming, and it sounded bigger than the last.

With the water level having dropped to her chest, Nang brought the baby down so she could look into her face. "I am so sorry," she said, crying hysterically. "I can't help you. I am so sorry."

Leaning over, Nang lowered her hands until the baby's body touched the water. She could hear the baby's lungs struggling for breath, see her little hands and feet thrashing for life, but there was nothing Nang could do. Screaming and crying at the same time, she let the baby go. The water carried her for a few yards, and then the tiny body disappeared beneath the surface. For a few seconds, Nang gazed at the spot where the baby had vanished, knowing that now even if she somehow survived this, she would never sleep another night. Then she spun just in time to see a second wave, this one forty feet in height, barreling down upon her. Not wanting to get pulled away from the truck, she ducked beneath the water so she could lie down in the bed.

The wave picked up the truck and threw it into the side of a building. The walls collapsed and the roof fell down on top of the truck. For a moment, all Nang could see were nails and wood, but then water flooded over her again, lifting the roof higher above the truck bed and taking it partially away. Nang was in great pain, but she didn't know which part of her body had been injured. Her only thought now was making it to the surface. Just like before, she needed to wait until the world around her slowed. She tried to be patient, but it was taking much longer than last time. Eventually panic took over and she began to flail her arms and legs. She got to where she could stand, but that was as far up as her body would go. It felt as if her feet were stuck to the bed of the truck. She lifted her left leg, and it came up just fine. Then she tried lifting her right leg, but it wouldn't move. She realized now that the pain she felt came from her right calf. Something sharp and heavy must have pierced through it, because she couldn't lift it even one inch. From this position, she couldn't get her head above the water to take a breath. Realizing that she would drown if she remained locked in her current position for another minute, she tried to tear her leg free despite the tremendous pain.

As she was on the verge of inhaling a breath of water, Nang's head broke the surface. Her leg was still stuck, but the water level had gone down. Only seconds after she took a huge gulp of air, however, her head was suddenly pulled back beneath the water. She could feel hands grabbing at her, and at first she thought demons were trying to take her life. Then, beneath the surface, she saw the faces of the old woman and the two children who had been in the truck with her. None of them had reached the surface yet, and they grabbed at her clothes in an attempt to climb up her body. On instinct, she began to push them away, certain they would drown her. When Nang fought her way back to the surface, she couldn't see them anywhere. All she could see was the roof of the house hanging over one end of the truck and water in every direction. Most of the buildings that had survived the first wave had been pummeled by the second. The village was gone.

It all became too much. Instead of trying to free her leg so she could climb up something tall or swim to safety, she just dog-paddled in place with her hands and her one usable leg to keep her head above water. A considerable amount of time passed, though she wouldn't be able to remember how much. The only thing she was certain of was that she heard the third wave coming. This time she couldn't bring herself to dive back under and hide in the truck bed. She couldn't do anything but continue to dog-paddle and shut her eyes. Without the truck's metal cocoon, however, the third wave ripped her away from the vehicle and whatever had speared her leg. As her body tumbled around and bounced off cars and chunks of cement, she tried swimming to the surface but hadn't the slightest clue in which direction to go. She could see the faces of her parents again, and now she called out to them with all her heart. She begged them to help her. As her body continued to rebound off sharp and dull objects, and after what seemed like ten minutes had passed, she became certain that she was already dead and gave up. No longer needing her arms to swim, she placed her palms together and prayed to Buddha.

Almost instantly, she felt what she would later describe as an invisible hand lift her toward the surface. Her chest struck something solid. Whatever she had hit was round and tall and allowed her to get her arms firmly around it. She stayed in that position for thirty seconds, not daring to move. A voice whispered to her. It sounded like her voice.

"You need to climb up this tree. You need to climb up now!"

Nang opened her eyes. It was a coconut tree, but she was still well below the surface. With water rushing around her, trying to pull her away, she climbed arm over arm, leg over leg, until her head came above water. She took a breath and then another. All she could see was the bark of the coconut tree. She looked up;

the top of the tree wasn't that far off, which meant that the water line was still at fifteen or twenty feet. Climbing the rest of the way seemed impossible. If her hands or feet slipped, she would fall back into the water and get carried away. She had no courage to do anything other than cling to the spot where she was.

Out of the corner of her eye, she saw a car go past her. She grew afraid that something would strike her in the back. She craned her head around and then let out a scream. A barrage of boats and large chunks of buildings came straight for her. If one of those objects hit her, it would either crush her against the tree or knock her back into the water. She looked back up, whimpering. To climb the tree was her only option. She remembered that she was no stranger to climbing coconut trees. When Wichien had gotten shot, she had climbed thousands of coconut trees to pay the hospital bills. She told herself that this was the last thing she had to do before she was safe. The thought gave her courage, and she began to climb again, arm over arm, leg over leg, until she reached the lip of the bushy head at the top. She carefully worked her way over the coconut clusters, eventually grabbing a concave branch and pulling herself the rest of the way up. Flopping down on the spiky leaves, she lay, trembling, as ants swarmed over her body. When she caught her breath and gathered a little strength, she sat up.

Her body had been dragged beneath the water more than thirty yards from the road. Directly below her she could hear the *oot, oot, oot* of pigs drowning in the water. She could see chickens and dogs struggling to stay afloat. She could see people who had latched on to pieces of wood and refrigerator doors go drifting by. She could hear what sounded like a thousand children calling out for their parents and a thousand parents calling out for their children. Everywhere, people cried out for help.

Three coconut trees stood before her, lined up in a row perpendicular to the beach. Halfway up the tree directly in front of her, Nang saw the elderly neighbor she had helped into the truck clinging to the trunk just above the waterline. The woman screamed. She saw an aluminum roof coming right for her, the corner of which would shortly saw her body in two. Nang's eyes snapped away for a moment to track down a voice that had risen above everything else. Standing on the roof of a two-story house, she saw the elderly woman's middle-aged daughter.

"Mama, you have to climb up!" the daughter shouted hysterically. "You have to climb up now!"

Nang looked back down at her neighbor, praying she would find the strength to follow her daughter's advice. The old woman lifted an arm as if she planned to climb, but then she brought it back down and continued to cling to the trunk at the waterline. The old woman began to scream louder now, as did the daughter. Nang, who could clearly see what would happen, grabbed the sides of her head and began to scream as well. The old woman looked one last time over her shoulder at the advancing roof, now only a few yards away, and then let go of the tree. Her body disappeared beneath the surface, but then she popped back up and began to flail her arms. A moment later, the roof struck the tree, clung for a second, and then rolled off to the same side where the old woman had been carried. Nang shouted for the old woman to swim away, get away from the roof, but she had no strength left to do anything other than keep herself above water. In a few seconds, the roof swept over the woman. Nang expected that the roof would wash by and then the woman would pop back to the surface, but that's not what happened. The roof sank. It had stayed afloat for god knew how long, only to sink the moment it had a life in its belly. In a matter of seconds, there was no sign of either the roof or the old woman.

Nang could hear her neighbor's daughter crying hysterically. She could still hear the *oot, oot, oot* of pigs drowning in the water and children screaming for their mothers. All she could see was death. She became convinced that everything happening was the work of evil spirits seeking some sort of revenge. Those were the thoughts that were with her when she saw a fourth and final wave coming toward shore. She couldn't take it anymore and turned her eyes down. The moment she did this, she noticed two things at once: The water had taken all her clothes, and she had a massive hole in her calf. With adrenaline shooting through her body, she had forgotten that she was injured, but now the pain returned to her at once. Inside the massive gash, she could see bone and, around the edges, shredded flesh and muscle. Blood surrounded her, dripping from the branches on which she sat. Feeling her head begin to spin, she latched on to the surrounding leaves. A moment later, she lost consciousness.

12 DANG

CHAPTER

Dang awoke that morning at five o'clock and felt like going right back to bed. There hadn't been many happy moments in Laem Pom since the battle with the Far East Company had begun, but the night before, the community had decided to forget its troubles for a few hours and throw a Christmas party just for fun. Though they were Buddhists, the Christian holiday gave their children a chance to dance and sing and have a good time. Dang had tried to leave the festivities at nine o'clock, but her children were having too much fun. She had tried to leave again at eleven o'clock, but again her children wouldn't let her. The festivities carried on well past midnight, and now Dang was paying the price.

She rolled out of bed and walked sluggishly over to her husband, who was busily washing little Kwan's clothes in the sink. Dang kissed her husband on the cheek and began the list of chores she needed to complete before heading out—ironing the kids' clothes, fetching water from the well so everyone could shower, and finally preparing breakfast. Normally she would blare the radio while she worked to ensure that the kids got up, but this morning she decided to let them sleep. She could still see the smiles on their faces from the night before. Watching them dash around the coconut trees on the beach with the other kids reminded her of her youth. The only thing that had changed in all these years was the manner in which they lived. In 1996, all the residents of Laem Pom had marched down to a nearby school that Mr. Chuan Leekphai, the country's prime minister at the time, was visiting. They told him that despite the wealth of Nam Khem, the leader of the village still hadn't strung electric poles out to their community, forcing all of their children to study by candlelight. It struck a chord with the prime minister, and a few months later the first electrical wires reached Laem Pom. Several families had purchased black-and-white televisions, and with the community having remained a close-knit family over the years, all the kids were invited into those homes several nights a week to watch cartoons. It certainly beat having to stay up late at night collecting tin on the beach as she had done, just for the chance to stay in school. Dang helped her daughter with her studies every night. She wanted to do the same for her son, but at fourteen he had surpassed her schooling long ago.

Finishing her chores by seven o'clock, she went to the bed, peeled back the mosquito net, and gently woke the children, who greeted her with loving smiles. She headed out the door a few minutes later with her husband. As on every morning for the past few months, Tueng had to use his truck to transport a group of construction workers to a resort being built on Bang Niang Beach, located thirteen miles south of the highway from Nam Khem. If he was lucky, the foreman would ask him to carry bags of cement and pound nails for the rest of the day. On most days, Dang worked transporting fish in her motorcycle sidecar to the restaurants she had contracts with. Business had been good, but she knew it could be better. Today Dang had set up an appointment to meet with the purchasing manager of the Bang Sak Princess, a five-star hotel/resort that had just opened up on Bang Sak Beach, located approximately six miles south on the highway from Nam Khem.

After briefly stopping by her parents' house next door to remind them to look after her kids, she hopped on her motorcycle and headed out. By the time she had reached the highway above Nam Khem, half a dozen cars had given her a long beep of their horns and blazed past her. She had always been a slow driver, but this morning she was exceptionally slow. She had a lot on her mind. If this deal went through, it meant that she could buy her family new clothes and finish tiling the floor of their home. But she knew getting a contract with a five-star hotel would not be easy. They would want to know that she could deliver a specific amount of prawns, shrimp, jack fish, and squid every day, even if that was not what the fishermen had caught. That meant she would have to make connections at many piers in the area, not just those in Nam Khem. To convince the purchasing manager that she was the right merchant for the job, she would have to rattle off numbers and figures off the top of her head. If the deal went through, it would give her family security it never had. She went over everything she would say again and again.

She reached the security booth at the Bang Sak Princess thirty minutes after she left home. Foreigners walked in and out freely, but because she was Thai, the security guard wanted to see her identification. She showed it to him, and a few minutes later another security guard came up on a motorcycle to escort her down to the offices. Dang had expected an elaborate setup in the main building, but because the hotel hadn't yet been finished, the offices were currently housed in a cluster of trailers on the north side of the hotel, not far from the beach.

Dang parked her motorcycle and, still rehearsing her speech, headed toward the trailer door. The security guard stopped her before she reached the steps.

"The purchasing manager hasn't come in yet."

"But we have an eight o'clock appointment."

He shrugged his shoulders. "You never can tell. He might come in an hour, or he might come in three hours."

"Do I have to leave, or can I wait over by the hotel?"

"No problem," the guard said. "You can wait wherever you would like."

Dang walked east, toward the main lobby. She ran into a group of her girl-friends who worked at the hotel. They began to chat, and soon Dang and her friends moved closer to the beach and took refuge under a tree. They chatted for a long time. Dang kept her eyes locked on the trailer off in the distance so she could spot the purchasing manager when he arrived. Some of the other women gazed mindlessly out to sea. At around ten o'clock, one of them noticed something strange. The tide had gone out, exposing rocks and leaving fish to flop on the sand. Dang had lived by the beach all of her life, and never had she seen anything like this.

"I'm going to record this," one of her friends said. She pulled out her brand-new cell phone, which happened to have a camera built in, and snapped a picture.

Dang stood up. Something was bothering her. It felt as if the ground was shaking, but at the same time she knew that it wasn't. A noise grew all around her, a rattling, chugging noise not unlike that of a train. Then she saw the wave.

"*Yed mae,*" she swore. "Run!"

Dang didn't wait for her friends. She broke out into a full sprint for the highway. It wasn't until she had taken ten strides in that direction that she realized just how far she had to go. The highway was 200 yards directly to the east. It didn't occur to her that the road was nearly as low as the terrain on which she ran and would therefore offer little protection from the wave and the wrath that it brought. The highway just seemed like a safe place, perhaps because it led to Nam Khem and her home. She looked over her shoulder at one point during the run, and she saw the wave crashing over the shore. Two ghastly images came to her at once—that of a devil hand reaching out to grab her, and the head of a massive cobra poised to strike.

She had made it less than thirty yards from the tree she had been sitting under when the wave struck her powerfully in the back. She went face-first into the soil, and then her body got ripped up and tossed mercilessly around and around. Something large bashed into her side, so she wrapped her arms over her head to protect it. Her best estimate was that she got tumbled and beaten beneath the water for two minutes. She made no effort to reach the surface; she just ended up there. Debris surrounded her, and she pushed it away with her arms. Before she could clear a spot in which to wade freely, something grabbed her legs, and the water pulled her back under. She got thrashed for a few more moments, and then she sprung to the surface again. She took another breath and got pulled back under again. This happened over and over, five, ten, fifteen times. Each time she came up, she felt fainter, like she couldn't go on. She thought of her parents and her children, certain these were the last seconds of her life.

Then one time she sprung up and realized that she wasn't out in the open. She had been pinned up against a cement wall. She thrashed her hands out before her as she had done on each of the other occasions, shoving away twisted metal and pieces of wood. Her arms had weakened, and the debris surrounded her. She figured it would close her in, blocking her route to the surface the next time she got pulled under. She began to scream, and a moment later she heard a man's voice above her. Looking straight up, she saw a hand extending down to her. It became clear where she had been carried. She wasn't pinned up against a wall, but rather against the side of the steps that led up to the lobby. The man was standing on top of those steps, trying to save her. She tried to reach up and take his hand, but the moment she did, she sunk below the surface. The water battered her over and over into the corner between the stairs and the wall of the lobby. She feared that the next time she came up, the man would be gone, but he wasn't. He still stood on the stairs, a worried expression locked on his face.

Dang's entire body radiated with pain. Her arms were limp at her side. "No, no," she called out. "Leave me here. I can't go on anymore."

"Sister, you have to come now," the man shouted.

"It's all right. Just let me drown," Dang said. She honestly didn't want to fight anymore.

The man pointed furiously to the west. "No, hurry up, hurry up! Another wave is coming!"

Dang, still flailing in the water, managed to look in the direction the man was pointing, and she saw a second wave hit the shore. Riding out in front of the wave, heading right toward her, was the trailer the hotel used as an office.

Her fear gave her strength. She reached up again, and this time she managed to grab the man's hand. Her feet scraped against the side of the stairs to help her up. Once her entire body lay on the sharp corners of cement, she scrambled on her hands and knees into the lobby of the hotel. It rested a good fifteen feet above the earth, but that mattered little. She was sure the wave she saw hit the shore would momentarily tear right through the lobby. Then the man scurried up a tower of scaffolding that had been erected in the lobby for some repairs. At the top of the tower, there was a gap between the wall and roof for ventilation.

Dang headed up after him, barely grabbing a hold of one bar before letting her other hand go to reach for the next. As she neared the top, she heard what sounded like a million firecrackers exploding at the same time. She crawled out of the gap at the top of the scaffolding and then twisted her body so that she could climb up and over the edge of the roof. Once on the tile, she rolled over to her stomach and looked down. The second wave had already torn by beneath her, stripping the lobby of its walls and depositing chunks of cement along with boats, cars, and hundreds of people at the bottom of the gradual hill on the other side of the highway. The massive body of water hovered there for a moment and then began to move back out, bringing with it the chunks of cement, boats, cars, and hundreds of people. A new image leapt to mind—that of a massive frog's tongue lashing out to capture its prey and then sucking it back in.

Dang began thinking about her family. When a third wave and then a fourth had pulled back out to sea, she could see a hundred twisted bodies strewn in the mud in all directions. Many of them were children and infants. She didn't know whether another wave would come or not, but that didn't matter anymore. She began to climb down.

"Wait," said the man who had rescued her. "It isn't safe yet."

Dang ignored him—she needed to get home, and she needed to get there now. When she reached the lobby, she ran down the steps and splashed into the knee-high water. Both feet caught in the muck below the surface, and she fell. Climbing back to her feet, she realized that her body hurt worse than she previously thought, especially her chest, which felt tight. She began to walk instead of run. Her shoes had been torn off, and sharp objects dug into the soles of her feet.

On her journey toward the highway, five cooks who worked at the resort joined her. They searched for the road together, but it was nearly impossible to find. The earth had been covered by fallen telephone poles, mangled cars, broken buildings. Hundreds of people writhed in the mud that covered everything. Dang tried ignoring the people, because there were just too many of them to help, but then she nearly stepped on a woman who lay crushed beneath a cement electricity pole.

"Please help me," the woman said weakly. "Please don't leave me here."

Dang bent down and tried lifting the pole, but it weighed several hundred pounds. "I don't know how I can help you. I have to go home and look for my family. They need me right now."

"Please, don't leave me here, sister."

Dang called out to the cooks, who had walked fifteen yards ahead of her. They quickly came over to her location, and when they saw the woman lying

crushed, they each took a corner of the pole and lifted. With all of them strain-
ing, Dang dragged the woman's body out from underneath the pole. Dang and
the cooks knew that it wouldn't be possible to take the woman with them, so they
carried her body across the invisible road and up the hillside on the other side.
Setting her down, Dang dropped to her knees and placed her palms together at
her chin.

"Sister, I am sorry I can't stay with you," she said. "I have to go find my children. I pray that you will be all right and that help will come soon."

Dang quickly left the woman. She climbed down off the hill and began
working her way north along the highway. Everywhere she looked, there were
dead bodies. She could see faces protruding from the mud and peering out the
windshields of cars that had been twisted into knots. She had told herself that
the wave had come just to the Bang Sak Princess, that it had affected only this
isolated area, but now she realized that that couldn't be true. Thinking of all the
family she had left at home earlier that morning, she prayed to all the gods in
the world that a miracle had saved Laem Pom.

Nam Khem lay six miles to the north, and with each step she took, it seemed
farther and farther away. Panic would consume her for a few minutes, and then,
a moment later, it would be replaced by a sense of hopelessness. She felt rational
thought slip away. Stones in the mud stabbed at the bottom of her feet, and she
kept tripping over electric wires hidden just below the surface of muck. Numerous times she stepped on a half-buried body, and on each occasion she knelt
down to apologize for their suffering and for her own survival. Then, remembering her family, she climbed back to her feet and began to run again.

As the first wave swept over the coastline in and around Nam Khem, Lieutenant Colonel Niphon Yanphaisarn sat at his desk in the Pangnga Police Station, located on the highway just down the street from the hospital. He had spent the last three days monitoring the ten-man detail he'd sent to La Flora Resort to protect the Royal Family. Sorting out all the logistics and laying out their duties had taken up a fair amount of his time, so this morning he sat at his desk to catch up on paperwork. Everything had been routine from the time he had walked into the station, but around fifteen minutes past ten o'clock, he heard a fellow lieutenant currently overseeing the detail at La Flora come over the radio.

"We have a giant wave approaching the shore. I need every policeman in the area to move people away from the beach."

Yanphaisarn peered at the radio in the corner of his office. The majority of men who worked at the station had a great sense of humor, and he thought the lieutenant was trying to play some kind of practical joke. Under normal circumstances, he would have thought it quite funny, but not with the Royal Family vacationing in the area. If things didn't run like clockwork, all their asses would be on the line. He glared at the radio for another minute, and when the lieutenant said nothing more, he got back to his paperwork.

Five minutes later, Yanphaisarn jumped in his seat as the lieutenant's voice came over the radio again. This time he was shouting.

"No, it's too late! It's too late!"

The radio went silent. Yanphaisarn walked over and stood above it, waiting for something more. He hadn't the slightest clue what was going on, but it sounded serious. A few minutes later, the lieutenant came over the radio for the last time. His voice was hardly recognizable.

"Send help here! Send help here!"

Yanphaisarn assumed there had been an attack on the Royal Family. He ran out into the main room, where fifteen of his subordinates had been listening to the same transmission. He pointed to six of them and told them to follow him.

They took two trucks, and as they headed south along the highway, Yanphaisarn noticed nothing out of the ordinary. The sky was blue, no wind. It wasn't until they passed the narrow, windy road leading down to the beach and Nam Khem that he saw the first sign that something was wrong. Dozens of cars and trucks, all packed with people, squealed off the road and onto the highway. Some headed north, while others headed south. All of them were in a hurry. It made Yanphaisarn wonder what the hell was going on. Because this portion of highway sat approximately twenty-five feet above sea level and because it was bordered on both sides by jungle, Yanphaisarn couldn't see the massive waves striking the shore or the destruction that they caused. He didn't see any sign of a mass-scale tragedy until the road dropped in elevation and veered closer to shore near Bang Sak Beach, and even then all he saw was a traffic jam on both sides of the road. To see the beach, he needed to travel a hundred yards further south to reach the bending dip in the road that left the jungle behind, but with traffic at a standstill, that wouldn't happen for some time. He pulled off to the side of the road and managed to maneuver his way around the traffic and park at the junkyard near the bend. He hiked the rest of the way on foot.

When Yanphaisarn rounded the corner, the devastation came into view. The entire highway had been overrun with fallen telephone poles, overturned cars, and lifeless bodies, some of which were buried neck deep in mud. The beach's long line of hotels, starting with the Bang Sak Princess, had all crumbled to the ground. In an instant, he forgot all about the Royal Family and the ten-man detail he had working at La Flora. There was no way he could reach them anyhow.

As Yanphaisarn tried to take it all in, a dozen people suddenly came running up to him. They pulled on his arms and shirt. They demanded that he help their father who was trapped, their sister who was dying, or their child who was missing. Yanphaisarn became overwhelmed and couldn't think of what to do. He had never received training for this type of situation. Eventually, he turned to the six men he had brought along.

"Go with these people, but bring back only the seriously injured. Leave the dead."

As his men went running off in every direction, Yanphaisarn saw a truck trying to flee the area nearly run over an elderly man. Not wanting the death count to grow higher than it already had, he jumped into the road and began directing traffic. When his subordinates had filled each truck with six people, one of them a pregnant lady who looked to be in bad shape, Yanphaisarn headed back to his truck so he could transport them to the hospital. Before he could climb into the passenger seat, however, a man came running up from the beach.

"Another wave is coming!" he shouted. "Another wave is coming!"

Having seen what a giant wave could do, Yanphaisarn instantly ran for the hillside on the east side of the highway, leaving the wounded behind in his truck. His subordinates followed right behind him. When they reached what they felt would be a safe elevation, they stopped and turned around. Yanphaisarn could see no sign of a wave out at sea, but he didn't want to take any chances. He waited on the hillside for twenty minutes, and when still no wave had come, he and his men climbed back down, got into the trucks, and began the drive back to the hospital.

From the passenger seat, Yanphaisarn looked back frequently to see how the victims were doing. Two officers had climbed in back to comfort them, but many of them didn't look like they would make it. Blood covered the bed of the truck, and some of the victims shook violently and vomited pools of black water.

Yanphaisarn still had no idea of the enormity of the disaster, and the hospital was no indication. Pulling up to the top of the ambulance ramp, he could see perhaps forty people lying on the concrete benches of the emergency room. At least ninety percent of them were Burmese laborers who had fled from Nam

Khem, which was much closer to the hospital than either Bang Sak or Bang Niang Beach. Because not many Thai or foreigners had arrived, the Burmese were getting treatment from the doctors and nurses and were in the process of getting moved into beds. Yanphaisarn and his men unloaded the men and women they had brought and carried them into the hospital. Then they climbed back into their trucks and began the drive back to the Bang Sak Princess. At this point, Yanphaisarn assumed they were looking at 100 or perhaps 150 dead. If there were more than that, he figured the hospital would have already filled up. He had no idea what he would face in the coming hours and days.

Doctor Wut Winothai finished his morning rounds at the hospital a few minutes before ten. For three days now, they had been treating approximately 500 outpatients a day, 75 more than normal, and instead of having the customary 100 patients admitted, the majority of the hospital's 177 beds were full. Fifteen doctors worked at the hospital, but with ten of them being specialists, the sudden surge of patients had kept Doctor Winothai and the four other general practitioners very busy.

With a few hours of free time ahead of him, Doctor Winothai exited the rear of the hospital, strolled down the cement walkway that led to numerous outbuildings, past the apartment complex that housed the majority of the hospital's 197 nurses, and then across a lawn to reach his one-room house, which was just as old and dilapidated as the majority of the equipment in the hospital. Over the past decade, Doctor Winothai had received a handful of offers to work elsewhere, but the thought had never crossed his mind. If he downsized to a clinic, he wouldn't be able to take himself seriously. If he upgraded to a larger hospital, he would get caught up in the bickering that resulted when more than two dozen doctors were forced to practice under the same roof. He found Takuapa Hospital to be a happy medium. Everyone here considered themselves members of one big, happy family.

Instead of taking his customary nap, he picked up the morning paper and sat down on the sofa. Thirty minutes later, lost in the current headlines, he heard the siren of an ambulance off in the distance. He set down the paper and listened more closely.

The highway out in front of the hospital was the main route for commuters, buses, and trucks heading north and south along the west coast of the isthmus. Because the highway was only two lanes, trucks attempted to pass buses, buses attempted to pass cars, and everyone attempted to pass the hundreds of scooters that puttered along the shoulder. Sometimes these attempts were just that, attempts. With there having been several mass accidents in the past, the hospital had prepared for a disaster where a hundred wounded people flooded into the emergency room at the same time. The doctors and nurses would break down into teams. One team would handle the patients that needed surgery, another team would work with the patients who were unconscious but not severely wounded, and another team would work with the patients who had suffered broken bones and superficial wounds. To keep their plan sharp, they held a drill once a year, where all the doctors and nurses would assemble in the lobby and break off into their teams. During the first mock emergency, because they had no loudspeakers or alarm system at the hospital, everyone had agreed that an ambulance would drive laps around the hospital with its siren blaring to alert everyone to the fact that there was an emergency. The moment they heard the ambulance make three laps, they were all supposed to drop what they were doing and convene in the emergency room.

The ambulance's siren faded into the distance, came back, and then faded in the distance again. When this happened for the third time, Doctor Winothai left his home and jogged back to the hospital. He arrived at the ER a few minutes after eleven o'clock and found it packed with men, women, and children who had large open wounds and badly broken bones. They sat on the cement benches and lay on the floor. He counted thirty-five heads, and he felt confident that the staff could give each person the care they needed. Then he went into some of the nearby rooms and saw that the beds that had been empty earlier in the morning were now full as well. These patients had the same injuries as the people in the ER, but they also appeared to have water in their lungs.

As Doctor Winothai moved among the crowd, he heard that a tidal wave had hit the coast, but he had no idea how big it was or how many people had been hurt. He met with the other doctors to develop a game plan, but not all fifteen doctors were present. One of their orthopedic surgeons had gone to La Flora Resort to look after the Royal Family. Two doctors had gone on vacation to Ranong, located along the coast 150 miles to the north. (One of them, Doctor Winothai later learned, had been killed by the tsunami.) And two more doctors were visiting family in Bangkok. They were also down nurses—currently, there were only twenty in the ER. Because it was Sunday, many of the nurses were off. Doctor Winothai suspected that the ones who lived in Nam Khem would start to trickle in, but at the time, he didn't know how badly Nam Khem had been hit or that several nurses would never be coming back. The doctors decided that trying to come up with a new plan wouldn't be in anyone's best interest. They should stick as close to their emergency plan as possible, even though the situation didn't fit the mold. To accommodate all the patients into the plan, they just had to tweak it a little.

The doctors and nurses broke down into two groups. The first group looked after the patients who had broken bones and superficial wounds in the emergency room. Doctor Winothai was part of the second group, which was responsible for taking the patients who had inhaled large amounts of water and couldn't breathe on their own into a back room, laying them down in beds, and then inserting tubes down their throats, which would then be hooked up to one of the hospital's six respirators. While the two groups attempted to get a handle on things and assess the most serious patients, the three surgeons among them prepared the operating room. The whole process was far from organized, but Doctor Winothai still felt confident that they could treat all forty or so patients in a timely manner.

About twenty minutes after disappearing into a back room with his patients, Doctor Winothai walked back into the ER and learned the true scope of the disaster. The 40 patients had turned into 200. Severely wounded people lay on the floor of the lobby, on the patio outside, and on both ambulance ramps. He tried to convince himself that handling 200 patients at the same time was still possible, but when he went outside and looked down the street, he saw what looked like a thousand more men, women, and children staggering his way. There were an additional 500 or so people packed into the beds of trucks and on top of cars. That meant the staff was looking at some 1,500 patients at the same time, and there was no telling how many more were on their way. The hospital didn't have enough beds, they didn't have enough doctors, and they didn't have enough supplies. He told himself that things couldn't get any worse, but then, a moment later, someone began to scream that another wave was coming. Everyone in the ER burst past the reception desk to reach the fourth floor, inciting mayhem. Doctor Winothai had no idea how they were going to get through this. Hundreds, if not thousands, would most likely die by nightfall.

Back on the sea in his longtail, Wimon attacked the third and fourth waves just like he had the second, by heading over them sidelong. The fact that he and Prakong were still alive was a testament to the fact that he had made the right decision, but in getting hefted two stories up and then violently dropped back down, his longtail had taken substantial abuse. Cracks ran down its length, some so menacing that he was surprised that they had not yet sunk.

"Prakong," Wimon called to his brother, who was still curled at the front of the boat. "Are you going to be all right?"

His brother nodded absently.

Wimon squinted out to sea, trying to spot anything irregular. The second wave had been the largest, the third slightly smaller, and the fourth no bigger than the first. Seeing no more monster waves and suspecting the worst had already come, he turned around and panned his eyes across the three miles of water leading to shore. Right in the middle of the expanse lay the remains of the twenty-four longtails that had been in the area before the tsunami hit. The majority of their captains had tried to head back to land when they saw the first wave, and from the looks of it, a few of them had made it just a mile shy of their destination before they got hit.

At least two dozen men were still alive and kicking in the water. With a quick jerk of his arm, Wimon cranked the motor to life. He swung the boat around and headed for the closest group of men. His plan was to pick up as many people as he could, power up onto shore, and then run up to the highway and hitch a ride back home. During the heat of battle, he hadn't given much thought as to how much of the coastline had been impacted. Now a vile feeling in his gut told him that the waves had swept over Nam Khem. If it was true, his wife, children, and mother wouldn't have survived. He held the tears at bay, because he knew once they started, they wouldn't stop. He needed to focus on the task at hand.

Less than half a mile out from the first group of men, still two miles from shore, Wimon felt his boat rear up. Every hair on his body stood up, and he kicked himself for having been so stupid; focusing all his attention on the drowning men, he hadn't been paying attention to what went on behind him. He let go of the longtail and covered his head out of instinct, but surprisingly he didn't get violently tossed to the tremendous heights that he expected. The wave lifted his boat five feet into the air and then put it back down. He spun around, certain the baby wave would shortly be accompanied by another monster. A hundred yards out, he could see a lump on the surface, but it was no bigger than the one he'd just gone over.

Not sure how big these waves would grow, he eased up on the gas and watched the first one make its journey into the beach. It didn't become a giant, but it did get larger. The waves during monsoon season were frequently too large to attempt a return to shore, and the series of waves now heading in were a good deal larger than those experienced during monsoon season. The lives of the men in the water depended on him, but Wimon felt that if he tried such a stunt, both he and his brother would join the men in the water. The waves were just too large for a longtail, particularly one in such bad condition.

He reluctantly turned his boat around and headed further out to sea to where the waves were less than three feet tall. After he waited ten minutes, it appeared as though the waves were getting smaller, and he headed toward shore again, only to encounter the same blockade half a mile out from the first group of struggling men. Over the next forty-five minutes, he made half a dozen attempts, but each time he retreated for fear of his boat splintering in two. Thoughts of his family suffering back in Nam Khem were eating him alive inside. On his short jaunts in the direction of the shore, he had seen devastation—crumbled buildings, overturned cars. If his wife and children hadn't seen the wave coming. . . .

He could hear their screams in the back of his mind and see their bodies trapped beneath rubble. Wimon also grew more concerned about Prakong. He hadn't moved or said a single word since they'd gone over the first wave.

Wimon continued with his attempts to reach shore, but at the same time he also began edging toward Nam Khem, in the north. He didn't want to leave behind the dozens of fishermen drowning in the water, but in his mind he didn't have a choice. His boat continued to take on water, and he didn't know how much longer they could remain afloat. Perhaps the waves were less intense somewhere else along the coast? He needed to reach his family. It was the only option he had left.

By one o'clock, approximately 2½ hours after the first wave hit, Wimon reached the narrow channel between Nam Khem and Kho Khao Island. He hadn't found a stretch of coastline along the way where the waves were less intense, and the waters off the coast of Nam Khem appeared somehow more intense than anywhere else. The big waves of monsoon season seldom lasted this long, and he started to believe that the current waves were never going to end, at least not for a couple of days. He was prepared to give it just a few more hours, but then he saw two men clinging to a piece of a wrecked longtail about half a mile from shore. Both men looked utterly exhausted, and every time a wave swept over them, they would lose their grip, flounder for a moment, and then cling again to the wrecked longtail. Wimon knew that if they were left out there for just a few more minutes, a wave would take one or both of them under for good.

After instructing Prakong to latch on to his empty water jug, which he did immediately, Wimon took a deep breath and began heading for the two men. Waves picked up his boat and then dropped it roughly back down. The hard part was keeping the nose aligned with the shore. If a wave caught the rear of the boat at an angle, it could whip them around sideways. Although that position had allowed them to scale the monster waves, it would end in disaster with these smaller ones. Wimon put his shoulder into the longtail, fighting the waves that came up upon him with speed. When he was twenty yards out from the two men, he slowed to a crawl.

"I can't come any closer," he shouted, worried that a wave would carry his boat into the already wrecked longtail and finally do his boat in. "You have to let go and swim to me."

The two men didn't hesitate. As they thrashed their arms and fought through the debris that surrounded them, Wimon edged closer and closer. When the men finally came up along the side of the boat, Wimon abandoned his post at the rear and ran over to lift them out of the water. The first man he pulled in was a forty-year-old laborer who had been swept off the shore of Nam Khem. The second was an eighteen-year-old laborer from the northern city of E-Saan who had been working at Jern-Jern Resort on Kho Khao Island. The two had started the morning off a mile away from each other, on two different landmasses, only to meet in the middle of the sea and cling to the same piece of wood.

The two men, both of whom had been stripped down to their underwear, struggled to their knees and then bowed at Wimon's feet. It made Wimon uncomfortable; such a gesture was offered only to the King. (Weeks later, the man from Nam Khem would go to live the life of a monk for seven days in Wimon's honor.) Without speaking, both men collapsed onto the bottom of the boat. Wimon went back to his position at the tail. He looked out to the sea and then toward the shore. Waves still rolled in, waves that could easily finish his boat off, but now that he was so close to home, so close to his family, he flooded the engine with gas and went for it.

My longtail is old and broken, he whispered to Buddha, *but I wish you could spare my boat until we reach the shore so that the people on board can live. I wish that you could be with me for the next little while and carry us the rest of the way.*

Having taken refuge on the second floor of someone's house after getting beaten and battered by the first wave, Watcharee, Wimon's wife, gazed out a window on the street below, looking for her daughters, Frame and Film, both of whom had been torn from her grasp. There was no sign of either of them. She fell to the floor when the second wave hit and remained curled there for the next ten minutes.

When the final wave passed and the horrendous noise of collapsing buildings had been replaced by the screams of men and women and children, she went back to the window to resume her search for her babies. She looked out on a world of total and utter chaos. The majority of the village was gone, and the thought of her children having been washed out to sea with the rubble and trash caused something to break in her mind.

"I've lost all my children, I've lost all my children," she shouted hysterically. "I've lost my babies."

Her outburst brought a woman to the second-story window of one of the surviving houses across the street. Watcharee nearly fell back when she saw her. She had been convinced that everyone other than those who had taken refuge in this house had been either seriously injured or killed. Seeing someone alive and well gave her hope that her children might have survived.

"Everything will be okay," the lady said.

"It won't be okay," Watcharee shouted back. "I lost my children."

"We will go looking for them, but we have to wait until the water goes down. You're in my sister's house right now. You can go to the dresser and put on some clothes. It will help you calm down."

Watcharee went to the dresser as she had been told and put on some clothes. When she returned to the window, the woman across the way had gone back into the house. Watcharee called her daughters' names again, but instead of searching for their bodies on the street, she looked to the other buildings that still stood. Fifty yards to the south, on the opposite side of the street, she saw five or six people hanging out of two second-story windows. Most of them looked absently down to the street or out to sea, but Watcharee saw one woman looking in her direction.

"I've lost my little girls," Watcharee shouted at her.

"I saved one little girl."

"What's her name?" Watcharee cried.

The woman vanished from the window. Watcharee couldn't figure out why she would do such a thing. She turned with the intention of running over there, but when she reached the stairs, she grew too frightened to head down and turned back to the window. Looking back at the other house, she saw Frame, her eight-year-old. Her body and face and hair were covered with mud, and where her skin was visible, Watcharee could see what looked like cuts and bruises, but she was alive. It was a miracle. A clothesline had hung her baby by the neck, and she had survived. It suddenly grew hard to breathe, and Watcharee had to brace herself to keep from fainting.

"Mama!" her daughter shrieked.

"Are you all right, baby?"

"Mama, I'm coming to you."

"No!" Watcharee shouted. "Don't move. I know you want to be with me, but you have to stay right there. It isn't safe to come down yet."

"Mama, you have to come get me."

"I'll come for you in a minute, baby. Try to calm down. Everything will be fine. Do you know where your sister is?"

"I don't know, Mama."

Her daughter covered her face with her hands. She was screaming and crying beneath them.

"Just stay right there. Don't move. I'm coming right back."

Watcharee ran across the room to the window on the opposite wall, the side that faced the beach. Waves continued to wash over the shore and onto the land, but they were not the monster waves that had caused all the death and damage. She didn't know whether the big ones would return, but the thought of getting hit by another wave was somehow less terrifying than the thought of being separated from her child for another minute. She went back to the street-side window and looked at the house where her daughter now was. The bottom floor was gone, as well as several of the support beams. It looked in bad shape, and if another wave came, it could easily collapse, trapping her daughter beneath the rubble.

"Frame, I'm going to meet you out in the street, and we're going to come back to this house," Watcharee shouted. "Can you do that? Can you still run?"

"I can run, Mama."

"What about your leg? Does it hurt?"

"It hurts, but I can run."

"Okay, wait until I get downstairs, and then you come down. When you see me come toward you, run toward me."

Her daughter nodded and then disappeared from the window.

Watcharee headed down the stairs, through the area where the kitchen had been, past the pole she had gripped on to, and then out into the street. The water had gone down to shin level, exposing dozens upon dozens of bodies. She needed to somehow hide them from her daughter's eyes, but then she realized that Frame had already seen too much. If they made it through this alive, she would never be a little girl again. Her innocence had been shattered. Nightmares would haunt her, and when she awoke, there would be no escaping their truth and terror. This day had happened; everything about it was real. It struck Watcharee now, standing in the middle of the street so close to the dead, that life as she had known it had come to an end. Wimon too was gone. His body now lay at the bottom of the sea. Her knees weakened and her bones suddenly hurt. A surge of hopelessness overcame her.

Then she saw Frame running toward her across the road. Her little arms flailing in the air, her bad leg trying to catch up, her mouth open but only a whisper of a scream emerging. Hopelessness vanished and love took its place. She scooped her daughter up into her arms and ran, crying, back through the kitchen area and up the stairs. In the room on the second floor, she hugged and kissed her daughter while searching her body for wounds at the same time. When she became certain that Frame had gone without serious injury, she had to conjure all of her strength to pull away. Frame needed to be held, and Watcharee needed to hold her daughter to convince herself that her flesh hadn't gone cold, that she wasn't imagining this moment, but Film still hadn't been found. She returned to the window and called down for her baby.

For the next hour, Watcharee called out for Film. She prayed that someone else, perhaps another woman in another house, had saved her as well. Occasionally someone would pass by down below, headed for higher ground, and Watcharee would ask them if he or she had seen a little girl. Some said they hadn't, some said they weren't sure, and some said nothing at all. After an hour had passed without a wave coming, Watcharee gathered the nerve to go down to the street and look for her daughter, but then a man off in the distance began shouting about another wave. When the wave didn't come, Watcharee gathered her nerve again, but then someone else began shouting about a wave. She started losing her mind. She needed her husband to come rescue her, make all this go away, so she went to the window facing the sea and searched for any sign of Wimon, even though she knew in her heart that he would never be coming back. She began to weep uncontrollably again when she saw the scattered remains of more than a dozen longtail boats drifting in the water. Wimon was her strength, her back, her pride. Who would carry them through all this suffering and pain?

Watcharee scooped Frame into her arms and retreated to a corner of the room, where they wept for all they had lost. Soon after, Watcharee heard a helicopter overhead. The man and two women who had been in the room with her this whole time stripped off their shirts and ran to the window facing the sea. They waved their shirts madly in the air and shouted at the top of their voices. The helicopter circled over them once, twice, and then Watcharee heard the beat of its blade fade to the north. Having sunk so deep into misery, Watcharee hadn't suspected the helicopter would stop to rescue them. No one would rescue them. Eventually another wave would come or they would have to head through the graveyard below on their own two feet to reach safety.

"I see a boat out at sea," one of the women said to Watcharee. "I don't know if it's your husband's boat, but you should come take a look."

Watcharee felt a flash of anger at the woman for getting her hopes up, but she joined the woman at the window nonetheless. Once again she had to brace herself to keep from fainting. About a quarter of a mile out at sea, she saw Wimon's boat heading for the narrow inlet on the north side of the village where he always docked. The waves were quite large, lifting his boat and slamming it back down, but she knew that if he had found a way to survive the monster waves, he could survive these smaller ones.

"Daddy is coming home!" she shouted at Frame, and then lifted her so she could see with her own eyes.

Wimon would rescue them and make everything all right. He would go searching for Film, and he wouldn't stop until he found her. He would make the family whole again. Watcharee planned to wait for him here, but then, just a few minutes later, she heard a man on a loudspeaker announcing that the area still wasn't safe. Watcharee ran to the street-side window and saw the people who had taken refuge in the homes across from her wading through the mud in the direction of a rescue truck off in the distance. When the man with the loud-speaker came into the area, Watcharee called down and asked him where he was taking everyone. He said Nam Khem Temple. After being surrounded by death and destruction for three hours, Watcharee couldn't think of any place she would rather be. She made the decision to take her daughter to the temple. Wimon would find them there.

As Wimon steered his longtail down the narrow inlet on the north side of the village, the waves died away. For the entire journey into shore, he had flexed every muscle and held on to a couple of massive breaths. He had reached safety now, but he felt no relief. In the mangrove jungle off to his left, he could see bodies suspended among the tangle of vines and branches and lying at odd angles on the ground. He had held on to the hope that the waves had somehow spared Nam Khem, but that hope was now crushed.

Why did this happen? he thought. *Life is so cruel.*

Nearing the dock where he parked his boat, he saw the rear ends of a few longtails protruding from the water. He could also see ten or fifteen bodies spread out on the flat area in front of the docks. If the wave had reached this far inland, it had also reached his home, which was only fifty feet from the beach half a mile south.

Wimon ran his boat up onto shore and then proceeded to unload his brother and the two men he had saved. He didn't have the courage he needed to make the journey home yet, so he sat down in the dirt next to his brother and placed his face in his hands. A few minutes later, he heard a strange noise and looked up just in time to see the upper rim of his longtail sinking into the water. The boat had survived four massive waves and countless smaller ones, only to sink moments after he had reached the shore. He knew then that Buddha had answered his wish, and it gave him hope that perhaps his other wish had been granted as well.

Wimon helped his brother to his feet, and they began walking in the direction of their homes. Before Wimon had taken ten steps, the man from Nam Khem whom he had saved called out to him.

"Uncle, where do you live?"

Wimon spun around. "Why? Why do you ask me this?"

"I want to know so I can come pay my respects."

"Thank you, but that does not matter to me," Wimon said. "If we see each other again, we will talk. Right now I have to try to find my family."

Wimon turned and headed south, but he stopped once he reached the main road. Heading east on the road would take him home. Heading west would take him to the temple, then the highway, and then the hospital. He wanted to head east, but he could see now that the village in which he had lived for the past twenty years was gone. There was nothing left. Where hundreds of homes had stood early that morning now lay nothing but a seemingly never-ending expanse of rubble, overturned cars, and boats.

"What happened here?" he said aloud. "Life is so cruel."

He wanted so badly to head home to look for the bodies of his loved ones, but he just couldn't take another step in that direction. His brother, who had still not said a word, began to cry again. They both stood there for several minutes, staring off at the empty space where Nam Khem used to be, and then a truck hauling survivors came up the road. Wimon searched the back for his mother, wife, and children. None of them were there.

"Don't go into the village," the driver said. "Anyone who survived has already gotten out. People say the waves will be coming back."

Wimon nodded. He helped his brother into the back of the truck, and then he climbed on top of the eighteen others. They crawled slowly up the road, around the fallen electrical poles, around the cars that had been twisted into knots, and past the hundreds of bodies lying in the mud. They drove past Nam Khem Temple and then bumped out onto the highway, which had by now filled with thousands of people trying to make their way to the hospital. As Wimon witnessed the horrors around him, one thought played itself over and over in his mind: *Why did this happen? Life is so cruel.*

15 NANG

Nang drifted in and out of consciousness on top of the coconut tree for nearly an hour. It hadn't crossed her mind to try to climb down or call for help. The only rational thought that still remained was the one that told her to keep holding on to the branches. She managed to do this while awake, and she somehow managed to do this while blacked out. There had been so many frightening noises around her that her mind had turned most of them off. Now something told her to turn her audio back on. There was a voice she needed to hear.

"*Mae yoo nai. Mae yoo nai.*"

It sounded like her son's voice. She sat up and saw the wound in her leg. The top of the coconut tree was covered in blood. There was so much blood that she knew she couldn't have much left in her body. She began to feel light-headed again.

"*Mae yoo nai.* Mom, where are you?"

Now she knew that it was the voice of her twenty-year-old son.

"Nueng, I'm here."

"I can't see you, Mom."

"I'm up here in this coconut tree."

Still clutching the leaves in both hands, she leaned forward so she could look down. She saw her son standing below her, his face streaked with tears.

"What are you doing up there, Mom? You have to come down."

Nang looked out to sea. Her eyes weren't clear enough to see that far, but in her mind the disaster was still unfolding. She expected waves to come and come until the tree on which she sat toppled over. "They will have another wave, Nueng. You must run from here to the high land."

Down below, she saw her son grow alarmed. He began to run, but instead of heading inland, he headed toward the beach. He reached a home that still stood, bounded inside, and in a moment he appeared in a second-floor window. He hovered there for a few seconds, looking out to sea, and then he came running back to the coconut tree.

"Mom, you have to climb down. There is no wave coming right now. You can make it."

Nang shook her head. The coconut tree had saved her life, and she was afraid to leave it. Bodies lay in the mud for as far as she could see, and she became certain that if she went down, she'd die.

"I can't do it, Nueng. I'm too afraid."

"But Mom, you have to come down. I need to take you away from here."

"I'm afraid, Nueng. It's such a far drop."

"But you know how to do this, Mom. You just have to come down the same way you went up."

Nang realized her son wouldn't leave without her. Gathering up her nerve, she turned over to her stomach and inched her lower body over a cluster of coconuts. For a moment she dangled, but with a few strong rocking motions, she managed to get her legs wrapped around the trunk. All the hours she had spent climbing coconut trees came back once again. Her hands grabbed at branches, one after the next, until she lowered herself enough to wrap both arms around the trunk. Then she slid down, her calloused hands and feet bumping over the ribs of the tree.

She collapsed into the mud at the bottom. Worried about being naked before her son, she covered her breasts and groin with her arms, only to realize that she hadn't been stripped completely bare. She still had on her bra and underwear. Her T-shirt had been ripped away, but the elastic collar remained around her neck. The same had happened with her pants. Both legs were gone, but the waistline had survived, as well as the inner lining of one pocket. When she saw the pocket, she reached down and gave it a pat. Inside, in a small purse, she kept a single tooth from both her mother and her father. She had seen their faces while submerged under water, and now she knew that having their teeth close to her body had allowed their spirits to join with her. They had been with her the entire time and had worked a miracle.

Her son quickly stripped off his shirt and guided her head and arms through the holes. As he helped her to her feet, he caught sight of the wound in her leg.

"Mom, you must ride on my back," he said, turning around and bending over. "I will take you and run."

Nang grabbed around his neck, and her son scooped up her legs. He began running down the same street all the cars had tried to escape on, only now most of them were gone, washed into buildings or deposited hundreds of yards farther inland. As they moved by the Jai-Yen-Yen Bakery Shop, Nang felt her head growing light again.

"Nueng, I can't breathe," she cried over his shoulder. "I think I'm going to die."

Her son began shaking her legs. "Mom, please don't faint. You have to stay with me. I will take you to see a doctor. Don't leave me."

Nang managed to stay awake. They reached the bend in the road where the motorcycle wreck had occurred, and then veered to the north, toward the highway. Five hundred yards up ahead by the school, they both saw a rescue truck and several men dressed in yellow shirts. Nueng shouted at the workers for help, but with electrical poles and other debris blocking the road, they couldn't maneuver their vehicle any farther west. Nang looked in every direction for other rescue workers to come help her, but there were none. In that moment, she thought the wave must have killed most everyone in the province. If it hadn't, surely there would be more than three rescue workers. (Later, Nang learned that the majority of help had gone to Bang Sak and Bang Niang Beaches to look for the missing members of the Royal Family and to help tourists who had been vacationing at the resorts.)

Nueng, though terribly winded, managed to carry her the rest of the way. After Nang got loaded into the truck, she expected that her son would join her, but he began running back toward the beach.

"Nueng, you can't go back there," she shouted.

He stopped and turned. "I have to go back to see if I can save anyone else."

"But if another wave comes, who will take care of me?"

"I will be fine. I'll come find you in the hospital."

As the truck pulled away, Nang watched her son head back into the chaos.

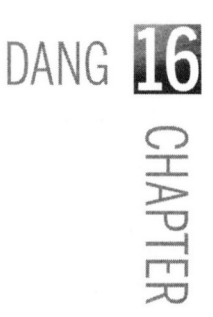
Although Dang was exhausted from fighting the wave and climbing to the roof of the Bang Sak Princess resort, she needed to reach Laem Pom. She needed to hold her children in her arms, but she couldn't run anymore. After half an hour of leaping over poles, slipping in the mud, and tripping over electrical wires strewn across the highway, her body and mind just shut down. Squatting, she wrapped her arms around her legs and buried her face between her knees. Ten minutes later, she heard a man's voice behind her.

"Sister, are you okay?"

Dang looked up and saw a young Thai couple. "I can't go on anymore. My body is bruised and my legs are so tight. I ran so far."

"Are you going to Nam Khem?"

"Yes. I need to find my children."

"Come on, sister," the man said.

He took Dang's right arm and helped her to her feet. His girlfriend took her other arm. Dang limped forward for twenty yards, but then her legs began to give out. Instead of setting her down, her companions lifted her entirely and began to carry her. Eventually Dang told them to put her down, and she walked with them. After half a mile, they began picking up their pace. Soon they were jogging.

In an hour and a half, they rounded a bend, and the road leading down to the village came into view. Dang had been praying that the wave had hit only Bang Sak Beach, but when she saw hundreds of trucks and cars packed full of broken people pulling out into the traffic jam on the highway, she knew that Nam Khem had not been spared.

Dang broke ahead of her traveling companions. She ran alongside the road with the intention of heading straight down the road leading to Nam Khem, but a policeman directing traffic at the intersection grabbed her before she had the chance.

"Don't go down there," he said. "There is nothing left of Nam Khem. Everyone is dead."

Dang opened her mouth to scream, but nothing came out. All around her were sirens, flashing lights, and panicked people. She shut her eyes and tried to make it all go away. The faces of her family appeared in her mind, and the harder she closed her eyes, the crisper those images became. She told herself that the policeman was lying, that he was a bad man trying to keep her from her children. She pushed the policeman out of her way and ran down the road.

Her lungs burned and her legs had tightened up even more, so when she saw a truck headed down instead of up, she climbed into the back. The truck drove ten yards, but then it came to an abrupt stop as a dozen cars jumped out of the opposite lane. In a matter of moments, both lanes had filled with eastbound traffic, forcing the truck Dang had climbed onto into a ditch on the side of the road. Realizing it would take hours to reach her home, Dang jumped out and began to run again.

She just kept running and running. When she passed the public health office, she knew that she had only a little bit to go. All she could think about was finding her children, yet her pace started to slow. On the road ahead of her, she could see fallen poles and mud and bodies. It became harder and harder to place one foot in front of the other. Eventually the jungle wall to her left vanished, and she had no choice but to look out across the village. It was just as the police officer had said; there was nothing left. Where houses once stood now sat massive boats, the kind that carried 20,000 pounds of fish and hundreds of men. Back on Bang Sak Beach, portions of the Princess Resort still stood, but that wasn't the case here. The monster wave had taken everything.

With her community of Laem Pom located south of the main village, on the opposite side of the rubble that stretched before her, she took a left on a road that ran parallel to the beach and headed for home. When the patch of jungle she had explored so much as a child came into view, she couldn't see her home or the homes of her neighbors. She saw only a twisted jungle blackened by muck that ran to the treetops. She stopped for a moment, just staring. Her cell phone began to ring. (Since she traveled everywhere by motorcycle, she kept her cell phone in a ziplock bag to protect it from rain; thus, it had survived being under water.)

Her hands trembled as she pulled her phone from her pocket, certain it was her husband or one of her children trying to reach her to tell her that they were alive and safe.

"Dang," said a man, his voice unrecognizable.

"Who is this?"

"It's Jui. I'm a cousin of your neighbor Meow. I'm in Bangkok right now, and I need to know if she is all right. I can't reach her."

"I don't know where anyone is. Everything here is gone."

"Dang, everything will be all right," Jui said. "At least you still have your daughter."

"No," Dang shouted. "I don't have her."

"But I can hear her crying in the background. I'm sure that's your daughter."

Dang's hand dropped from her ear, her eyes darting in all directions.

"Kwan," she shouted, "Mama is here."

When she heard no reply, she stopped and listened. There were screams and shouting off in the distance, but none of them could have been mistaken for the cries of a little girl. She suddenly grew terrified that her daughter was dead, that the crying the man had heard was her daughter's spirit trying to call out to her over the phone. She shoved her cell phone in her pocket and continued toward Laem Pom.

She stopped when she reached the barbed wire fence the Far East Company had erected directly behind her community. She could see her neighbor's six-year-old daughter, Janya, sitting with her back to the fence and her hands cupped to her cheeks. Dang pushed through the knee-high water toward her, but when she got close, she began to scream. Janya wasn't leaning up against the fence; she had been shoved into it by the wave. A strand of barbed wire had somehow gotten wrapped around her neck, and it had sliced deep into her throat. The little girl had tried to free herself, and she had died in that position. Dang couldn't imagine how long she had suffered before the end. She pulled on the barbed wire, trying to loosen the noose, but she succeeded only in sawing the razor wire deeper into Janya's throat. Not wanting to sever the girl's head, Dang backed away. She was still screaming; the blood of her neighbor's child covered her arms and legs and face.

Dang forced herself away. She walked further down the fence line and found dozens of her neighbors tangled up in the razor wire. After trying to pull several of them free but only managing to mangle them even more, she stopped touching them. Then she saw her auntie. She had been washed into a portion of the fence the Far East Company had covered with sheets of aluminum rather than barbed wire. Her auntie's face had been sliced off by a sharp edge of one of the sheets. Another sheet had stripped all the muscle and tissue off one of her legs. Dang recognized her only because of her shirt.

Somehow, Dang continued on. Wading through the water, she moved away from the fence and toward her home. On the way, she found a baby drowned in the water. She picked up the baby girl and brought her over to the roots of a tree that were not submerged. After cleaning the baby's face and body, she saw the body of a three-year-old boy who had died clutching a coconut leaf in his arms as if it were his favorite blanket. Not far from him, she found more children, all of them dead. She went to each and shook them.

"Nui, Nui," she said, "Auntie Dang is here. You need to get up and talk to me. I love you so much—you know that. You can't leave me now."

When they didn't answer, she carried them to a safe place, cleaned their bodies, and said a prayer. Having no strength to carry their bodies to the temple, 1½ miles away, she began collecting sticks and baskets floating in the water. When she found a dead body, she planted a stick in the earth next to it or placed a basket by its side so rescue workers would know where to look.

After an hour or more gathering the bodies of children, Dang finally reached the location where her house had once stood. She called hysterically for her children, her mother, and her father, but she got no answer. She found the body of her elder sister, Whipharat, and she shook her body just like she had the children. Refusing to accept that her sister was dead, Dang demanded that she get up and talk to her. Her sister didn't move. She said nothing. Crying, Dang planted a stick by her side and walked away.

Next she found the body of Roong, another neighbor. Then there were more bodies, all of them her neighbors in Laem Pom. Their entire community was gone. Everyone dead. Dang sat down in the mud. She had no reason to go on.

A good while later, she spotted a rescue worker a few hundred yards to the north, headed toward the main streets of the village.

"Older brother," she called to him. "You must come help me."

The rescue worker looked at her for a moment, but then he turned his back and continued toward the heart of Nam Khem. Dang had been out here for hours. Her whole body was covered in blood. She needed to find her children, but she came to the conclusion that if she remained in Laem Pom another minute, she too would die. She went and sat in the mud by her sister for a few more minutes, and then she headed back toward the narrow road that would take her up to the highway and to the hospital.

Her mind gone numb after seeing so much horror, she wouldn't remember what she saw along this walk or even if she talked to anyone. The only thing she knew for certain was that at some point she saw her husband in the back of a truck halfway up to the highway. He too was covered in mud, and she would later learn that he had ridden a plastic fuel container for more than half a mile and then climbed a cluster of bamboo trees to reach safety. They embraced each other for what seemed like half an hour, then headed back to Laem Pom to find their children. They found more bodies and did their best to clean each one, but when the sky began to grow dark and they still hadn't found their kids, hope began to fade. They both cried as they headed toward Yanyao Temple. It was there that they would find the dead that had already been collected.

CHAPTER 17 PUEK AND LEK

Puek and Lek reached Khao Phrapichai Mountain, the highest point on Kho Khao Island, thirty minutes after dashing away from the chaos at the intersection in the back of a truck. Lek had never been here before, and standing at the bottom and gazing up, she realized that it wasn't a mountain at all, but rather a large hill. The jungle had been cleared on the hillside, perhaps for a future crop of rubber trees, and the hundred people who had already arrived were sitting near the top. Judging by the train of cars that stretched down the road and into the distance, hundreds more would soon arrive. Lek wanted to lead Puek up so they could get some rest and be out of harm's way, but first they needed to find the father of the boy Puek held in his arms. At the intersection, both father and son had fallen off the back of the truck. The father had chased behind them for twenty yards and handed his boy to Puek. He had said he would meet them here.

As the adrenaline that had been shooting through her body for the past hour began to fade, Lek grew terribly concerned about her father, who had been milling around the house when they left that morning. If the west side of Kho Khao Island had gotten hit, then Nam Khem had probably been hit as well. Their home was near their beach. Losing his hand had made her father old before his time anyway, and now that he was on in years, he had a hard time shuffling down to the store. He didn't have the strength to run like they had or even climb a tree. She feared he was dead.

"Where's my child?" she heard a man shout.

Lek spun around and saw the father who had chased after the truck. Puek outstretched the boy he'd been holding in his arms since they'd left the intersection. "That's not my boy," the man said. "That kid is Burmese."

Puek panicked. Somehow, he had picked up the wrong boy in the back of the truck. He set down the Burmese kid, who instantly went running up the hill. Puek's hands began to tremble and he spun in all directions, as if trying to search for the man's son with the eyes he no longer had. But a moment later, the correct child came running down the hill and leapt into his father's arms. Puek produced a warm smile for their reunion, but now he couldn't get his hands to stop trembling. He felt like he was going to vomit.

Lek took Puek by the arm, and they climbed the hundred yards to the top of the clearing. Sitting down and facing east, Lek could see the rooftop of the jungle below and the sea off in the distance. Being able to watch for another wave felt reassuring, but what she truly wanted was to be on the west side of the island so she could see Nam Khem. To do that, she would have to climb through perhaps a quarter of a mile of dense jungle to reach the top of the hill, and she didn't have the strength. A large percentage of the people huddled on the hillside either lived in Nam Khem or had relatives there, and none of them had the strength to make the climb either. Everyone just sat cross-legged in silence, gazing out to sea.

Lek suddenly remembered her cell phone. She pulled it from her pocket and quickly dialed her father's number. The network was busy. She then tried to reach her younger brother Jui, who lived in Nam Khem with his wife and two children, but the network was still busy. After trying for half an hour straight but not managing to get through to anyone, she decided to save her batteries and try again later. She kept her mind from dwelling on the fate of her family by watching the people streaming in. There were five villages on the island, 1,000 residents combined, and it appeared as though all of them had decided to come to the mountain. Hundreds of Burmese, who had been working to build Jern-Jern Resort and Jom Tien Resort, also turned up. And then hundreds of Europeans who had been vacationing on the island arrived. In just a few hours, the hillside had become a refuge for more than 1,000 people.

Among the crowd, Lek spotted a ferryboat captain who shuttled people between the mainland and Kho Khao Island. Thinking that he might have news of Nam Khem, she headed down to him. He told her that he had been on his boat between the two landmasses when the wave hit. Dozens of boats had capsized, and hundreds had died in the channel. Men and women drowning in the water had cried to him for help, but with a second wave only minutes away from reaching him, he hadn't stopped. He suspected that most of those in the water had washed further out to sea. As far as Nam Khem, he didn't know what had become of the village, but the damage was severe. He doubted that anyone had survived.

Lek went back to Puek and put her arms around him. She cried on his shoulder. Her misery deepened as the wounded started to pile up around them at the top of the clearing. The sight of all the blood and gore made her stomach weak, but she couldn't let the wounded suffer on their own. She went to a foreign man whose body had been badly bruised. She offered him the inhaler that she kept in her back pocket, and when he turned it down, she bent over to rub balm on his body to ease the pain. He pushed her away and then got up and stormed off. Frightened, Lek decided that she wouldn't offer him any more help. She went to another foreign man with the intention of rubbing his body with balm, but he shouted at her not to touch him. It became clear that for some strange reason, the foreigners didn't want to be touched, so she went around offering massage to the Thai men and women, all of whom were more than grateful.

When Lek returned to Puek an hour later, she found him in a bad state. He had been sitting there by himself, listening to the cries and screams of a thousand people. She put her arm around him, trying to imagine what it had been like running from a danger he could not see. The scene on the hillside was far from tame, but she knew that in Puek's mind it must be ten times worse. He couldn't see the sunshine, the greenness of the jungle, or even the light blue of the sea off in the distance. He could hear only people's terror and pain. She worried that he would slump into serious depression, but luckily they both were soon distracted by a job to do. The leader of the island arrived with a truckload of food that needed to be prepared.

When Sudjit Rinphanit arrived with the ten-wheel truck loaded with pilfered food, he instructed a few of his employees to take the food to three different spots on the hillside and set up kitchens. Then he got on both his cell phone and his walkie-talkie and began the lengthy process of calling for help. Eventually he managed to reach the sheriff in the district office and informed him what had happened. He also spoke with two colonels, one from the police department and one from the military, both of whom were dear friends of his. All three of them promised to send help as soon as humanly possible, but with the disaster being so widespread, they didn't know when that would be.

Rinphanit had decisions to make, the most important of which concerned the wounded. Unfortunately, there were no doctors or nurses on the hillside. With many of the wounded looking like they would die before nightfall without treatment, he sent one of his employees to the public health office, located on higher ground near the ferry launch, with the intention of bringing a doctor back to the mountain. His employee returned empty-handed. The ferry launch had been struck hard, and dozens of wounded men, women, and children had already found their way to the public health office. The two doctors, who on a normal day saw nothing more than a few cuts and bruises, were madly trying to stitch a hundred open wounds. Since the doctors couldn't come to the mountain, Rinphanit decided to send the seriously wounded to them. He put drivers into two of his trucks and had them transport the injured to the public health office. He came across a foreign man whose body had been carted out to the mountain. Upon closer examination, Rinphanit realized it was the same man who had refused to leave the beach out in front of his hotel. Guilt swept over him; he should have tried harder, picked him up and carried him away if he had to. From the look of the man's body, he had suffered a horrible death.

Rinphanit felt tears well up in his eyes. He began walking toward a more secluded spot, but a foreign man on the verge of panic stopped him before he could slip away. At first, Rinphanit hadn't a clue what the man was trying to tell him, but then he saw him point to an old woman lying in the grass not far away. Rinphanit assumed it was his mother. Her body had been beaten and battered, and she looked as if she were already dead. As he moved closer, he saw her chest slowly rising and falling. In the barrage of foreign words the man produced, Rinphanit recognized one: "hospital." He assumed the man wanted to head to the ferryboat launch and attempt to take his mother off the island. If Rinphanit's mother had been lying in the grass in such bad shape, he would have done the same. He tossed the man the keys to one of his cars.

Rinphanit hoped that they would find a way to the mainland, but at the time, he had no idea how bad the ferryboat launch had been hit. It was completely gone, as were all the boats in the water. The foreign man returned with Rinphanit's car a few hours later. His mother lay dead in the backseat.

The stress of the situation began to wear on Rinphanit. He would run up the mountain to fulfill someone's request for more water, come down the mountain to organize different tasks for his employees, and then run back up the mountain to fulfill someone else's request. He was exhausted, both physically and mentally. He worried about family members he had in Nam Khem, and he still hadn't found his sister, who had been seen near the ferryboat launch just before the wave struck. Just as he began to feel like he needed to take a step back from the madness and catch his breath, he spotted Puek sitting high up on the mountain with his wife, Lek.

Rinphanit had been certain that Puek hadn't made it. He had known Puek for more than twenty years, since before Puek had been promoted to captain and reaped all kinds of success. Rinphanit had spent a lot of time with Puek during his year of bad luck, in which he had lost his vision, his son, and his boat. To see his old friend alive flooded his heart with warmth. He quickly ran over to him.

"We were together when we were happy," he said, "and now we are together when we suffer. May we always be together."

He watched Puek's face light up at the sound of his voice. After a few words, Rinphanit scurried off into the jungle and cut down a banana leaf, into which Puek and his wife could place the two spoonfuls of rice his staff members were doling out to each person on the mountain. Then he called over his daughter and asked her to fetch two blankets for Puek and his wife. Rinphanit wanted to stay and comfort his friend, but there was no time. In every minute of every hour, there was someone who needed something from him, and he did his best to fulfill those needs. Then, at approximately four twenty p.m., the first helicopter arrived, dropping packages of food.

When Rinphanit saw the packages land, he instantly knew that it would not be enough to feed a thousand people in the hours or days to come. He pushed the thought to the back of his mind to take care of more immediate matters. His staff had already cleared a landing spot in anticipation, and the moment the helicopter touched down, Rinphanit slid open the rear doors and began loading the first batch of wounded inside. After seven people had been placed in back, the helicopter took off, headed for Takuapa Hospital, above Nam Khem. Rinphanit suspected that before dark, the helicopter would be able to transport the majority of the wounded, but the rest of the people would probably have to sleep on the mountainside. They would need food, and lots of it, so he strapped life vests onto a few of his employees, gave them the keys to two of his trucks, and then prepared to send them back to his resort to raid the kitchen. As he gave them their instructions, shop owners from around the island told the workers to head to their stores to get even more supplies. No one worried about money or who would pay for the food. At that point, the only thing people cared about was saving lives.

To Lek, sitting high up on the mountain with Puek, Rinphanit looked like a great colonel commanding his army. He had transported the majority of the wounded off the mountain, catered to everyone's needs, and then, shortly after five p.m., he had sent a group of strong young men back down to his resort to get food.

While the men were away, Lek left Puek's side and walked over to a local woman who made a living turning wood into charcoal and then selling it around town. She had been sitting in the same position for hours, cradling her breasts with both arms, crying softly to herself. Lek asked her why she was crying, and the woman told her a heart-wrenching story. Her husband had given her their son to run with, and he had scooped up their daughter and followed her. Her husband hadn't run fast enough, and the wave took both him and her daughter away. She had gone back to look for them. She couldn't find her husband, but she had found her daughter's body dangling in a tree.

"I wrapped her body in a blanket," the woman said. "I didn't know what to do, so I carried my baby up here."

Lek's eyes suddenly focused on the lump under the blanket at the woman's side, and instantly she broke out into tears. She sat down next to the woman and put her arm around her. They cried together for more than an hour.

During this time, Lek watched the commotion on the hillside. She began to feel more and more sympathy for the foreigners. Her life had always been tough, and as a result, she was accustomed to hunkering down in a patch of grass without food or comfort. The majority of foreigners had come here expecting to stay in nice hotels and eat in fancy restaurants. The stress of the situation had taken its toll on them. While Thai children ran around the mountain, playing games, the foreign children just kept crying. The Thai men and women, though suffering horribly, kept to themselves and were quiet, while many of the foreigners seemed confused and angry. When she returned to Puek, he also felt bad for the foreigners, so they decided to give one of their blankets to a foreign family huddled close together to their left.

Later in the afternoon, Rinphanit's employees returned from their supply-gathering mission. They carried everything up the mountain and laid it out on the earth. While one group of men and women began cooking, another group went around to the foreign families to distribute the tents that had been collected from the hotel. An hour later, everyone ate a hearty meal of eggs, rice, and sausage. While Lek and Puek searched for a softer patch of earth in anticipation of the night ahead, they came across a middle-aged Thai woman cradling the lifeless body of her elderly mother in her arms. They decided to sit close to her so they could offer her support during the night, but she was beyond comforting. She refused to let go of her mother, claiming that the feel of her skin was the only thing keeping her together. Both Puek and Lek worried about her, but there was nothing they could do. As they night wore on, they watched the woman deteriorate to the point where she could no longer speak. It dropped Lek into a deep depression. She began wondering how much more she would have to endure. She had lost her son, her husband had lost his sight, and now an unimaginable disaster might have claimed the life of her father. She wondered what she could have possibly done for her life to have been filled with such torment.

THE HOSPITAL 18

While making his second trip from the Bang Sak Princess Resort to the hospital, Lieutenant Colonel Niphon Yanphaisarn got stuck in a traffic jam on the highway just north off the turnoff to Nam Khem. Having eight severely wounded men and women in the back of his truck, he tried jumping onto the shoulder of the road to bypass the wait, but a hundred other cars had already beaten him to the punch, and now the shoulder had backed up as well. Still a mile from the hospital, Yanphaisarn heard a commotion in the bed behind him. He spun around and saw the elderly man they'd picked up going into convulsions. The officers in back tried to hold him down, but the man's arms and legs flung wildly around the bed. This went on for about twenty seconds, and then the man died. As an investigator, Yanphaisarn had seen hundreds of dead bodies, but seldom had he seen someone die before him. It struck him hard. He spun back around and searched for the fastest route to the hospital.

Things were beginning to fall apart. There were trucks filled with injured people pulling out of Nam Khem and speeding north, toward the hospital. There were families racing south, trying to reach their relatives in Nam Khem. There were mobs of frantic people running and screaming everywhere. Yanphaisarn began to realize that the scope of the disaster was much larger than he had first thought, and this became even more evident when he reached the hospital fifteen minutes later. What seemed like a hundred cars had been abandoned out front, and when he and his men carried the seven wounded they had collected toward the ER, he found dozens of injured men and women lying on the lawn out in front. He wondered why they remained outside when a hospital lay right in front of them, but as he climbed the ambulance ramp, he learned the answer. The hospital was full. The beds had been filled with foreign victims, the Burmese workers he had seen on his first visit had been moved to the floor, and Thai people lay everywhere. Yanphaisarn didn't want to put the victims he had rescued down on the floor, but he didn't have a choice. Never had he seen such chaos.

He headed back outside and then just stood there, trying to decide what to do. The ten men he had sent to protect the Royal Family were missing, and hundreds of wounded still lay in the mud at the Bang Sak Princess. He considered just heading south and picking up as many bodies as he could, but he knew that the drive back to the hospital might take hours. Judging by the hundreds of cars coming from both the north and the south, the traffic and panic would get only worse. Feeling lost and confused, not knowing where to begin, he suddenly stepped out onto the highway and started directing traffic.

Inside the hospital, most of Doctor Wut Winothai's patients who had been sleeping soundly in their beds before the tsunami struck had discharged themselves by noon. Some returned home to check on their loved ones. Some left because they had lost all hope of any further treatment, and still others left because the wounded men and women and children on the floor appeared to need their beds a whole lot more than they did. Doctor Winothai felt relief when they were gone. The staff currently had more than 2,000 people to treat, 600 of whom were seriously injured and had been admitted. With the hospital having only 177 beds, patients lined the floor of every room of every building, including the abandoned building they hadn't used in years. Patients spilled out into the hallways and down the ambulance ramp in front of the emergency room. The staff even had wounded on the front lawn.

Doctor Winothai ran from one side of the hospital to the other, cleaning and stitching gashes of all shapes and sizes, but then the hospital began to run out of supplies. First went the gauze, then the alcohol, and then the painkillers. The cafeteria soon ran out of food. When they ran out of something, they tried to use something else in its place. For gauze they used pieces of cloth, and for alcohol they used another antiseptic. Just as they started to run out of the alternatives, local pharmacies began delivering crates of supplies. The one thing they couldn't afford to run out of—which they didn't, thanks to the pharmacies—was antibiotics. Every cut, whether it was a massive wound or a little scratch, festered in a matter of hours due to the bacteria the tsunami had stirred up.

It got so bad that eventually Doctor Winothai started sending people away. The hospital had six respirators, which pumped air into the lungs of those who could no longer breathe on their own, but they had more than fifteen patients who needed to be hooked up to them. Doctor Winothai had only two choices—watch them die, or attempt to save their lives by packing them into an ambulance and sending them off to another hospital, all of which were hours away. And many of those who were lucky enough to get hooked up to a respirator still didn't make it. In addition to having inhaled large amounts of water, they also had sand and mud and other debris in their lungs. In the larger hospitals, the staffs had bronchoscopes, which could wash all that harmful matter out, but Takuapa Hospital didn't have one. And even if they did have one, it wouldn't have been enough. They needed fifteen of them. And if they had fifteen, they still wouldn't have had enough specialists to run them. All Doctor Winothai could do was hope that his patients got rid of the matter on their own—several of his healthier patients coughed violently, and in the murky water they expelled were leaves and pine needles and sand.

The three surgeons in the hospital performed one operation after the next, but with more than a hundred patients needing surgery, they couldn't even make a dent. If they worked fast and without complications or breaks, Doctor Winothai figured each surgeon could perform one operation per hour. He did the math and realized that by the end of the day, they would still have more than fifty patients who needed operations, and that didn't include those among the hundreds still pouring into the hospital who would need surgery as well. The only thing they could do was start sending them to other hospitals with the hope that they survived the journey.

The madness carried over to the x-ray room. To treat the patients who had drowned, Doctor Winothai needed an x-ray of their lungs to see how much water they had inhaled. The surgeons needed x-rays of their patients' broken bones before they were laid onto the operating table. Normally they had five x-ray technicians working their two machines, but two of the technicians were on vacation and one had died in the tsunami. The two remaining technicians worked as fast as they could, but it was impossible for them to x-ray 200 people in any reasonable amount of time. As a result, more patients got sent away.

Doctor Winothai felt on the verge of a meltdown. Every time he entered a room, he got asked by three or four nurses to check this patient or that. Every time he set out to accomplish a task, he got bombarded in the hall and acquired three more tasks. At all times, he had a list of ten or twelve things he needed to accomplish locked in his head, and all it took was for someone to give him one more thing to do for that whole list to come crumbling down. The nurses did the best they could, but there weren't enough of them either.

As Doctor Winothai moved from place to place, he kept having two recurring thoughts: *Our emergency plan has fallen to shambles* and *This is the greatest disaster Thailand has ever known.*

When Wimon climbed off his boat and saw the wreckage of his village, he lost nearly all hope that his family could have survived, but one of the first people he saw upon walking through the hospital doors was his mother. His heart felt like it would burst as he ran forward and embraced her. He learned that it was his mother's devotion to Buddhism that had saved her life. She had gone to the temple that morning to make a merit. When she came out of the hall and heard that massive waves had just swept over Nam Khem, she thought she had lost four of her children to the sea and instantly fainted. Her chest hurt a little from her fall, but now that her Wimon had come back, she felt much better. She hugged and kissed him and then whispered a magic sentence into his ear: *"Your wife survived."*

Wimon gave his mother one last kiss and then went running through the hospital, trying his best not to bump into the doctors and nurses speeding down the halls but doing so nonetheless. Finally he peered into a room and saw his wife lying next to Frame. His wife had stitches on her shoulder and bandages covering what he would later learn to be a broken collarbone. Frame had scrapes on her body and mud in her hair, but otherwise looked fine. He went and lay down next to them, already weeping because he could see on both of their faces that something awful had happened.

"Where is she?" Wimon asked.

His wife took his hand. "The water took her away from me."

"Has anyone found her body?"

Watcharee shook her head and then buried her face in her husband's chest.

Wimon tried to climb to his feet to go find Film, but he found that he couldn't. He felt like something had snapped in his mind. He couldn't talk or stand up. All he could do was weep like a child. Never had he seen this amount of cruelty cast upon the world. His daughter's life had only begun. She had been filled with such happiness and innocence. Her biggest concern in this world was getting a slice of watermelon. He was sick with grief.

About an hour later, his brother Nikhom walked into the room with his son. Wimon just stared at them as if they were ghosts. After the first wave struck, Nikhom's boat had vanished. Wimon had been certain that the wave had torn their longtail apart and they had drowned. He asked his brother how he had made it, and Nikhom told him that he had gone over the waves sidelong. Hearing that brought goose bumps to Wimon's arms. It told him one very powerful thing—his family were survivors. Nikhom was still missing his wife and his four-year-old grandson, Boat. Just before dark, Wimon left the hospital with Nikhom and they hitched a ride back to Nam Khem to find those they loved, praying that they too had somehow survived.

Walking across the rubble in the area where their homes had stood earlier that morning, Wimon stumbled upon Boat—he'd been crushed under a cement electric pole. Hesitantly, he called his brother over. Nikhom held it together the best he could. By the time they had moved the pole and placed Boat's body into the back of a rescue truck, it had already gotten dark. Wimon and his brother headed back to the hospital. With the main lobby now overflowing with people, Wimon took his mother to stay with a friend at the public health office and then returned to his wife. He spent an hour by her side, but eventually he could tell he was beginning to get in the way of the doctors, so he headed back outside, found a patch of grass in front of the hospital, and lay down. He cried softly to himself the rest of the night, trying in vain to put whatever had broken in his mind back together.

Having survived the massive waves by finding refuge in a coconut tree, Nang finally arrived at the hospital. A few minutes after rescue workers dropped her off, she got escorted to a corner of the ER by one of the twenty nurses running in every direction. The nurse seemed very sweet, and she did a thorough job of cleaning the grime and dirt out of the massive hole in her leg. But instead of calling over a doctor to stitch her wound, the nurse put a makeshift patch on top of it to stop the heavy bleeding.

"Will I get to see a doctor?" Nang asked.

"Do you think you can wait?"

Nang looked around at the other people lying on the floor. She was in a great deal of pain and still felt faint, but she could see nearly a dozen people in her immediate area who looked on the verge of death. There were men and women foaming at the mouth. Several people appeared to be foaming at the eyes.

"I can wait a little while," Nang said.

The nurse patted her on the shoulder and then charged off into another room. Nang curled her arms around her chest and waited, but an hour later she still hadn't seen a doctor. It wasn't that doctors weren't available. In the last hour, she had seen a handful of them come into the ER to treat the foreigners, many of whom had only minor scrapes. The doctors had also helped Thai people, but apparently only those who teetered on the brink of death. It made Nang concerned that she would never get treated, but she was too weak and timid to speak up. Eventually she began to feel as though she was getting in the way and moved to a less crowded room.

Nang began to nod off. She would sleep for ten or fifteen minutes, and then some sound would awaken her. Finally, her son returned from his journey collecting survivors down on the beach. They huddled together for the remainder of the afternoon, through the night, and then well into the following day. She didn't get to see a doctor in that time.

As the afternoon progressed, Doctor Wut Winothai started running into serious problems with the foreign patients, as did the four other general practitioners. Doctor Winothai cleaned their wounds with great care, but when he finished and needed to move on to the next patient, they wouldn't allow him to leave. Since very few of the nurses spoke English, the foreigners all wanted to speak with a doctor. Some would demand that he lead them to their family members in another part of the hospital. Others had lost their money or jewelry and wanted him to help them find it. Doctor Winothai was in the business of helping people, and he found it very hard to turn down their requests. His Thai patients began to suffer as a result.

He had his limits, of course. When the same foreigner made the same request three times in a single hour, Doctor Winothai decided to put his foot down. He continued to help the foreigners, but he stopped going over to them every time they wanted to see a doctor. It had a negative side effect. Several of the foreigners began shouting until a doctor finally went over to them. Doctor Winothai realized that everyone under his care suffered more than just the wounds on their bodies. They needed emotional support. More specifically, they needed emotional support from a person in a position of authority. They wanted to hear from a man who had spent six years in medical school that everything would turn out fine. Doling out emotional support was one of Doctor

Winothai's specialties, but with more than 2,000 wounded people lying in every room and hallway, lifting his patients' spirits was the last thing on his list. He knew that it would have negative repercussions in the future. The hospital would get complaints from foreigners and Thai alike saying that the doctors didn't care, but at least Doctor Winothai would be able to sleep at night knowing he had saved as many lives as he could.

The doctors eventually held a meeting about what to do with their foreigner predicament. They came to the conclusion that just healing patients in the hospital would be hard enough without having to run trivial errands, so they decided their best plan of attack was to discharge the foreigners as fast as possible. It meant treating them first, which would appear to the doctors' Thai patients as if they were favoring the foreigners, but the doctors all felt that in the long run it would result in better treatment for their Thai patients.

They started by patching up the foreign patients who had minor injuries and sending them on their way. Then they moved on to the foreign patients who were more seriously injured. They placed them in beds and got them fixed up to the point where they could travel, and when helicopters began arriving in the late afternoon, they began shuttling them out to private hospitals. It went quite smoothly, because the majority of the foreigners had insurance. Doctor Winothai and his fellow practitioners didn't view this as unethical; the foreigners would get the personal attention that they needed, and with nearly every private hospital in the country being better equipped than Takuapa Hospital, they would receive treatment closer to what they were accustomed to in their own countries. In addition to this, the private hospitals also had officers who could contact their embassies and arrange further help.

To be fair, every time a helicopter came in, Doctor Winothai would ask his Thai patients if they wished to be transferred to a private hospital with the foreigners, but very few took him up on the offer. Most of them didn't have insurance, and those who did have insurance didn't want to leave their families and friends, even if it meant that they might die. As a result, seven foreigners went out with each helicopter, and the complaints from other Thai patients rolled in. It got to the point where Doctor Winothai and his fellow doctors had to decide whose lives they would save. Each foreigner who left opened up another bed for a Thai, but that still left hundreds of Burmese patients lying on the ground. When Doctor Winothai sat down and treated a wounded Burmese, he used the same methods and the same antibiotics as he did on the men and women from his own country, but he didn't sit down and treat them nearly as often.

The reasons were many. For hundreds of years, Thailand had been a proud, independent country that never much cared for its neighbors. Cambodians were considered lower than them. Laotians were considered younger brothers to the Thai, which meant that the Laotians had to pay them respect. The Vietnamese couldn't be trusted, and the Burmese, historically, had been their enemy. They tolerated the thousands of Burmese who illegally crossed the border, because they needed the cheap labor, but to treat a wounded Burmese while a Thai patient lay bleeding didn't seem right to him. It wasn't something Doctor Winothai was proud of, but he had to make a choice: Treat men and women who lived next door, or treat a group of Burmese workers who had illegally entered his country. There had been a lot of hard decisions during the course of the day, but that wasn't one of them.

Images of the bodies she'd seen wrapped up in the barbed wire fence still clung to Dang's mind when she walked into the hospital with her husband well after dark. They moved from room to room, looking for their children and the other members of their family. In one of the last rooms, Dang saw her mother lying on a bed. Dang wanted to run to her and hug her with all her might, but her body looked in such bad shape that Dang kneeled down at her side and took her hand instead. Her mother's eyes fluttered open.

"Dang," she whispered. "I thought you were dead."

"Mama, are you all right? You look in so much pain."

"I'm all right, baby. Don't you worry about me."

Dang looked deep into her eyes. "Where is our family, Mama?"

Her mother's eyes turned away. "I was with your father. He saw the low tide and went running to the beach to warn people. He didn't worry about his own life. When he came back to get me, the wave hit him. I fainted and woke up here."

"Did he survive?"

"I don't see how he could have, baby," her mother said, trying to hold back her tears. "I think your father died."

"And what about my children?"

"Your younger sister, she escaped with your niece and nephew on a scooter."

"Did she take Kwan and Arthorn?"

Her mother started crying. "She tried calling to Kwan. She saw Kwan start to run. No one knows. Your sister went back looking for her when the water was gone. She shouted her name but couldn't find her."

"But she could be all right? She could have run away."

"Baby," her mother said, squeezing her hand, "I don't think she could have survived."

"And what about my son?"

"You know. . . . The people here—when I got here, I asked them for twenty baht," her mother said, trying to avoid the horror by focusing on trivial facts. "They gave me forty baht, because I didn't have anything left."

"Mama, what about my son?"

Her mother's body began to tremble. "I don't think he survived."

Dang lost control. She let go of her mother's hand and crumpled to the floor. Tueng knelt down and put an arm around her. He too wept uncontrollably.

"Tueng," Dang said. "Now we have nothing left."

"But we don't know for certain. We mustn't give up hope. If you give up hope, I don't know what we will do. You have to be strong now. We don't know anything for sure."

Dang labored to her feet. She kissed her mother and then headed out into the emergency room. She stopped everyone she knew, and some that she didn't know, to ask if they had seen her son or daughter. Everyone in the lobby said that they hadn't, so Dang went outside where more groups had gathered and asked the same question. After a hundred people said they hadn't seen anyone in her family, a man who owned a restaurant where they frequently ate said that he might have seen her son.

"He's about fourteen, right? He drives a Honda Zonic motorcycle?"

"Yes, yes."

"I'm not sure if it was him, but the kid I saw had short pants and no shirt."

"Yes!" Dang shouted.

"If that was your boy that I saw, then he is still alive. A lot of people have gathered at the district hall. You might want to go there looking for him."

Holding her husband's hand, Dang crossed the highway and ran a few hundred yards to the north. She pushed her way through the crowd of hundreds that had gathered on the lawn in front of the district hall, but after making several laps, she still hadn't found her son. Eventually, she decided to go back to the hospital. After searching every room twice, she went to the district hall again. She went back and forth with her husband for the rest of the night, shouting her son's name. As the next morning broke, her husband pulled her into his arms. They could keep checking the hospital and the district hall, he told her, but at some point they also needed to go to Yanyao Temple and search among the piles of the dead.

After directing traffic out in front of the hospital for more than an hour, Lieutenant Colonel Niphon Yanphaisarn was relieved by a couple of traffic police. With the highway backed up in both directions, going back to the Bang Sak Princess was out of the question. He went to the station instead. He got on the radio and put out an all points bulletin for all off-duty policemen from every station in the area to report to work at once. Then he gathered up all he needed to make reports on dead bodies, asked three of his subordinates who always assisted him on such inspections to join him, and headed over to Yanyao Temple.

Twenty bodies lay on the ground in front of the temple. A doctor from the hospital arrived to assist Yanphaisarn with the lengthy process of examining the bodies and writing up the reports, but before they began, Yanphaisarn separated the deceased into two piles. At one side of the yard, he placed the foreigners, and on the other side, he placed the Burmese and Thai. He hoped that the identification process would go quickly, but as he moved the bodies around, he noticed that the looting had already begun. The rear pockets of many men and women had been slashed with a knife and their wallets removed. Yanphaisarn wanted to get the bodies released to their families as quickly as possible, but with many corpses now lacking ID, the process would take much longer.

With no time to waste, he assigned a number to each body and created a folder to correlate to each number. They began with body #1. The doctor worked to determine the cause of death, and Yanphaisarn and his men filled out the necessary paperwork. They wrote down a description of the victim's clothing and jewelry and where his body had been found. After taking a fingerprint and photographing the victim, they placed all the paperwork into the folder and moved on to body #2.

They had finished approximately seven bodies when they heard a rumor that another wave was coming. The doctor and all of Yanphaisarn's men dropped the folders they had been carrying and went running toward neighboring buildings to reach the second floor. Yanphaisarn headed for the bank behind the temple and hovered on the front stoop. At the first sign of danger, he planned to shoot out the glass doors and head up to the third floor.

When no wave materialized, everyone regrouped by the bodies. While making their hasty escape, however, they had haphazardly tossed all the folders into the air. Paperwork was scattered about the yard, and after spending half an hour trying to put the papers back into the right folders, they realized that it would be much easier to just start over. This time they had examined ten bodies before another rumor circulated and all the folders were dropped.

As the afternoon dragged on and they still hadn't made much progress, hundreds of people started wandering into the temple, looking for their loved ones. At first Yanphaisarn thought it was quite convenient, because it would make the identification process go that much quicker, but then family members wanted to remove their deceased relatives before he'd had a chance to complete his report.

The Muslims were especially difficult, because under their religion they had to bury the dead before sunset.

Yanphaisarn felt horrible arguing with men and women who had just suffered such a heartbreaking loss, but he couldn't just release the bodies to people who claimed to be family members. The government paid upwards of 40,000 baht to a family that had lost a relative, and in all the commotion, Yanphaisarn knew it would be all too easy for someone to steal a stranger's body and then claim it as a relative. Then the family the body truly belonged to would never get to burn their loved one and hold a funeral ceremony. They would never get to collect the money they had coming to them.

As long as they didn't have any more rumors circulate, Yanphaisarn hoped to finish his work over the next five or six hours so he could release the last of the bodies to the families by midnight. But each time they finished with one batch, another batch would come in. By seven o'clock, he had more than 250 bodies before him. At eight, more than 300. He heard over the radio that Bang Muang Temple, which was located closer to Nam Khem, had the same number. And yet the deceased continued to roll in by the truckload. Eventually, Yanphaisarn stopped separating the foreigners from the Thai and Burmese. In addition to no longer having the time to do this, they had also run out of space at the temple to use as a divider between the two groups. Outwardly, he kept doing his job, but inside he was falling apart. The waves had come and gone in less than twenty minutes. How many more lives could they have claimed? A hundred? A thousand? This made no sense at all.

In the evening, Doctor Wut Winothai grew worried again. Pharmacies had been bringing by boxes of supplies all afternoon, but now the donations had begun to taper off and the hospital was running out of supplies again. Just as he began to give up hope, the hospital in Surat Thani sent a handful of much-needed surgeons, nurses, ambulances, and an officer to help with logistics.

Since the operating room was only large enough to handle the surgeons currently at work, the surgeons from Surat Thani began loading up the ambulances with the most critical patients and taking them back to their hospital. Doctor Winothai had hoped it would lessen the burden, but patients continued to arrive by the dozens. Every nurse and every doctor had been going full steam for close to sixteen hours. Nearly everyone working in the hospital had lost someone they knew or loved to the massive waves, yet no one was ready to quit. Doctor Winothai would have worked straight into the next day and the day after that, but thankfully he didn't need to. Around one a.m., the trucks packed with wounded stopped arriving. He took it for what it was—a temporary lull. With the night pitch-black and the electricity down, rescue workers were probably just unable to find any more survivors buried beneath the rubble. At first light, they would resume their search, and the injured would start flowing into the ER once again.

After making a couple more rounds, Doctor Winothai got one of his fellow doctors to cover for him. He headed out the rear entrance and sluggishly crossed the few hundred yards to his home. He took a quick shower and then climbed into bed. But he couldn't sleep. He kept hearing screams and cries in his head. He tossed and turned for three hours, trying to force his mind to shut down. When it refused, he climbed out of bed, put his clothes on, and headed back into the chaos.

At four a.m., Lieutenant Colonel Niphon Yanphaisarn got a call from his boss. Yanphaisarn still had to write up reports on the majority of the 400 bodies that had now piled up at Yanyao Temple, but his boss wanted him to head out to La Flora Resort to look for the body of the King's grandson. Yanphaisarn finished the report he was working on, and then he hopped in his truck and headed over there. He expected he would have to park at the Bang Sak Princess and then walk the rest of the way, but when he arrived, all the big debris had already been cleared from the road. There were more than a hundred policemen and a hundred soldiers in the area, all of them looking for the King's grandson.

Before climbing out into the darkness, Yanphaisarn grabbed his camera off the passenger seat. If he came across a body, he would snap a photo to make the report process much easier later on. Heading through the rubble toward the beach, he spotted a policeman he recognized from another station beating some bushes with a golf club to see if he could find anything inside. Yanphaisarn headed over to him.

"Inspector Yanphaisarn," the man said. "What are you doing here?"

"I'm helping look for the grandson. If you find any bodies, let me know so I can take pictures and write up the appropriate form."

"How many cameras did you bring?"

"Just one. Why?"

The man lifted his golf club and swung it in a circle.

"Because in this small area around us, I've found more than thirty bodies. All of them foreigners."

Yanphaisarn squinted into the darkness, and as his eyes began to adjust, the bodies of dozens of men and women came into view. As he realized that this was just one small section of one beach, the scope of the tragedy began to sink in. They were not looking at a few hundred dead as he had thought earlier in the morning, or even a thousand dead as he had thought when he'd left the temple not half an hour before. Thousands upon thousands had lost their lives.

After finishing the film he had in his camera and loading his truck with bodies, Yanphaisarn headed back to Yanyao Temple to drop the bodies off and get more film. Along the way back, he saw a train of headlights off in the distance. A few seconds later, more than fifty rescue trucks passed him. He breathed a sigh of relief.

THE HUNT
FOR THE MISSING

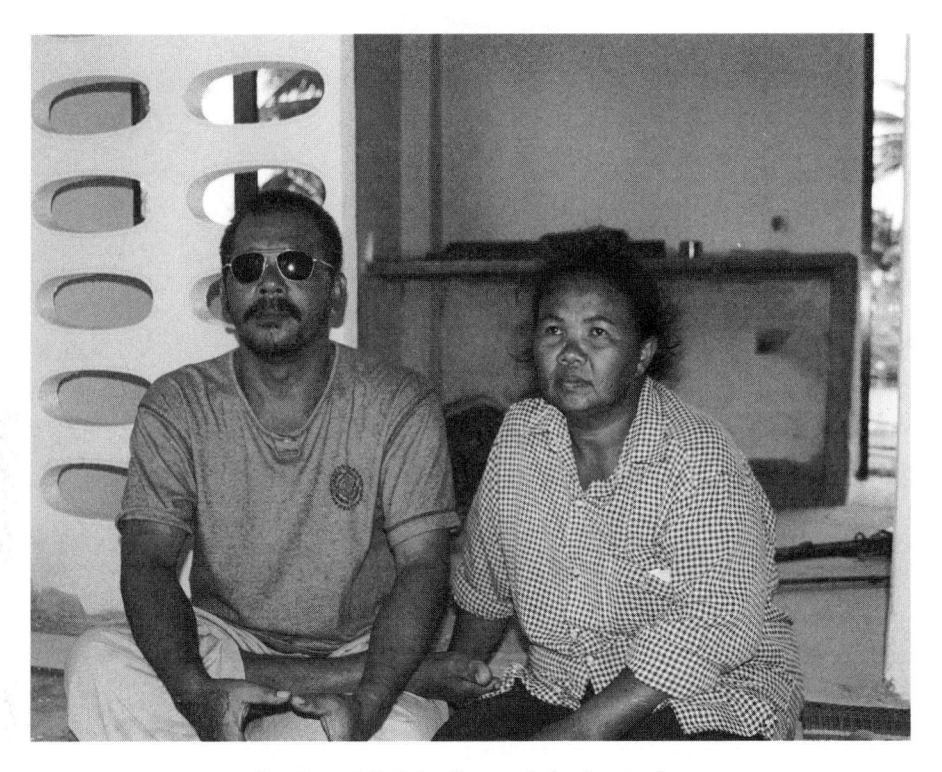

*Puek and Lek in front of the home that
Compassion in Action helped to build.*

CHAPTER 19 DANG

As the sun came over the horizon, Dang still hadn't found her eight-year-old daughter and her fourteen-year-old son. During the night, she had made more than twenty trips from the subdistrict hall to the hospital, the hospital to Yanyao Temple, and Yanyao Temple back to the subdistrict hall. She called their names everywhere she went, dug through the bodies piled in the backs of trucks in search of their faces, and asked everyone she saw if they had seen her little girl and boy. The man who said he'd seen her son running from the wave had given her a shred of hope, but now that hope began to fade. No one else had seen anything.

At eight a.m., she hitchhiked down the highway, reached the narrow road leading to Nam Khem, and then walked down to her community of Laem Pom to look for their bodies. With the rescue workers focusing on the village, the dead she had marked with baskets and sticks the previous afternoon still remained. She bypassed those she knew were not her relatives and found a dozen more of her neighbors buried in the mud and tangled up in the barbed wire fence the Far East Company had erected two years before. Around noon she began to feel faint, and she realized that she had not eaten in more than twenty-four hours. Relief workers were handing out little packets of food and bottles of water in the village, so she left her community to sit down in the shade and eat. She took one bite out of a sandwich and had to spit it back out for fear she would vomit. She didn't try eating again—she sipped on some water instead. When she no longer felt light-headed, she headed back toward Laem Pom and saw an intimidating-looking man standing by the barbed wire fence.

Thinking the man had come to search for relatives of his own, Dang attempted to walk past him. He quickly blocked her path.

"Dang," the man said, "don't even think about coming onto this land."

"How do you know my name?"

"I know your name, I know where you work, and I know the names of everyone in your family. This is not your land anymore. Your home is gone. You have nothing here, and I won't let you past me."

Dang felt confusion sweep over her. Later, she would learn that this man's name was Boonsri Boonthongkum, a local thug who had been hired by the Far East Company to claim their land. But now she knew nothing other than that this man was stopping her from accomplishing her mission.

"I need to find my children," Dang said. "Right now I am missing seven people in my family. I'm missing my daughter, my son, my father, my younger brother, my sister, my nephew, and my aunt. I need to go to my home to find their bodies, so please let me pass. I beg you."

Boonthongkum grabbed her arm and squeezed it tight. "Dang, you will lose your life if you try to go home. The tsunami might not have taken you from this land, but I will."

Dang thought about running past him, pushing him over, striking him until he fell, but she had the strength to do none of those things. She remembered what had happened to Mr. Nithat Siribenjakul, the man who had been hired by the company to convince the residents of Laem Pom to leave and then flipped sides. They had murdered him in cold blood. The look on the thug's face said that he would do the same to her. Fearing for her life, she pulled her arm out of the man's grasp and then ran back toward the highway.

She went to the hospital, to find her mother getting rolled out the front doors in a wheelchair. The doctors had given her an injection and a bottle of antibiotics, and they were now sending her on her way.

"My mother still isn't well," Dang said to the doctor.

"We don't have enough room here," the doctor returned as sympathetically as he could after having worked nonstop for the past twenty-four hours. "You're going to have to take your mother to stay at the district hall."

Too weak and shaken to argue, Dang nodded and then wheeled her mother down the street. But when she got to the district hall, there was no room out on the grass in the shade, so she had to put her mother on the cement under the sala. There were no pillows, blankets, or mats, but there wasn't much Dang could do. There was no help to be found anywhere.

After spending the next several hours wandering around in a daze, looking in this truck and that for her children at Yanyao Temple, Dang felt her cell phone vibrating in her pocket. She pulled her phone out and pressed the talk button.

"Mama, is that you?" her son said, and instantly Dang collapsed to her knees. "I've tried to call you so many times. You have to come pick me up."

"Where are you, baby?"

"They took me to the hospital in Surat Thani."

"Is your sister with you? Do you know where she is?"

"I'm sorry, Mama," he said, crying now. "I couldn't help her. I don't know where she is."

"It's okay. It's going to be all right. I'm still looking for her, baby. We're going to find her. I'm going to come pick you up right now."

"Please hurry. I'm scared."

Dang hung up the phone and ran straight for the district hall. Her uncle had come in his truck early in the morning to help the family out. They got on the road twenty minutes later. When they finally arrived at the hospital, Dang found her son standing in the lobby, dressed in hospital clothes. He had bumps and scrapes on his arms and legs, and he was holding his chest, but he didn't have any serious injuries. The second she picked him up, they both broke into tears.

"The wave hit me and made me crash into a roof," he said through his sobs into her ear. "Then it took me from the roof into a coconut tree, and I hurt my chest. I grabbed that tree so tight. I saw one woman drowning, so I grabbed her and we hugged the tree together. When the water went down, I walked into

Nam Khem, looking for you. A big truck with ten wheels picked me up there and took me here. I kept thinking how alone I was. I thought I lost everything, everyone was gone already. Then I asked people here to use their phones. I called you so many times, but I could never reach you."

"It's okay. I'm here now."

"Mama?"

"Yes, baby."

"Tomorrow we have to find Kwan."

"We'll do that. First thing in the morning."

20 WICHIEN AND NANG

Wichien had been trying to reach Nang for the past thirteen hours. He had been on the bottom of a river on the gulf side of the isthmus, collecting sand used for ceramics, when the tsunami had occurred. He hadn't realized disaster had struck until his boss called him into the office later that day to watch the news. Wichien had seen footage of the devastation on Phi-Phi Island and Patong Beach, on the island of Phuket, but there wasn't any mention of Nam Khem. His boss had taken him to the bus station at first light, and now he had been sitting on a bus for what seemed like an eternity, trying to get home.

Still a few hours away from Nam Khem, he managed to get through to his son on his cell phone. Once he was certain that his son had been unharmed, he asked Nueng about his mother.

"She is in the hospital," he said.

"Is she going to be all right? Please tell me she will be all right."

His son wouldn't answer.

When Wichien got off the bus at the main intersection above Nam Khem at three p.m., his son was waiting for him with tears in his eyes. Together they rushed to the hospital. Wichien suspected he would find Nang in a bed, getting looked after by a doctor, but instead he found her huddled in a corner of a room far away from the main lobby. Her face was now swollen to twice its size, and her cheeks were a grotesque blue. She had cuts and scrapes all over her body, and when he lifted the bandage covering the massive hole in her leg, he could see torn muscle and what looked like bone. At first he didn't even think that the lady before him was his wife; she looked nothing like the young girl he had fallen in love with many years before. Never had he seen Nang with such a broken look on her face.

He hugged her gently and kissed her forehead. "How long have you been here like this?"

"Since after it happened," she said weakly.

"Why haven't you seen a doctor? Why do you sit here like this?"

"I don't know who I can go see."

Wichien felt anger well up inside of him at how his wife had been neglected, and he stormed into the main lobby and then off into the surrounding rooms. Everywhere, he saw foreign men and women who had much less serious wounds lying in bed and getting cared for. Wichien approached the first doctor he saw.

"My wife is lying down without a blanket or a mattress. Why haven't you done anything for her? Why are you helping all the foreigners first?"

"We have to look after them. They are our guests," the doctor replied.

"What about the Thai people? You believe that the Thai people should die first? A lot of people from Nam Khem got hit by the waves. Why don't you look after them? Do you want to let them die here?"

"Where is your wife?" the doctor asked.

Wichien stopped shouting and led the doctor to Nang. Upon seeing the wound in her leg, the doctor called for some nurses to help him, and they brought her into a room and placed her on a bed. In less than an hour, two Japanese doctors entered and examined her. They had arrived with eighteen other doctors from Japan earlier in the day, and they had their act together. They had come with their own equipment and a mountain of supplies—boxes of alcohol, gauze, bandages, and antibiotics. They brought enough to fill the entire storage shed of the hospital. They worked only with wounds, and they worked with them well. They would put their gauze, medicine, alcohol, and antibiotics into a basket, and then two of them would approach a single patient.

While one of the doctors massaged Nang's feet to get her to relax, the other one cut off some of the dead skin and decided that she needed an operation to take the infection out of the wound. Nang almost refused, fearing the pain, but eventually she agreed. (Later she would be glad that she had gone through with it. In the weeks to come, she saw more than a few men and women whose minor cuts had become infected and caused them to lose their limbs.)

Just before dusk, Wichien left his wife's side for an hour and headed down to Nam Khem to retrieve their money and documents. A few times he lost his way, because there were no longer any landmarks to help him. After half an hour of working over and around the debris, he entered his neighborhood and saw that his home still stood; at least, part of it still stood. The front and back walls were gone, and everything on the bottom floor was stripped away, but the roof was still intact, as was the second floor. If his wife had taken refuge there, instead of running, she wouldn't have suffered so horribly, but there was no way she could have known.

Wichien didn't like being this close to the beach, but he needed to retrieve his money, his wife's jewelry, the deed to his home, and all the other documents he kept in a small box in his bedroom on the second floor. The moment he climbed up to his loft, however, he noticed that he had come too late. Someone had already been there. They had stolen not only their box of valuables but also their rice cooker, television, radio, clothes, and shoes. They had even taken their coat hangers. To rub salt into the wound, the thieves had defecated on his floor before they left.

Wichien took a seat. Since he'd been shot in Burma, he had lived an honest life, going to Nam Khem Temple once a week. He had worked so hard for so long, and now his wife lay in the hospital, his home had no walls, and all their valuables were gone. He began to cry. Eventually, he went back to the hospital. There he remained by his wife's side for the next fifteen days as she slowly recovered from her wounds. He never wanted to see Nam Khem again.

When Puek and Lek crawled out from underneath their blanket at dawn, the woman behind them still cradled her dead mother in her arms. Not much had changed from the night before. A dozen or so people squatted in the surrounding jungle to relieve themselves, but the majority of those who had taken refuge on the hillside sat cross-legged with a blanket wrapped around their shoulders, shivering even though it wasn't cold. Exhausted and hungry, Lek focused her thoughts on her father and home.

After half an hour had passed, they heard the hollow thumping noise of a helicopter off in the distance. Nearly every man and woman on the hillside stripped off their shirts and began waving them wildly in the air. The helicopter, which didn't spot them at first because of the encompassing jungle, circled back and landed at the bottom of the hill. The soldiers on board unloaded hundreds of small care packages that contained water, dried food, a toothbrush, Band-Aids, antibiotics, painkillers—everything that was needed to sustain life at that moment. Once the goods had been unloaded, Rinphanit helped place the wounded who hadn't been evacuated the previous afternoon into the back.

The helicopter headed east for Takuapa Hospital, and when it returned twenty minutes later, it brought a doctor and nurse. They quickly climbed out of the helicopter and began checking the hillside for any seriously wounded victims. When they didn't find any, they returned to the soldiers at the helicopter. A few moments later, seven foreigners were loaded aboard and taken off the island. The helicopter came back in twenty minutes, and as another seven foreigners were loaded aboard, a Thai man rushed down to the soldiers. He shouted that the foreigners shouldn't get special treatment; they should devise a fair way of deciding who would leave first. The soldiers didn't listen. They continued to escort the German and Swedish tourists to the helicopter each time it returned. Though Lek and Puek wanted to return to the mainland to see what was left of their family and home, they agreed with the soldiers. Both of them had spent their whole lives sleeping in the dirt and getting bitten by mosquitoes, but it was all terribly new to the foreigners. They also realized that in the coming months, it would be people from places like Sweden and Germany who would return to Thailand to help the people whose lives had been demolished. The foreigners were good people; they just weren't built tough like the Thai.

Lek watched the helicopter come and go well into the afternoon. At first, it returned approximately every half hour, but then it began landing every five or ten minutes. She had heard that people were getting dropped off at the district office, and she couldn't understand how the helicopter went there and back so quickly. The district office was more than six miles away. She figured it had to be dropping people off much closer, perhaps in Nam Khem, but that suited her just fine. The quicker she could reach her home, the better.

At around four p.m., when fewer than fifty people remained who wanted to get taken to the mainland, Lek and Puek got their chance to climb aboard. A few days prior, Lek would have been scared to death of a helicopter ride, but right now she would have jumped off a bridge if it meant learning what had happened back home in their absence. One way or another, she had to know.

What Lek thought to be one helicopter was actually three. While making plans for breakfast and running up and down the hillside to distribute water, Sudjit Rinphanit had managed to get through to some of his friends in the government on his cell phone. He told them that they needed to offer more help than they had the previous afternoon. They responded by sending three helicopters, hundreds of care packages, and a doctor/nurse team. It improved the process considerably, and when the last seven people who wanted to leave the island had crawled aboard the final helicopter in the late afternoon, the pilot waited for Rinphanit to get in back as well. Rinphanit took one look at the remaining 300 men, women, and children, all of whom lived on the island and had nowhere else to go, and he told the pilot he wasn't coming. The helicopter took off, and Rinphanit walked down to his people.

"Are you going to stay?" a man asked.

"I'm going to stay."

"Then I'm staying too."

A woman stood up. "I'm staying as well."

"Me too," said a teenage boy.

In a matter of minutes, all 300 of them had stood up and said that as long as their leader remained by their side, they would remain on the island and attempt to rebuild their lives. Rinphanit wiped a tear from his eye. He went around and hugged as many of them as he could, and then he got to work. He pulled aside a couple of his workers and told them to go around to the different restaurants and collect more water. Their next mission, he explained, was to head down to the ferryboat launch and collect the dead bodies.

As Rinphanit neared the launch on the east side of the island, the side that faced Nam Khem, he saw there were bodies everywhere. As he began loading them into his truck, he received a call from Mr. Nawin Chidchob, the minister of transportation. Mr. Chidchob wanted to send another helicopter to the island to bring him back to the mainland, but once again Rinphanit refused to leave. A few hours later, he got a call from the governor of Pangnga Province. He, too, tried to get Rinphanit to come back to the mainland, but Rinphanit held fast to his promise.

"You need any help?" the governor asked.

"I need hundreds of body bags," Rinphanit said. "If you can spare them, I would also like some rescue workers to come get the bodies. We should bring them to Yanyao Temple as quickly as possible so their family members can find them."

Thirty minutes later, two helicopters brought hundreds of body bags and more than a dozen rescue workers. Rinphanit was shown how to properly wrap the bodies in plastic, and they worked together collecting the dead until deep into the following day. When the majority of those who had perished on the island had been gathered, Rinphanit found the number staggering, nearly 500 in all. Rinphanit eventually found the bodies of his sister and his niece. He gave them both a beautiful funeral ceremony and burned their bodies before the end of the week. They would remain forever with him in spirit.

A few moments after climbing out of the helicopter at the district hall in the late afternoon, Puek and Lek were surrounded by family and friends who fell all over them with hugs and kisses. They'd been going crazy looking for them. Lek's older brother, younger sister, and her younger brother Jui, whom Lek had been so worried about, were all there. Ko Sa and several other fishermen joined the group as well. They had all gone down to sift through the rubble earlier in the morning. The group clung to the hope that both of them had gone to Kho Khao Island to give massages, but then someone said they had seen both of their bodies lying in one of the ponds in Nam Khem. They had spent most of the afternoon crying together, only to see them step off a helicopter alive and well.

They all retreated to the shade of a tree to celebrate the happy homecoming, but within fifteen minutes, the surrounding misery slowly brought them back to reality. Lek turned her eyes to the ground and asked about their father. Her brothers and sister sat in silence for the longest time, and then they told her that it didn't look good. They hadn't yet found his body, but there was nothing left of their home, and they doubted he could have made it. He was old and crippled, and he had most likely been carried away. Lek nodded, and then she got up so they could all resume the search. She asked one of Puek's old fishing friends if he could take Puek to stay at his home tonight, and the man kindly agreed. She kissed her husband good-bye, and they left each other's side for the first time since disaster had struck.

The family broke into two groups to cover the most ground. Lek went to the hospital and then to Yanyao Temple to look among the bodies piled on the ground and in the backs of trucks. Her sister checked the bodies at Bang Muang Temple and Nam Khem Temple. When they reconvened later that night, empty-handed, they all headed down to Lek's home in Nam Khem and spent the next two hours wading through the muck and darkness, calling their father's name. When it grew pitch-black out, they went back to the subdistrict office and slept together in a huddle on the ground, holding one another.

The following morning, they got right back to it. Lek went around to all the relief workers and asked them if they'd seen a man with one hand and a tattoo on his chest. She went to policemen and doctors and nurses and asked the same. She left her cell phone number with everyone. She checked the temples and then rechecked them. Then, on Tuesday afternoon, fifty hours after the waves had come, she got a call from a volunteer working for the Portektueng Foundation. He said he'd found a man with one hand and a tattoo on his chest stuck under the roots of a banyan tree. He'd just brought the body to Yanyao Temple, and she should come and see if it was her father.

Twenty minutes later, Lek stood gazing down upon the body of her father. She lost control. Her father had wanted to spend the last two months living with her brother in Bangkok, but she had insisted that he come live with her. She had only wanted to spend time with her daddy, something she had rarely gotten to do while growing up. Now he had died because of her selfishness. It ate a great big hole in her heart, and she knew the guilt would remain with her for the rest of her life.

Her sisters led her out of the temple as her brothers loaded their father's body into the back of a truck. Later that evening, they all made the drive to the temple in Ranong, 150 miles away. Lek had wanted to cremate him in Nam Khem, but Yanyao had been burning bodies day and night, and there would be no way to keep his ashes separate from those who had been burned before him. They arrived to Ranong well after dark, and the monks had already laid out the chairs and the coffin. They cleaned their father's body with water, dressed him in his favorite clothing, and then laid his body in the coffin. They placed his palms together with a lotus flower between them. Incense and flowers surrounded him. And then the four monks began to pray:

You sleep at night and get up in the morning, but now you will get up no more.
In the morning you stand up, but now you will stand up no more.
This will happen to everyone. No one can avoid this.
Now you are in peace.

22 THE POLICEMAN AND THE DOCTOR

More than 2,000 bodies had piled up at Yanyao Temple. Lieutenant Colonel Niphon Yanphaisarn had written up hundreds of reports so that family members could claim the bodies of their loved ones, but after forty-eight hours without any sleep, he finally hit the wall. He headed home shortly before midnight on Tuesday, only to hear his wife retch the moment he walked through the door. The smell of the dead had worked deep into his clothes, hair, and skin. He showered under the hose on the front lawn and put on fresh clothes, but when he went back inside, his wife said he still hadn't gotten rid of the smell. He curled up on the back porch and tried to get some sleep. The sun awoke him a few hours later. He tried to ignore the heat crawling over him, but then his boss called. They needed him down at the station.

A stack of reports nearly a foot tall sat on his desk. While he had been working with the bodies at the temple, his subordinates had been out making arrests. In less than forty-eight hours, they had caught seventy looters. Since none of his subordinates were qualified to do investigative work, the reports had come to him. He began sifting through the files and saw that the robbers hadn't just come from nearby provinces, such as Surat Thani, Krabi, and Nakhon Si Thammarat. They had come from provinces in the north, northeast, and northwest. A large percentage of them were Burmese who had come into the country illegally. Their looting activities also varied. Laborers working on construction sites had stolen electrical wires and metal faucets—anything they could dump onto a scale and sell wholesale. Others were hotel staff members who had broken into rooms after the wave hit and stolen all the foreign guests' valuables. Still others were men and women who had thrown a plastic card around their necks and pretended to be volunteers helping to collect the dead bodies. They went looking for bodies, all right, but instead of loading them onto trucks, they'd strip them of their jewelry and wallets.

The more Yanphaisarn read, the more disgusted he grew. They had stolen chairs and tables and anything else they could get their hands on. One of the more organized groups had driven a truck up to a scooter shop, smashed in the door, and then driven off with fifteen Hondas. Yanphaisarn knew that for every one they caught, a hundred more got away. With the majority of the police searching for the King's grandson and collecting the dead bodies, the looters pretty much had free reign. Only the unlucky or the completely stupid had gotten caught.

After looking over all the files, Yanphaisarn took a deep breath. This would take weeks. In each case, he had to interview the accused to get their side of the story, head to the scene of the crime and interview any witnesses, write a detailed report, and then send the case along to the prosecutors. He felt his time could be much better spent helping to identify the bodies, but this was what his boss had wanted him to do. So he plucked up the top folder, read it again, and then went to the jailhouse to interview the man who had been arrested.

"How many bodies did you rob?" Yanphaisarn asked him.

"No, no, I just came looking for my relatives."

"Then why were you found with twenty wallets?"

"I picked them up to see if they belonged to my relatives."

"Half of these wallets belong to foreigners. You have a foreign relative?"

The man opened his mouth to speak, but then he quickly closed it.

Yanphaisarn felt like slapping the crook. He'd been so consumed by the fortune he was making, it had never even crossed his mind to take the money and ditch the wallets. In some cases, with men and women who had been found with Rolex watches and diamond rings, he knew it would be hard to prove their guilt, because the previous owners of the valuables could no longer testify. Luckily a large number of those arrested had been in the possession of drugs as well, so at least they could get them on those charges. Yanphaisarn assumed that because of the shaky evidence, most of the looters wouldn't get more than three years. If it were up to him, he would have locked them up for ten.

The day fell further apart when Yanphaisarn went back to the station. Sitting in his office was a man who claimed to be a volunteer working for the German Embassy. He had heard that passports and jewelry had been collected from German tourists, and he needed Yanphaisarn to hand them over. Yanphaisarn had a bag full of foreigners' passports and jewelry under his desk, but he wasn't about to hand it over, not to someone who claimed to be a volunteer working for the Embassy. Yanphaisarn said he didn't know what the man was talking about and sent him away. Twenty minutes later, a volunteer working for the Swedish Embassy came by, then another volunteer from the Germany Embassy, then another Swedish volunteer, then a German one again. At one point, two Swedish volunteers demanding to collect valuables showed up at the same time, and they didn't know each other. Yanphaisarn found it impossible to believe that foreign embassies would have sent five or six people to achieve the same mission. He told each volunteer the same thing—he wouldn't release any passports or jewelry until the items had been properly documented, and once they had been properly documented, he would release them only to someone who could prove they actually worked for the embassy. Having been a police officer for more than twenty years, Yanphaisarn didn't trust anyone. Chaos turned people into crooks.

Yanphaisarn eventually told his subordinates to send away anyone claiming to be a volunteer working for an embassy, and then he sat down to begin writing up his reports on the looting cases. Halfway through the first case, he got called out into the main room. He reluctantly headed out of his office, only to see a massive line of people that stretched from the reception desk, out the front doors, and then into the street. Everyone in that line held several sheets of paper that needed his signature so they could collect money from the government. Some documents were to verify that they had lost their mother or father or son, and others were to verify that they had lost their car or motorcycle or home. By the end of the week, there would be more than 30,000 cases, and with each case needing at least three documents bearing his signature, he would have to scratch his name more than 90,000 times.

When Yanphaisarn's twenty-four hours at the station were finally up, he went home, showered outside in the yard, and then returned at once to Yanyao Temple. Doctor Pornthip, a famous DNA specialist and author of many best-selling books, had arrived a few days before and set out to establish a better system of identifying the bodies and releasing them to family members. Yanphaisarn had hoped that this new and improved method would have the report-writing process streamlined, but it didn't. Now, four days after the tsunami, the bodies had begun to rot. Dressed in boots, smock, and mask, Yanphaisarn spent all day wading his way between bodies swollen to twice their size. Most of the bodies were no longer recognizable, and with fingerprinting having been rendered obsolete, due to the skin on the fingertips having sloughed off, it meant that DNA testing would have to replace the simplistic method they had previously employed. To make matters worse, the 2,000 bodies had now become 4,700 bodies. It hadn't reached the point where mass graves needed to be dug, but it had gotten bad. He feared many of the bodies lying on the ground would never find their way into their families' care or even receive proper funerals. It broke his heart to think of how many souls would linger.

Only two foreigners remained at Takuapa Hospital on the afternoon of Tuesday, December 28, and that made things a whole lot easier for Doctor Wut Winothai and the other general practitioners. Supplies were also trickling in at exactly the right time. A few hours before they ran out of surgical gloves, a box of surgical gloves came in. An hour before they ran out of alcohol, a box of alcohol arrived. Just as they started needing Formaline to preserve the dead bodies, that came in as well. Logistically, everything looked good.

On the treatment side, things didn't look as good. The day of the tsunami, they had tried their best to stick to the emergency plan they had developed. A major component of that plan was to clean people's wounds, stitch them up, and then quickly release people from the hospital so the doctors and nurses could deal with the more serious patients. It would have worked perfectly for a car accident, but this wasn't any car accident. The murky water of the waves had worked down into every cut, scrape, and gash. Normal seawater contained several different types of bacteria, but the water of the tsunami had hundreds, most of which had come from the raw sewage it picked up off the roads. By the time Doctor Winothai realized that everyone who had open wounds needed to be operated on, the staff still had only three surgeons. As a result, they had no choice but to clean the wounds with alcohol and then stitch them up. Now the people who had been stitched up returned by the dozens, with infections. When the surgeons reopened the wounds, the infection had already eaten the patients' muscles. Doctor Winothai and his fellow doctors would have stitched up hundreds more that day, but luckily they had run out of thread. It became clear that those who had been treated less had actually been treated better.

By late Tuesday afternoon, the number of returning patients had grown to nearly a hundred. Those who had left the hospital two days prior with just minor cuts now had festering wounds. Some had developed the beginning stages of gangrene. Many patients had developed blood infections, and others had developed pneumonia or lung infections.

Never in Doctor Winothai's wildest dreams did he think the infections would have taken hold so fast. He pumped his patients full of antibiotics, but there were just too many different types of bacteria to kill. By evening, they had to amputate arms and legs. Before the end of the night, people started dying. It was hard for Doctor Winothai to take, because he knew if they'd had the right antibiotics and enough time to put everyone on the operating table on the day of the tsunami, all of their lives could have been saved. It made him wish he'd paid more attention to the patients with small wounds. That awful day made him wish a lot of things.

The morning after the tsunami, Wimon rose off his patch of grass in front of the hospital at sunrise. He went inside to visit with his wife and elder daughter, both of whom were recovering, and then he headed down into the village. He walked the cement foundation of his home, which was all that remained, lifting portions of the collapsed cinder block walls to see if his three-year-old daughter lay trapped beneath. When he didn't find her, he tried to retrace her steps of the day before in order to discern where her body might have been carried. He walked to the main road, looked under more rubble. He began to weep as he looked further inland. On the east side of the road, just behind a long row of buildings that no longer stood, sat the largest of Nam Khem's tin-mining ponds. The homes that had been built right on the pond's edge had collapsed into the water and sunk to the murky bottom fifty feet below. It became clear to Wimon that anyone along the road who hadn't been shoved into something planted firmly on the ground had been carried into that pond.

He walked to the edge and looked down. A dozen bodies lay just beneath the surface, and deep down in the depths he thought he could see a dozen more. He couldn't imagine a more horrible way to die, and he began to weep harder. His little girl was down there.

Why isn't anyone helping us? he shouted in his mind.

When he had come down this morning, he had expected to see hundreds of soldiers and rescue workers. With the bodies of thousands of residents from Nam Khem already piled at Yanyao and Bang Muang Temples, it should have been clear to the world that Nam Khem had gotten hit just as hard as, if not harder than, the tourist beaches to the south, but since all the news reporters had converged near the area where the King's grandson had perished, it seemed that nearly everyone had forgotten about Nam Khem. Wimon had been looking for the leader of the village, Sathaien Petklieng, since he had stepped off his boat the previous afternoon, but he hadn't seen the man's face once. Twenty years prior, when their leader had taken the position over from his father, he had promised to be there for the people in their time of need. Wimon couldn't understand where he had gone off to in their most critical hour. If they didn't get the people out of the ponds in the next few days, their bodies would start to change. The thought of his not being able to recognize his little girl made him sick with fear. He prayed that soldiers would arrive with water pumps.

He left the pond where Film had most certainly lost her life and began picking through the rubble again. After seven hours of this, he found the body of his sister-in-law, Nikhom's wife. He helped a rescue worker uncover her, but just as they were getting ready to lift her into the back of the truck, a car sped up and warned them that another wave was coming.

Wimon looked out to sea, and although he couldn't see a wave on the horizon, the whole ordeal the previous day had been so terrifying that he couldn't help but run. He left his sister-in-law's body where it was, and he raced in the rescue worker's truck, up toward the highway. Once they were up on higher land, Wimon grew angry. He'd seen people over the last two days stealing jewelry and picking the pockets of the dead, and he knew that the wave scare was most likely a rumor started by thieves who wanted to go to Nam Khem and rob homes. He became sick with anger—and even more so because Petklieng was nowhere to be seen. Their leader had abandoned them, left them to the vultures.

When no wave came, Wimon headed back down into the village and got the body of his sister-in-law. It was dark by then, so he brought her body to his brother and then spent the evening going back and forth between Yanyao Temple and Bang Muang Temple. He lifted the lid on every coffin, unzipped every plastic bag, checked in the back of every truck. Eventually security guards at the temples would no longer allow him inside. With the hope of locating his daughter's body gone for the day, he returned to his patch of grass in front of the hospital and tossed and turned with uneasy sleep and nightmares.

The following morning he headed back into the village once again, but the little sanity he'd managed to hold on to the previous day was now gone. There was just too much death and suffering. And the thought of his daughter hovering in the darkness at the bottom of the pond haunted every second of every minute. The day before, he'd been thorough in his search, checking his home and the surrounding area, but now he just wandered aimlessly. He pulled at his hair as he walked, and then he would suddenly break out in tears and have to crouch down and wrap his arms around his knees to keep his body from trembling. One minute he could hardly lift his feet, and the next he'd get bursts of energy and run in circles. He screamed and wailed the entire time.

A reporter approached him sometime in the late morning and asked him if he was one of the local people. Wimon told him that he was, that he had lost eight in his family, most of whom were probably trapped at the bottom of a massive pond behind his home. The reporter asked him if he would do a radio interview, and Wimon said he would. People needed to know what had happened in Nam Khem. They needed to know so they would send help.

The reporter picked a quiet spot under a tree where they could sit down. Over a cell phone, Wimon talked with a man sitting in a broadcast booth somewhere in Bangkok. He told the man and his listeners what had happened to him out at sea, what he had found when he returned, and how Nam Khem had been forgotten. He hoped that it would bring rescue workers and soldiers, but he knew that one radio program would not be enough to get the word out.

The reporter sitting at his side put a hand on Wimon's shoulder after the interview had finished. "Is there anything I can do for you?"

"Yes," Wimon instantly returned. "You can get me in touch with Mr. Sorayuth."

Sorayuth was the most popular reporter in Thailand.

"Why do you wish to speak to him?"

Wimon didn't answer—his thoughts raced in so many directions he now found it hard to speak. But in the back of his mind he knew if he got the message of what had happened in Nam Khem to Mr. Sorayuth, he would be able to help. He had friends in the government and military. When Mr. Sorayuth spoke, people listened. In a matter of days, they would get help from around the country.

The reporter pulled out his cell phone and walked a short distance away. In a few minutes, he came back.

"I called Mr. Sorayuth's station, and they said he will talk with you. He has a team of reporters in Khao Lak right now, and Mr. Sorayuth is talking with people over live feed from Bangkok. You need to go to the Bang Sak Princess Resort."

Wimon thanked him and then ran to the public health center. From there, he jumped on a truck headed for Khao Lak. When he arrived, he saw hundreds, if not thousands, of government workers wandering through the debris in search of dead bodies. He saw hundreds of reporters standing around news vans, on which were mounted massive satellite dishes. If only the Phuyaibaan, the village leader, of Nam Khem were here, the village would have received the help that it needed, but Petklieng had apparently gone AWOL. Wimon no longer felt confident leaving the fate of Nam Khem in Petklieng's hands. He felt it was his duty to get the village help. And if there was anywhere he could do that, it was in Khao Lak.

Soon after, Wimon was sitting down, rigged with a microphone. He was talking to Mr. Sorayuth over the airwaves. He talked about his experiences, not making a lot of sense, jumping around in time. He just couldn't seem to get his head to function quite right. The one thing he made sure to say clearly, however, was how many people had died in Nam Khem. He said that the number of dead was more than 3,000.

"Impossible," Mr. Sorayuth said. "That is unbelievable. I heard only 300 died there."

Wimon shook his head. "It is true. No one knows, because no one has gone to the village. It has been forgotten."

"What do you need?" Mr. Sorayuth asked.

Wimon thought about what the village needed, but all he could think about was his little girl trapped at the bottom of the pond with a hundred others.

"I need four water pumps to drain the ponds."

Mr. Sorayuth gave him six.

Dang kept her promise to her son. The morning after picking him up from the hospital in Surat Thani, she took his hand and led him down into the village to find his sister. The tragedy had happened less than forty-eight hours before, and bodies still lay scattered in the mud. At several points, Dang tried to get her son to turn back, worried how such sights might affect him, but there was no discouraging him. He was stricken with guilt for having lost track of Kwan when the wave hit. He wanted his sister back.

"Kwan, where are you?" Arthorn shouted as they walked through the village. "If you are here, let me know. Please answer me!"

Her son steered directly toward their home in Laem Pom, the last place he had seen Kwan alive, but as they drew close, Dang saw the company's bodyguard, Mr. Boonthongkum, standing at his post by the main entrance. Not wanting to give her son anything more to worry about, Dang hadn't told him about her little encounter the previous day. Now she had to. When she explained why they couldn't go home to look for his sister, her son tried to run forward and challenge the man. Dang held him back. Taking his hand, she led Arthorn past the entrance to Laem Pom and then down the east side of the barbed wire fence. They got as close as they could to their community without crossing the property line the Far East Company had established. As they picked about the grass and jungle, looking for the dress Kwan had been wearing that morning, Boonthongkum walked down the opposite side of the fence. When Dang saw him coming, she pulled her son away from Laem Pom. She could still hear the threat Boonthongkum had made the previous day—*"The tsunami might not have taken you from this land, but I will."*

Dang had always solved her own problems, but this problem was too big and dangerous for her to tackle on her own. She headed directly to the Nam Khem police station up along the highway and talked with the senior officer, Mr. Phosayanon.

"I'm not sure if you are aware of my situation, but I live in Laem Pom," Dang said. "Right now—"

"I'm aware of your situation," the officer interrupted. "A representative of the Far East Company has already come to see me. He said that you have been trying to trespass on their land. I filed a report noting that you've made frequent attempts to trespass. You are not welcome there."

"Well," Dang said, "will you take *my* report?"

"No. I will not help you."

Dang knew what had happened, but she found it hard to believe. The company had bought off the police. Anger welled up inside her. At this moment, she cared nothing for her land—she needed to find her daughter and father and everyone else that had vanished from her life in a blink of an eye. She needed to find them and give them a proper funeral.

"Yed mae," she shouted, the Thai equivalent of "fuck you." "If you will not help me, fuck you."

Dang left the police station and, pulling Arthorn along behind her, went to the subdistrict hall. She tried telling an officer there of her problem, but she got the same response. Not knowing where to turn, she approached a reporter from Channel Seven News and told him everything that had occurred. Sympathetic to her plight, the reporter confidentially gave her the personal cell phone of the governor. Dang called and begged him for permission to return to her land to find her family.

"I know about this case, and I don't want to talk about it right now," the governor said. "Right now all I want to talk about is what to do about the dead bodies."

"If we don't talk about the land issue," Dang returned, "then how can I go and get the bodies? That's all I want. I just want to collect the bodies of my family. You have to understand that. I want nothing more."

"I don't want to talk about it," the governor said again, and then he hung up. Dang tried calling him back, but he had turned off his cell phone.

Later that night, feeling defeated, Dang took her son to sleep at the camp that had been set up in front of the subdistrict office. Her son, worn out from the traumatic day, fell asleep instantly, but Dang's eyes remained open deep into the night. She stared up at the stars and thought about all she had lost, wondering how she could go on. Around two a.m., she heard her son talking in his sleep.

"Kwan, where have you been?" he mumbled. "I have been looking for you. Where have you been?"

Dang hovered over him for a moment, wondering what to do. Should she let him visit with his sister in his sleep? She wondered what they were doing, what Kwan looked like in his mind. Was she smiling? Was she asking for her mother? Her son looked so happy in that moment, but Dang knew that any happiness he now felt was only fleeting. She shook him gently until his eyes fluttered open.

"Kwan isn't with us," she whispered. "We haven't found her yet, baby."

Dang watched the happiness slowly fade from her son's cheeks. He looked older now, much too old for a fourteen-year-old boy. It broke her heart into a thousand pieces.

"It hurts so much waiting for her to come back," he said. "She was always teasing and yelling at me. Sometimes we fought, but we loved each other so much. I want to play with her again. I want you to bring her back to me."

"I'm trying, baby," Dang said, wiping the tears from her face. "I'm trying as hard as I can. You're going to have to be strong for me, all right? You have to be stronger than you have ever been. Can you do that?"

Her son nodded, and then Dang kissed him on his cheek. She remained awake by his side for the rest of the night, waiting to see if Kwan would visit him again in his dreams. She should have let him sleep.

For four days and three nights, Wimon had worked with volunteers to drain the water from the pond behind his home with the pumps Mr. Sorayuth had so graciously given him. They had pulled more than sixty bodies from the watery grave, but he still hadn't found his daughter. The water level had gone down thirty feet, but there was another thirty feet to go. Even the six pumps just weren't enough.

Mr. Sorayuth had been talking about Nam Khem on the television and radio for the past several days, and help had finally arrived in force. Various departments of the government had come to clean the roads, the Red Cross had begun to shelter and feed the residents of the village, and rescue workers flooded through the streets to collect the bodies and bring them to the temple. Wimon no longer felt abandoned, but they still needed more help, particularly with the ponds. There were five ponds total in Nam Khem, and if the one he had been working on was any indication, there were still hundreds of bodies below the surface of the others. To direct the government help in the right direction, the leader of the village just needed to make a few phone calls, but Wimon still hadn't seen Sathaien Petklieng. All Wimon knew for sure was that at the current rate, it would take a month to drain every pond. By that time, there would be nothing left of the bodies but bone.

As it turned out, Mr. Sorayuth came to Wimon's rescue. During their interview several days prior, Wimon had said that the death toll of Nam Khem was more than 3,000. Mr. Sorayuth had a hard time believing that, so he had come to the village to see the devastation with his own eyes. When he arrived, the first person he sought out was Wimon. They met down by the beach, and Wimon told him that they needed more pumps. Wimon's desire to help his people touched Mr. Sorayuth deeply. He told Wimon that he would get his pumps, but he also asked if there was anything he could do for Wimon personally. Did he need money? Did he need a new home?

"I would like to talk to a psychological doctor," Wimon said. "If it is at all possible, I would like many, many psychological doctors to come to Nam Khem to heal the people. Right now we are so depressed, so confused. There are many people here who have thought about suicide, including me. I feel it would help us all a great deal."

"I'll see what I can do," Mr. Sorayuth said, smiling warmly. "You are a very strange person, Wimon. Most people would ask for money, but you are not self-ish. I would like to talk to you again in the future."

They parted ways. A few hours later, ten more water pumps arrived and Wimon got back to work on the pond behind his home. The pumps chirped away until only muck lay at the bottom of the hole, but still Wimon hadn't found his daughter. The rescue workers began packing up the pumps to head off to the next pond, but Wimon begged them to stop. He was sure there were more bodies buried in the mud at the bottom, and he needed people to go down there with him. When they refused, Wimon went down in on his own and searched every inch of the mud. He came back up three hours later, empty-handed and devoid of hope.

He joined the rescue workers at the next pond, working alongside them during the day. At night, he left the village and went back and forth between the temples up along the highway to search for his daughter among the rows of dead. Each day, he felt another piece of his mind slip away, and soon he began breaking out in uncontrollable sobs. When he had thought his daughter was at the bottom of the pond, it had given him focus, some place to look. Something to live for. He realized now that she could be anywhere, and it was quite possible that he'd never find her. No funeral, no good-bye. Just this horrible feeling that accompanied the knowledge that her body lay out there in the heat of the day and the darkness of night, crying out to come home.

On the afternoon of January 5, he received a call from his wife and went to her at once. He kneeled beside her bed, and she showed him a picture of a little girl she'd found hanging on the bulletin board in the hospital. Wimon stared at the twisted, swollen face for several moments, trying to see who it was. He'd seen so many bodies over the past week that he had become immune to the emotions death could cause, but now he began to wail and scream. He had found Film, and all the warmth she had filled him with during her three short years flooded into him right alongside all the pain this world had to give.

They went to Bang Muang Temple an hour later. When Wimon saw his daughter curled stiffly on the ground, he scooped her up and held her. He said his good-byes, as did his wife. They performed the funeral ceremony later that night. Wimon prayed that her next life would be better than the last. If it were up to him, she would be a princess until the end of time.

The day after the funeral, Wimon called Mr. Sorayuth and told him that he had found his little girl. Since his interview ten days prior, people around the country had been sending letters to the station, asking how Wimon was doing, asking whether he had found the eight members of his family. Wimon, always thinking of others, didn't want them to worry anymore. He told Mr. Sorayuth that he would be just fine, but the moment those words came out of his mouth, Wimon knew he had just told a lie. With four members of his family still missing, the misery hadn't yet come to an end. Shortly after his phone call to Mr. Sorayuth, he went to the village to continue the search. Thoughts of suicide grew stronger and stronger in his mind. Since he was a little boy, he'd suffered through ten natural disasters. In the past, he had never focused on what he had lost and looked only to the future, but he didn't know if he could do that anymore. His heart felt so heavy with grief; the brutality of the world overwhelmed everything else. Then Mr. Sorayuth granted Wimon his wish. Seventy psychologists arrived in Nam Khem, many of whom stayed for weeks. Wimon was criticized by people in the community. They told him that he should have asked for a boat, a house, something that could have improved his life. Wimon gave them all the same answer: "Having my mind back is all I truly need to get through this. I'm willing to work for the rest."

Dang crept through the jungle with her husband. For seven days now, the thug hired by the Far East Company had stood guard at the mouth of their community. Dang had spent most of her days and nights at the temples, but now the rows of bodies had begun to change. She knew that time was running out for her to find her daughter and father, and this morning she had convinced Tueng to sneak into Laem Pom with her. They came through the jungle from the east to hop the barbed wire fence. If they were quiet, they might have a few hours to search before being discovered.

To reach the fence, they had had to skirt a small pond. Because she had spent so much of her time at the temples, the smell of death had been permanently etched into Dang's nostrils, but her husband immediately picked up the strong odor.

"Someone died here," he said.

Dang crouched in the grass. Through the tangle of brush she could see the guard a hundred yards to the northwest. He might see them if they started looking around, but she decided that it was worth the risk. Crawling on their hands and knees, they pushed the grass aside and checked in bushes. They took deep breaths of the putrid air as they crawled, attempting to silently track down the bodies. Tueng headed over to a tree clinging to the pond's southern bank and then froze. In a moment, he waved Dang over.

Grass sprouted from between the network of roots that wove down the bank, and on top of the grass and roots lay a sheet of aluminum bolted to a large piece of wood, clearly a portion of someone's roof. At first, Dang didn't see anything abnormal, but then she spotted a man's leg protruding from under the square of aluminum and draping into the water.

"Tueng," Dang said, "that might be my father."

Her husband leapt into the shallow water, no longer caring about the noise he made. He tore away the grass that rose around the metal sheet, but when he went to lift the sheet itself, it wouldn't budge. He looked underneath and saw that the man was still gripping the piece of wood. Tueng reached under and pried the arms away, and then he flung aside the metal blanket.

Dang crawled down the bank so she could take her father in her arms. Shielded from the sun, his body hadn't swollen like those at the temples. He still fit into his clothes, and his arms and legs were free of open wounds and broken bones. The only mark on his body was on his forehead, which had been brutally caved in by something heavy. She tried not to look at it. She kissed him on the cheeks and nose and eyes, remembering how he used to playfully shout at her when she jumped over his coconut trees as a child. He had come to this patch of jungle more than thirty years prior to raise his family. He had been a slave in the tin mines so his children could eat. He had worked his fingers to the bone to build them a home. Through his selfless actions, he had taught her about loyalty and pride and the importance of family. He had lived a long life and his time had come, but that didn't comfort Dang's heart. The best man she would ever know had left this world, and a piece of her had gone with him.

"We need help lifting his body," she said. "We need to take him to the temple."

Tueng reluctantly left her side and went running into the village. He returned twenty minutes later with three rescue workers, who were free to move in and out of Laem Pom, and a truck. Dang simply needed help lifting her father's body, but the rescue workers had other plans. For the past week, the different foundations had been competing to collect as many bodies as possible. The foundation with the highest numbers had the best chance of receiving additional funding.

"You can't take this body yourself," a rescue worker said.

"What do you mean?" Dang asked.

"How can you be sure that this is your father? We're going to have to take him."

Dang had asked for help lifting her father because she hadn't thought she could stand on her own. Now anger gave her the energy to stand and fight. "Even though my father is an old man, he had perfect teeth," Dang said. "He has a bad fingernail from hitting it with a hammer, and he has three scars on his backside from lying in bed for months when he was very ill."

The foundation worker stepped forward to examine the body.

"Don't touch him!" Dang shouted.

She crouched down at her father's side. With trembling hands she pulled his jaw open and showed the rescue workers his perfect row of teeth. She lifted his left hand and showed them the nail that had never quite healed. She rolled him over and pulled down his pants to show them the three scars.

"Now let me take my father to the temple," she demanded.

The rescue workers did as they were told. After Doctor Pornthip conducted a DNA test at Yanyao Temple, Dang loaded her father into the bed of a truck and took him to Phatthalung, the province in which he was born. Dang wanted to honor him properly. In Phatthalung, she gave him a five-day funeral ceremony, the best that her small savings could buy.

Shortly after the ceremony, Tueng went to Bangkok to ask his relatives for some money so they could buy food and other necessities. Not two hours after he had climbed onto a bus, Dang noticed that she was being followed by a man. Whenever she turned around to see if he was still there, he would point his finger at her and smile. After four hours, a different man she had never seen before replaced him. Dang went to the subdistrict hall, hoping to lose him in the crowd, but when she found a place to sit down, the man sat down not far from her. He bought a bottle of whiskey and shared it with the people around him. Every time Dang looked at him, he smiled and pointed his finger.

Dang grew sick with fear. A massive wave had swept over her life and claimed most of the people she ever loved, and yet she still had to deal with the

Far East Company. Half a dozen camps had been set up for the victims, and over the next few days she moved back and forth between them with her mother and son, but the men always managed to find her. Eventually she stuck close to friends, hoping the men wouldn't try anything as long as she was around a group of people. While all this distracted her a little bit, it didn't do anything to diminish her grief. At one point, she started weeping. A friend sat down next to her.

"You're thinking of Kwan, aren't you?" her friend asked. "Don't think too much about it. Your daughter was a good person, and she will have a better life when she is reborn again. I lost two children, but there is nothing I can do about it. The government gave me 20,000 baht for each of their lives. In a couple of years, I will get pregnant and have another child. Life will go on."

Dang's face turned angry. She couldn't believe that her friend was actually content with the money the government had given her in exchange for the lives of her babies. Kwan meant everything to her.

"Get away from me," Dang said. "Or I'll hurt you."

The woman scurried away, but a young Christian girl who tried telling her about the cycle of life replaced her. Dang told her the same thing—that if she did not leave, she would punch her.

Dang's mother began to worry, and she called over one of the psychologists Mr. Sorayuth had brought under Wimon's request. The psychologist tried talking to Dang, but she refused to talk to him. Eventually the doctor went back to Dang's mother.

"I fear that she will get worse and worse," the doctor told Dang's mother, handing her a bottle of little yellow capsules. "Try to talk to her, and give her this medicine."

Dang took the pills. They allowed her to sleep for one or two hours, but she always awoke screaming for Kwan. She would break into uncontrollable laughter one moment and then begin to sob the next. People tried to tell her that she would soon have another house and some money, but she didn't care about any of the material things she'd lost. She wanted her daughter back.

Tueng tried holding her when he returned from Bangkok, but she pushed him violently away. "I can hear Kwan crying out to me," she shouted at him. "Why don't you do something about it?"

"Dang, there's nothing we can do."

"*Yed mae,*" she swore at him. "I lost my daughter, and I can't even get onto my land to find her body. If you are going to be like this, just go away from me. I want a divorce."

Dang got up to leave, but her husband wouldn't let her. He truly loved her. And when Dang thought about it, she soon realized that he had lost just as much as she had. He was just handling it better, and that saddened and angered her. At all hours of the day and night, she suffered. All she thought about was Kwan, alone out there in the dark.

PART FOUR

THE ROAD TO RECOVERY

Dang with her husband and son.

 PUEK AND LEK

After the funeral ceremony for Lek's father in Ranong, Puek began hearing things. It started with children crying out for their parents, but then the screams were accompanied by the dreadful sound of the wave. He could hear buildings collapsing and a roar of water so loud he thought it would take his soul. The first several times the noises came, he had gripped Lek's arm and begged her to tell him if the wave had come back. Lek, who had been his eyes for eight years, would shoot a glance in all directions and tell him everything was fine. Puek eventually realized that the noises were just figments of his imagination, but he couldn't seem to block them out. Living in darkness, he was trapped in a permanent nightmare.

Puek didn't feel comfortable returning to Nam Khem, and he convinced Lek to go with him to their hometown of Prachuap Khiri Khan. A few hours off the bus, they went to the temple. Puek wanted to visit the monk who had warned him about his string of bad luck eight years prior, but the monk had passed away not long after Puek had lost his vision. Instead he went to the monk who had treated him so kindly when he had lived in the temple for five months at the age of twenty-two to honor his mother.

"What is it that you would like?" the monk asked him.

"To have good luck," Puek said. "To have a better life than what we've had."

The monk prepared some holy water. Puek and Lek kneeled before him, and the monk prayed as he splashed their bodies with the water. He told them that they would have better luck from that moment on and that they should return home and begin the climb toward a stable life. Two days later, Puek and Lek caught a bus to Nam Khem and went directly to the district office. Hundreds of tents had been erected nearby, but when they went into the main office to make inquiries as to how to get assigned one of the tents, they learned that there were no more vacancies. As they stood there, trying to figure out what to do, Lek's younger brother Jui approached them with a smile. The tents had gone quickly, he told them, but he had stood in line all day to get them one. He had even set it up.

Worn out from traveling, Puek and Lek located their tent and crawled inside. Within fifteen minutes, both of them were sound asleep. They awoke the following morning an hour after daybreak, drenched in sweat. The tent was sweltering; it was no place to be during the heat of the day. After getting dressed, Lek took Puek by the arm and led him to the shade of a tree. A mess hall had been set up, and she went to get them both some food. She came back an hour and a half later with half a plate of dried noodles. Puek asked her why there was so little food, and she told him she hadn't gotten there fast enough. They both agreed to wake up an hour earlier the following morning to ensure that they got in the front of the line.

This routine would last several months. Early in the morning, with Puek sitting under the tree, Lek would grab two plates and go running to the mess hall. If she managed to secure a place at the front of the line, she would get two full plates, but if she got stuck near the back of the line, she would be lucky to get one full plate for both of them. Running to get food made Lek feel like a beggar, and it didn't take her long to realize that something fishy was going on. The government gave the mess hall 100,000 baht a month to feed the people in the camp, but most of the food they ate came out of cans that had been donated. And when they didn't eat canned food, they ate ramen noodles. So if the mess hall got most of their food for free, and the little food they purchased was inexpensive ramen noodles, where was the rest of the money going?

The process of handing out donations was just as suspect. On a regular basis, truckloads of mattresses and rice cookers and hot pots would come in from abroad. The items would be placed in three piles under an awning, and then three massive lines would form out front. One of the piles would always be larger than the others, so Lek had to be careful which line she stood in. She tried her hardest to pick the right line, but by the time she got to the front, all the donations would be gone. She spent countless hours each day just standing in line, and still she hadn't received a mattress, a rice cooker, or a hot pot to warm water for tea.

Part of the problem was that hundreds of people were cheating. Families from all over Thailand had come to the area, pretending to be victims, so they could get the donations being handed out. They would dress up in rags and then break into three or four groups and head out to the different camps. They would tell anyone who cared to listen how they had lost their homes and families, when they actually lived in a village in the northeast and had never before been to the south of Thailand. When a family member received word that a truckload of donations was coming into his camp, he would call his relatives in the other camps and they would run over. Two or three family members would stand in each line to ensure that they got mattresses and rice cookers and hot pots. Lek suspected several men and women in her camp of pulling such a scam, and one day she went around to their tents and took down the zippers. Inside each tent she found a pile of rice cookers, fans, televisions, and radios. Their tents had been filled with so many appliances that there was hardly any room left to sleep.

There was so much corruption going on that Lek had to be vigilant at all times. She kept on her body the money the government had given her for her father's life and the loss of their home. She tried to spend as little of it as possible, because she didn't know how long it would have to last. With the resort on Kho Khao Island having been destroyed, it would be some time before they could start giving massages again. They had also lost their fish farm; the pladuk that hadn't been carried away by the wave had floated belly-up to the surface of their well shortly thereafter.

Three weeks after they had arrived at the district office, soldiers finished building 300 rickety plywood homes in and around Nam Khem. Lek filled out the necessary documents in the hopes that they could move into one, but just as with the donations, she hadn't been quick enough. Lek and Puek wished the families that had received one of the homes the best of luck as they moved out of the miniature tent city, but it didn't take long for the majority of those families to return. When Lek asked why they had come back, their answer was the same—they had stopped receiving donations. Apparently, people didn't feel as sorry for those living in plywood homes as they did for those living in tents. Lek was devastated. Even if they moved to a better place, it would actually do more harm than good. She began to wonder if she and Puek were destined to spend the rest of their days as beggars. As for Puek, he still hadn't gotten rid of the dreadful noises in his head.

28 DANG

CHAPTER

Something had to change. For the past two weeks, Dang had dragged her husband and son from one temporary housing camp to the next in an attempt to hide from the men following her. Her husband had asked several times to just choose one of the camps so they could start eating something other than ramen noodles, but Dang knew it wasn't that simple. In order to register with one of the camps and become eligible to receive donations, she had to show proof of residency. Dang had lived in Nam Khem since birth, but she had no documents to prove this. In order to receive the money the government officials were doling out to the families who had lost their loves ones, homes, and vehicles, Dang needed to show them documents signed by the village leader. Dang figured that since Mr. Sathaien Petklieng had sided with the Far East Company in their land dispute, there would be no way he would sign her documents. The rest of her neighbors in Laem Pom felt the same. As of yet, no one had tried to collect anything.

After a long talk with her husband, Dang realized that her pride was getting in the way. On January 10, she filled out the necessary forms, detailing all she had lost, and then got into a line that stretched out of the tent Mr. Sathaien Petklieng and his staff had erected near the beach in Nam Khem. She tried not to appear desperate, even though she was, and when it came her turn to stand before their leader, she casually slid the forms across the table.

"Phuyaibaan, could you please sign your name on these documents?" she asked. "I am a victim who lost my house and possessions."

Petklieng, who had been trying to convince Dang for the past few years to turn her land over to the company, picked the documents up, looked at them for a moment, and then set them on the table and slid them back to her without signing his name. Sensing a fight coming, he stood up and began to walk away.

"Wait," Dang called after him. "Why won't you sign?"

When Petklieng ignored her, Dang felt rage bubble to the surface. She began to shout, "I lost a lot of people in my family, just as you lost a lot of people. I can feel that it has made me a better person, but it has only made you worse. You have a dirty heart. Let one of your policemen come catch me. I don't care."

Petklieng just stood there, speechless.

Dang went back to her family in the camp, but after five more days passed, she began to realize that soon they would be starving. She had grown up hungry, drinking the water the rice was cooked in as a substitute for milk, but they didn't even have that much. Her family was stuck eating dried noodles for breakfast, lunch, and dinner. There were only so many noodles they could eat before their bodies started to break down.

She wasn't in this alone—nearly every family from Laem Pom was caught in the same predicament. Petklieng, who was aligned with the Far East Company and wouldn't do anything to jeopardize their claim to the land on Laem Pom, wouldn't sign any of the residents' documents. Dang gathered up all the paperwork from twenty of her neighbors and brought them to the Kamnun, the county chief. His signature would be just as valid. She found the Kamnun, Somkiet Maharae, at the Bang Muang Camp.

"I don't know if you remember me, but at the last election, you came to my community, asking us for our votes," she said. "I've come to ask if you could please sign these papers showing that these twenty families live in Nam Khem. I have everyone's documents, house registers, and ID cards. All we need is for you to sign your name."

"I won't sign," Maharae said. "I can't give my signature, because I don't want to get into trouble. The people who live on this land, when they hand me a document to sign, I always get into trouble."

"What are you talking about?" Dang asked. "I am a victim of the tsunami. I am a victim who lives in village #2."

"I am sorry," he said. "I still can't sign."

Dang threw up her hands and stormed off.

After she walked for ten minutes, she finally calmed down. She realized that she should have tried harder to convince him, because now she had only one choice left—go back to Petklieng. She doubted that he would even see her, especially after what she had said to him the week before, but she had to at least try. Twenty families were counting on her.

She went straight to the tent in Nam Khem. Petklieng was busily signing documents, but when Dang reached the front of the line, he said he was about to take his lunch break and walked away.

"I can wait," Dang called after him.

She grew more desperate by the minute. How would she possibly get him to sign the documents now? Then an idea came to her. She knew exactly how she would do it. Since Wimon had talked with Mr. Sorayuth live on television, a flood of reporters had been coming to Nam Khem. One such television reporter was filming Petklieng at this very moment. They had been joined by some kind of politician from Bangkok. Dang didn't know whether he held a big position in the government, but she supposed for her plan to work, it didn't really matter. She would make her leader sign the documents by putting his reputation on the line. She went right over to them.

"Phuyaibaan, Phuyaibaan," she said, walking into the live interview. "I am a victim who lives in Nam Khem. You know that I live here, because your relatives came to my house to get my vote. Would you please sign these documents for me?"

Her leader looked up at her. Dang tried to tell him with her eyes what she would do if he didn't sign his name, but he already knew. It was written all over his face. He had hatred in his eyes. He signed each of the documents while smiling into the camera.

Dang returned to the camp and handed the families their signed documents, but the victory was short-lived. Not long after Dang had sent in her forms, she got a check from the government for only 9,500 baht ($235) for her lost home. Most of those who lived in Nam Khem, even some of those who had only been renting houses, received 30,000 baht for their homes. It told Dang that either the company or her leader had longer arms than she ever could have imagined. From this point on, she and her family would have to fight for scraps.

For fifteen days, Wichien sat by his wife's side in the hospital as her body and antibiotics fought off the infection that gripped the wound in her leg. He fed her, washed her, and took her to use the bathroom. After he'd headed home the day after the tsunami, only to find his money and possessions pilfered, he hadn't had any urge to return to Nam Khem. But now that Nang was smiling again and holding conversation, his attitude changed. He wanted to go home so they could get on with their lives. (He also wanted to stand guard so thieves couldn't steal his cupboards and pipes, if they hadn't done so already.)

They had a little money to begin the uphill battle. On January 4, an assistant of the governor had come to the hospital and handed out 5,000 baht to people who had been injured. A few days later, Wichien had gone to the school along the highway and gotten 20,000 baht from the government for his damaged home. The Princess had set up a fund for the victims, from which he had received 9,000 baht. And during his wife's stay in the hospital, numerous foundations had come by to donate 1,000 baht here and 1,000 baht there. In all, he had almost 50,000 baht ($1,250), but after having put nearly 500,000 baht into his home over the years, he knew that it wouldn't be enough to rebuild the walls and replace the stolen items. Not knowing when he would be able to work again, he realized they would need to save most of their money for food.

They left the hospital in the late afternoon of January 12, and just outside the front doors, Wichien spotted a very old rice cooker sitting on the lawn. He hurried over and scooped it up under one arm. He felt ashamed to be seen carrying something that had probably been discarded by a very poor family, but without it, he and Nang would most likely go hungry.

They hitched a ride into Nam Khem and discovered a ghost town. There were soldiers and government workers moving from place to place, but the town's residents were nowhere to be seen. Some of them stayed at the temporary camps because they were frightened of another wave, and others stayed at the camps because they could get donations. On their walk home, Wichien talked with a few of those who had decided to return, and he learned that hardly any donations had reached the village. This made Wichien furious—in order to get aid, you had to look and act like a beggar.

Wichien carried his wife upstairs and laid her down in bed. Both of them were exhausted, but they still couldn't sleep. Nang would doze off for five or ten minutes, and then she would wake up from a terrible nightmare in which another monster wave crashed down over their home. The sea had drawn her to Nam Khem when she was nineteen, and now it had taken everything. She began to think about her mother, how she had left without her permission. If only she had listened to her mother and stayed home, none of these terrible things would have happened.

Although Wichien had been far away when the tsunami occurred, his time in the hospital, seeing all the pain and destruction caused by the wave, made him afraid too. When neither one of them had fallen asleep by midnight, Wichien told his wife that he would go out and stand guard. He put a chair on his front stoop and spent the remainder of the night gazing out to sea and eyeing the dark streets for silhouettes of men who had come to thieve. At dawn, Nang came down and assumed the watch post. Wichien went upstairs to get some sleep.

Two days later, they began working on their home. They scraped out the thick layer of mud that had hardened on their downstairs floor. They tossed the portions of their walls that had crumbed to pieces and saved the chunks large enough to reuse. Around noon, Nang took a break and walked up to the road where the wave had hit her. She saw the truck she had climbed onto badly mangled far in the distance. An image of the baby she had held in her arms tried to tunnel its way into her thoughts, but she forced it away. She didn't know what she would say to the mother if she had survived. What could she say?

Twenty yards south of the coconut tree that had saved her life, a group of rescue workers pumped water from the massive pond. Several of her neighbors were still missing, and she went over to see if she could identify any of the bodies they pulled from the water. Not wanting to interrupt the workers, she watched from a distance. She spotted two men, one foreign and one Thai, making their way around to the different people in the area. In a few minutes, they approached her. The foreign man handed her a piece of candy, and then he spoke to the Thai man so he could translate.

"My friend can see that you have a wound on your leg," the translator said. "He would like to know how you are doing. Is there anyone in your family still missing?"

"My neighbors lost many people in their families," Nang said. "Everyone in my family survived. I still have some pain in my leg."

"Do you need any help from God?"

Nang wasn't sure what he meant. "I would like to stay in my house rather than the camps, but the first floor has no walls. We need so much stuff to rebuild—bricks and tiles and two doors. My husband thinks the doors are the most important."

The translator relayed this information to the foreigner, and they spoke among themselves for a few moments in English. The translator turned back to her.

"If you can wait for a few moments, we can go with you to your home."

Nang nodded in agreement.

The foreigner snapped a few photos of the bodies being hauled out of the pond, and then Nang led them to her home. The foreigner, still with camera in hand, began taking pictures of the outside walls. Then he went inside and took pictures of their floor and roof and bedroom. Nang wasn't sure what this was all about, but she suspected that the man wanted to help her. Why else would he take pictures of her home?

The foreigner and his translator hung around for a few more minutes, talking among themselves, and then they thanked her and left. Nang expected that they would return with some type of help, money or building supplies, but when they hadn't returned by evening, she put them out of her mind.

The foreigner and his translator returned four days later, and they brought with them a large group of men, all from America. They came inside to examine the damage to their home. After everything had been inspected, the translator approached Wichien.

"Do you need some help from God?"

"If God can help me fix my house," Wichien said, "I would like that very much. I don't have anywhere to live. I want to make my wife happy and stay here, but we need to repair everything. You can see we have a long way to go."

One of the Americans spoke to the translator.

"Our God will help you," the translator said.

After that, they left again. They returned a few hours later with two plywood doors and a couple of tiles to replace the ones that had been stripped away by the wave. "This is help from our God," the translator told Wichien. "Do you want to become a Christian?"

Wichien looked at Nang; neither one of them knew what to say. All their lives they had been Buddhist. They were quite happy with their religion, and never before had they thought about becoming Christians. They had no idea what Christians even believed in. However, warmed by the foreigners' generosity and ecstatic to have a door that would keep out robbers and mosquitoes once they had rebuilt their walls, they didn't have the heart to turn them down. The Americans were the only ones to have helped them since they had returned to their home.

"My friends say you don't need to give them the answer right away," the translator said. "They will come back and visit you again soon."

They did just that. The following day, they stopped by several times. They brought bricks during one trip, cement on another, and then, in the late afternoon, they brought more tiles. Each time they came, they made it very clear that they hadn't brought the gifts—God had. Wichien and Nang didn't know what they meant by that. As the days went on, the men started bringing fewer and fewer supplies. Ten days after their first visit, Wichien told them that he would become Christian, out of fear of losing the only support they had. He told them Nang would become a Christian as well. This made the men very pleased.

Nang argued with Wichien that night after the group had left. She didn't know anything about Christianity. She was a Buddhist. She loved going to the temple and praying with the monks. When the wave had taken her under, she had called out to the great Buddha. He had saved her from certain death, and now Wichien wanted her to abandon him? She argued fiercely, but Wichien put his foot down. There hadn't been a single Buddhist who had come to help them in their time of need, he said. It had become clear to him that if they became Christians, they would continue to get help from the Americans.

The following day, the Americans delivered two Bibles that had English written on one side of the page and Thai on the other. They pointed out which sections they wanted Wichien and Nang to read, telling them it would help them to get to know God. Nang sat down with the book later in the afternoon and spent many agonizing hours gazing at the pages. She'd gone to school for only a couple of years, and all the big words confused her. She began to wonder how much she would have to read before the Christians were happy.

They came again on Saturday with a bundle of fruit. They asked if Wichien and Nang had been reading the Bible, and Wichien told them that they had. Before the Christians left, they told them that Nang and Wichien both had to go to church the following morning. They would send a car to pick them up. Nang told Wichien that she didn't want to go, but he said they had to. Nang lost sleep that night. She had endured a lot during her life, including getting sent by her family to Bangkok at thirteen and getting beaten by the husband of the family she worked for, but this was somehow harder to endure. Her faith had been the glue holding her together through her many hardships. She didn't feel any of this was right.

A van pulled up to their house the next morning, and when the back door slid open, they saw that several more people from Nam Khem had converted to Christianity in the last week or two. Wichien and Nang climbed into the back with them, and they were all taken to a massive tent that had been erected up along the highway not far from the district hall.

There were a few things that Nang liked about church. They had a television and music playing, which one wouldn't find in the temple, and there were also a bunch of kids running about. It made her feel warm after having spent the past days in her abandoned village. She even liked the four songs that they got to sing in Thai. The first one was for their King. The second was a song to thank God. The third song was to bless God. The fourth song—she didn't quite know what the fourth song was about, but it had something to do with God.

After the singing, she was asked to pull out her Bible. A man instructed her to open to a specific page, and then together they read three or four chapters aloud. Because of her difficulty pronouncing some of the words, she found it very embarrassing.

Each Saturday, the Americans came to her home to remind her and Wichien about their church appointment. The following morning, a car always pulled up out front. During one of these trips to church, while Wichien thanked God for all that He had brought, just as he did a hundred times each day now, one of the foreigners sensed that Nang wasn't entirely pleased with her new religion. He asked, through the translator, if everything was all right.

Since Nang couldn't tell him outright that she didn't want to be a Christian, not with Wichien in the car, she avoided the question by telling him of her other worries. "I'm stressed," she said. "As you know, we've hired a technician to help rebuild our home, but we ran out of money to pay him. We owe him 15,000 baht."

The translator relayed her words, and then the foreigner had him give her a wonderful message. "He said God will bring you so much more than He already has. He said he will ask God to give you more than 15,000 baht."

Although Nang had brought up money only to avoid the larger question, she grew excited that her debt would get taken care of. She waited for several weeks, but God never brought her the money.

It was hard for her to spend three hours in church every Sunday, but she did it because it was important to Wichien. Three weeks into their new religion, however, she had an awful dream in which a close neighbor who had lost her life in the tsunami came to her. *"I'm starving,"* she said. *"I'm out here all alone, and I'm starving."*

Nang awoke in a panic. She didn't know if Christianity had a ritual to get food to those who had passed away, and if it did, she didn't care to learn. She would go to the temple and make a merit. She told Wichien of this dream, expecting that he would argue with her about going to the temple, but he was just as concerned. They both suspected that it was against the rules of Christianity to go to the temple, so they decided not to tell anyone. That afternoon they brought the monks at Nam Khem Temple plates of food. As Nang watched the monks eat the food, she grew very happy. Her friend would be all right now.

They ran into friends before they left, and they all wondered why they hadn't seen them at temple for many weeks. Wichien told them that they had become Christians.

Nang assumed that their friends wouldn't understand—after all, she didn't fully understand. But with the Christian group having made their way around the community, within a month's time more than a hundred villagers had converted in hopes of receiving some type of aid in their time of need. There had never before been a Christian church in Nam Khem, but the Christian group planned to build one.

Right in the center of the village for all to see.

30 DANG

A month after the disaster, on the morning of January 27, Dang received a call from Doctor Pornthip, the famous DNA specialist working to identify the bodies at Yanyao Temple. They had found her daughter.

They had found something, but they hadn't found Kwan. As Dang stared down at the twisted pile of flesh on the ground, she could not see her daughter. She had pictured what this moment would be like every hour of every day for the past month, but she realized now that nothing could have prepared her for this. She couldn't gaze into Kwan's eyes and say good-bye. She would never again look at her wonderful smile. Her little girl had left the body lying before her long ago, and Dang hadn't been there to hold her hand or give her spirit encouragement to pass on to whatever lay before her. In the moment, standing there looking down, she didn't know how she would find the strength to go on. In the past weeks, people had told her that she was lucky because she had survived, but she knew now that those who had perished were the lucky ones. She had died a dozen deaths that day and every day since. For those who lived along the coast, there had been no escaping the wave. It was just a matter of time until those twenty minutes claimed all their hearts and minds.

In the days that followed the funeral, Dang retreated to quiet places to replay memories of her daughter before they had a chance to fade. Every now and then, she would pull out the two pictures she now carried in her wallet. The first was of the innocent girl she had always known, and the second was of what Kwan had become. She began talking to herself. The words she whispered were not kind. In her mind, the Far East Company and Sathaien Petklieng were to blame for what had become of her daughter. She would have found Kwan if only they had allowed her back into Laem Pom. She would have found her before her body could bloat and her skin could fall off, before she had become unrecognizable. Dang never wanted to forget what they had done out of greed.

Her anger grew every day, especially when she walked down to the village to gaze upon her community from afar. Instead of seeing the patch of jungle where she had raised her children and had hoped to watch her grandchildren grow up, she saw a mountain of garbage. The leader of the village, still doing what he could to deter her and her neighbors from returning home, had ordered all the rescue workers to dump into Laem Pom the trash and rubble they picked up from in and around the village. This had been going on for three weeks, and the mountain of refuse had grown tall. To make sure no one disrupted the mountain, Petklieng had posted a sign forbidding the removal of trash.

The warning did little to stop desperate residents from looking through the trash heap for scrap metal to sell. As long as the junk collectors didn't live in Laem Pom, the security guard hired by the Far East Company let them pass. A week after her daughter's funeral, Dang received a call from one such person.

The man told her that he had found the body of a girl around twelve years of age at the bottom of a small pond the trash had overflowed into. He had called Dang because he thought the community of Laem Pom would want to know. It was most likely the daughter from a family that lived in the area.

Dang put on her shoes to run over there and retrieve the girl's body, but Tueng held her back. He said that with the company's bodyguard still standing at his post, it was just too dangerous. Dang knew that he was probably right, but she didn't care. All she could think about was Petklieng and the faceless Far East Company. How evil were these people? They were willing to deprive a mother of finding her daughter. They were willing to bury a little girl beneath a pile of trash. And for what? For a piece of land? Someone had to stop them. Someone had to tell the world what they were doing.

"In the morning, I'm calling reporters," Dang said to her husband. "I'm calling every reporter who will talk with me. I'm going to tell them everything that has happened here. People need to hear about this. When reporters go out there and see the girl's body buried under the trash, people will know what we have been going through. They will support us."

"If you think that's the right thing," Tueng said, "then I will support you."

Dang knew it was the right thing, but she never got to make the calls. Two hours after she had gone to bed, her cell phone began to ring. It was the man who had found the girl. Dang had no idea what he would want at such a late hour, but she knew it wouldn't be good.

"They've brought out a backhoe," he whispered over the phone. "I'm out here right now, and they've brought in a backhoe to get rid of all the evidence."

"What about the little girl?" Dang asked. "Are they trying to take her body?"

"I don't know. She's at the bottom of that pond. I don't think they found her."

"Thank you," Dang said. "I'll pass the news on to everyone else."

The next morning, Dang did just that. Weera, a man who had lived in Laem Pom for twenty years, grew so upset that he immediately stormed down to Laem Pom, past the security guard, and then over to the trash pile, which had shrunk considerably overnight due to the work of the backhoe. He hefted chunks of rubbish and kicked scrap metal out of his way. It wasn't until he had been there for thirty minutes that he spotted something ten feet below the surface of the small pond. Heaps of trash had fallen into the pond, and it could easily have been a cinder block or a piece of someone's home, but something in his heart told him it was neither. The harder he looked through the water, the more certain he became. The Far East Company or the leader of the village had removed the majority of the trash, but they had also removed the little girl's body. All that remained was her head.

Weeping now, Weera dove into the water and swam down to the bottom. He retrieved the remains and brought them all the way to the temple.

A few nights later, Dang sat down with her husband. "Tueng, do you think I am going crazy?" she asked. "You have been giving me this medicine, and it hasn't helped."

"Of course I don't think you're crazy," he said, and then tried to hug her. She kept him at bay with her hands. "It's just . . . I just want to have you back, that's all. I want you to be who you used to be. I want us to be a family again," Tueng confided.

"If you don't think I'm going crazy, then please don't make me take this medicine anymore. From this moment on, I'm done taking it. I need my strength so I can fight the company. Will you fight with me?"

"Dang, calm down. Think about things before you say them."

Dang leaned forward and gently took her husband's shoulders. She looked him in the eyes so he could see that she wasn't crazy, that she meant every word she was about to say. In the back of her mind, she could see the statue of Jan and Mook, the two heroines who had taken up arms and saved the country from an invading force centuries before. "Now I have nothing and I must fight. If I walk toward it, will you walk with me? I don't expect to make it through this, and that scares me so much. I need to know you will support me whatever happens. That you will be there with me until the end."

Tueng grabbed her and hugged her tight. He put a hand on her head and talked in her ear. "I have only you and our boy left," he said. "I will walk with you even if we have death in front of us. I will take you and our child, and I will walk forward. I will always love you the same. If I have to leave you, it will be because death has taken me away. If death does not take me, I will be by your side forever."

"Then I will fight," Dang whispered. "I will fight them with all the strength that I have."

31 WICHIEN AND NANG

CHAPTER

Ten days after his wife left the hospital, already on his way to becoming a devout Christian, Wichien got a job working for Sathaien Petklieng, the village leader. In exchange for delivering sacks of rice to the soldiers working in the area, shuttling equipment to the subdistrict office up along the highway, picking up trash, and doing whatever other chores were asked of him, he received 175 baht (five dollars) a day from the Phuyaibaan, who got an allotment of money from the province to help get the village back on its feet.

Starting each day at the tent where the leader and his assistants conducted their business, Wichien noticed something unusual right from the start. Trucks would drop off sacks of rice intended for the victims who had decided to return home rather than stay in the camps. To receive one of these sacks, a resident had to go to the tent and sign his name on a list. Because Wichien worked at the tent, he got the opportunity to sign his name at the top of almost every list, but he never received a sack of rice. He would go back to the list, only to find someone had taken his name off it. Certain that his Phuyaibaan wouldn't do such a thing, he began watching the leader's assistants more closely.

One morning when he came to work, he saw a group of people at the tent signing their names on a list. Wichien approached the leader's assistants and asked them what the list was for. They told him they didn't know.

"People are standing before you signing this list," he said. "How can you not know what it is for?"

They looked back and forth at each other, and then they sent him on an errand. Before leaving, Wichien took a closer look at the people who had gathered, and he noticed that they were all family members or friends of the leader's assistants. A shipment of something or other had come in—whether it was food or appliances, he didn't know—so the leader's assistants had called everyone they knew to come down and get the donations. The people of the village would get to collect the scraps; that is, if there were any scraps left to get. This happened four times during his first week of employment. Later on, he noticed that the leader's assistants had stopped calling their family members down and began signing their names on the list for them.

Wichien held his tongue for as long as possible, but when a truck brought seventy sacks of rice to the village and still he didn't get one, he approached his leader.

"I live here. You know this," Wichien said. "My house is not far from this tent, and yet I have no rice to eat. I have my house deed. I have all the documents to show that I live here. Why can't I get any rice?"

Petklieng patted him on the shoulder. "Okay, Wichien, you will get some rice. I will write down your name and sign my signature next to it."

Wichien got a sack of rice, but he never saw any of the bigger items that came in, like rice cookers or hot-pots. He would watch a shipment come in, the leader would send him on an errand, and by the time he got back, the shipment would be gone. Soon Wichien grew nervous every time he got sent on an errand.

Despite the corruption going on, Wichien never blamed his leader. The Kamnun, chief of the entire county, did nothing for the people here. One day Wichien heard that the subdistrict office had received a large donation of money for the people of Nam Khem, but they never saw any of it—all that money just disappeared. The two subdistrict officers didn't do anything either. Only the Phuyaibaan of Nam Khem tried to help the people. He had missing family members to find and a business to run, but he spent every morning and afternoon sitting in the tent by the beach, signing documents for the people, many of whom grew quite nasty with him. They shouted at him about how they were being treated unfairly. They complained that the soldiers were building only one house on their property, whereas before they had had five houses. They shouted that he was doing nothing for his people, that he was a terrible leader.

Wichien watched his people go mad. When foreigners came to hand out monetary donations, instead of forming an orderly line, many people just ran up and snatched the money without so much as a thank-you. It made the Phuyaibaan look bad—it made all of Nam Khem look bad. Wichien knew that not all the people taking that money were from Nam Khem, that in fact many of them had come from villages in the north and only claimed to be residents, but there was so much chaos that no one had the time to check to see who lived where. The goal of those who came was to help people, not to play detective, but after a few days in Nam Khem, many of them didn't want to come back.

Wichien grew so tired of the shouting matches that broke out in the Phuyaibaan's tent every morning and afternoon that he tried to quit. "I don't want to work this job anymore," he told his leader. "I can't handle the arguments. People have lost their minds, and now I feel I will lose mine as well." But the Phuyaibaan refused to let him quit, and it made Wichien feel special. He held his leader in the highest esteem.

Nang wasn't so sure about Petklieng's intentions. She owed 15,000 baht to the workers she had hired to help rebuild her home, and when the money the Christians said God would deliver never arrived, she went out and got a job. A company based out of Chon Buri Province had generously offered to help clean up the piles of trash and rubble around Nam Khem, and they paid their workers 200 baht per day. Nang got hired on as a trash collector, but the money wasn't enough, so she started cleaning people's homes as well. In addition to getting hired by a few of the friends and relatives of the leader's assistants, she also got contracted by her Phuyaibaan's wife to clean the home they were renting.

While cleaning her Phuyaibaan's home, she discovered a stockpile of donated items. There were piles of rice cookers, gas stoves, dishes, bowls—everything one would need to restart their life—stored in a corner of his home. The old rice cooker Wichien had found outside the hospital had broken. She had been boiling rice in a pot for the past several weeks, but it never turned out right. When Petklieng came home, she confronted him.

"Phuyaibaan, all I have in my house is an old rice cooker that doesn't work," she said. "I was wondering if I might have one of the many rice cookers you have stored in your house."

Petklieng offered her a big smile. "Don't worry. I will put your name on the list. One of my assistants will call you as soon as we hand them out."

"Thank you," Nang said, but she didn't leave. She stood there for several moments, staring at the leader's stockpile.

"I will donate all this stuff to the people who live in Nam Khem," he said a shade too quickly. "The people at the camps can't get this stuff, because they already have donations coming to them. I'm just waiting for the right time to give it out."

Nang nodded and walked away. Realizing things had become dog-eat-dog, she went to the tent every time she learned a shipment had come in. When all the donations had been handed out and she remained empty-handed, the leader's assistants would say she would get something tomorrow—but the tomorrow they talked about never came.

CHAPTER 32 DANG

Dang was finally given a chance to be heard. The government had set up an organization to help the victims of the tsunami, and they invited Dang to Bangkok to tell her story to the parliament. It was a tremendous opportunity, but Dang was also very concerned. Those who controlled the Far East Company held high positions in the government, and it could easily be a ploy to lure her away from Laem Pom so they could finally finish her off. But things had gotten to the point where she no longer had a choice. Her community needed help. If the company planned to kill her, they would do it whether or not she went to Bangkok. She agreed to the meeting.

On February 14, a government van with tinted windows pulled up to the camp where Dang had been staying with her husband, Tueng, and son, Arthorn. When Dang slid open the back door, she saw ten men dressed in suits and ties huddled inside. Her heart beating wildly in her chest, she kissed her husband and son good-bye, a part of her assuming it would be for the last time, and then crawled inside.

The van took them to the airport so they could catch a flight to Bangkok. Dang had never been on an airplane, but she bit her lip and boarded with the others. In Bangkok, the ten men stayed in one hotel room, and Dang stayed in another by herself. Being alone in a hotel room in a strange city frightened her. She kept thinking of the first day the soldiers had come to her community, how they had tried to kill Baw. She kept her eyes locked on the door, expecting an assassin to barge in at any moment. She subdued her fear by focusing on the speech she would present to the members of parliament.

Her fear vanished completely as the sun came up. She grew excited at the thought of finally being able to tell her story to people who could make a difference. She showered, combed her hair, and then laid her clothes out on the bed to smooth out the wrinkles. At eight o'clock, she was escorted from her room to another van. An hour later, she stood in front of the parliament in a massive government building in downtown Bangkok. She had prepared an eloquent speech, but it went right out the window. She had planned to remain strong and maintain her composure, but the moment she opened her mouth, the tears began to flow. She told them everything, starting with the first day the soldiers had come and concluding with how the company had severed the young girl's head with a backhoe in an attempt to hastily remove the trash that had been dumped onto their land. She told them about her daughter and her father. She told them how the Far East Company had used her community's suffering to claim the land of Laem Pom, and how it had kept so many of them from finding their loved ones. She even showed them the two pictures of her daughter that she carried in her wallet.

Dang didn't expect that the parliament would work a miracle and all her problems would go away. She had never trusted the government and still didn't. They were always saying one thing and doing another. They always promised the world during election, and then those promises dissolved soon thereafter. More than anything, she had just wanted to tell her story. It felt wonderful to let it all out.

They told her that they would send a representative to Laem Pom to inspect the situation. Dang took it as an empty promise, but the whole process of going to Bangkok and sharing the problems of her community had given her strength. She went back to the van, back to the airport, and then back to the camp, where all her neighbors eagerly awaited her return and any good news her trip might have brought. Once everyone was gathered around, she told them word for word what had been said. Those who trusted the government were ecstatic. Those who didn't waved their hands and began walking away. Dang called them back—she had more to say.

"Who will fight with me?" she asked. "I am going to return to Laem Pom in a few days, and I don't care who will try to stop me. If you want to go with me, fight with me, then bring me your documents, your ID cards, and your house registers. Give everything to me, and sign your name on this list."

"But a bodyguard still stands out there," one man said. "He won't let us past. All of us have already tried and been turned back."

"He might be able to stop one of us," Dang said, "or even a few of us, but he can't stop all of us."

After getting the names of those willing to charge headlong into battle, Dang organized a meeting at which she required each of the families to put 1,000 baht into a hat to start a community fund. From now on, they would all live together, sleep together, eat together, and work together to rebuild their homes and lives. Because the Far East Company was so strong, the only way they would survive was to stick together. At the same meeting, she also suggested that only one member from each family return with her to Laem Pom. The reason for this was twofold. First, Dang was quite certain that the leader would do everything in his power to stop donations from reaching Laem Pom. He would try to starve them off the land. The only way they could get by was for two or three people from every family to stay at the camps and collect as much food as possible and then take it to Laem Pom. The second reason was that if the Far East Company did resort to murder, having only one person per family in Laem Pom would ensure that entire families didn't get slaughtered.

For the next week, Dang worked out all the logistics. She would need people to cook, people to build, and people to purchase supplies. She held meetings where she assigned the tasks to her neighbors. They had 40,000 baht, which wouldn't carry them far, but Dang suspected it would be enough to feed them for a week and get the first poles in the ground. People were concerned about filling their bellies, but they were more concerned about how the company might retaliate. Dang gave them as much encouragement as she could offer. She wanted to tell them everything would be fine, but she didn't want to lie. She hadn't a clue how matters would play out.

Exactly two months after the tsunami, on February 26, Dang formed the twenty-seven families into a group and went over the plan one last time. Their only intention was to reach their land. If someone tried to stop them, they wouldn't get physical. They weren't even going to cuss. They would just keep marching straight onto their land. Hugs went around, and then they got on their way. They headed down the windy road leading to Nam Khem, across the village, and straight toward Laem Pom. The bodyguard the company had hired stood guard at the entrance, but he didn't make an attempt to stop them either verbally or physically. There were just too many of them. After two months of jumping from camp to camp, two months of groveling for handouts like a beggar, Dang finally went home.

They set up camp in the spot where Aussie John's home had once been built. He was now gone, but the foundation of his home still remained. They planted poles around the cement edges, tied strings between the poles, and then made shabby lean-tos out of plastic bags. Before they could finish constructing their sleeping area, police flooded into the area. As they went around to make arrests, Dang confronted the head officer.

"You say we can't stay here, but the case is still in court," Dang said. "If the court says we must go, I will leave without a fight. But right now you can't arrest us. We are just trying to rebuild our homes on our land. We haven't done anything illegal. If you arrest us, I will make sure the government hears about it. I will tell anyone who cares to listen what you have done."

The head officer stopped his men. They remained in the area for the next two hours, but by nightfall the last of them had gone. Dang suspected that since the police officers hadn't been able to get rid of them, the Far East Company would send someone else. It would be all too easy for a hit man to come to this secluded area under the cover of darkness and solve the company's problems with a single bullet. Her neighbors probably weren't in danger. Dang was now their leader, and if the company came to collect a head, it would be hers. But for the first time since the tsunami had come, she wasn't afraid. She had come to the conclusion that she would gladly give her life. If she was killed, reporters would descend upon Laem Pom and tell their story to the world. She would gladly give her life if it meant that her people could finally get on with their lives. She didn't expect to make it through the night.

Dang awoke at sunrise. They began the morning just like they would every morning to come—with a community meeting. Dang told everyone that they were now more of a family than they had ever been. If anyone had a problem, they could come to her day or night. Then everyone broke off to fulfill their appointed duties. A few women went about setting up a makeshift kitchen. A couple of men hopped into a truck and headed toward the lumberyard to purchase building supplies. Others walked around Laem Pom, mapping out the areas where they would build their new homes. Dang ran back and forth between everyone, delegating, solving problems, and making sure everything ran smoothly.

When an official-looking car headed down the dirt road leading to their camp on the afternoon of February 28, Dang was certain that the Far East Company had returned to take their land. To her surprise, the man who climbed out of the car was Mr. Chaowarit Yongjaiyuth, who worked for the prime minister. The two found a quiet place to talk, and Dang begged him for fairness and justice. She told her story just as she had to the parliament, and again tears ran down her face.

"Daughter, you can come and rebuild your homes," Mr. Yongjaiyuth said, smiling at her. "You have lived here for thirty years—how could you not have a deed? I will ask Colonel Surin to come help you. He will contact the land office and inspect how the Far East Company got the deed for this land. If you need any help, just contact the soldiers in Nam Khem. They will help you."

Dang thanked him a dozen times. She relayed the information to the rest of her new family, and they all celebrated that night. Now that she had permission to stay in Laem Pom, she felt nothing could stop them. When Petklieng paid her a visit a few days later, she kept her chin high. He told her that she was in line to receive one of the hundreds of homes soldiers had built in Nam Khem over the past months, as were all the other families that lived in Laem Pom. Dang had never applied for one of the houses the soldiers were building, and neither had any of the other residents. They didn't want to live in the village— they wanted to live on their land. She told this to Petklieng.

"Why do you make it so difficult?" he asked. "Dang, your family had five houses in Laem Pom, and that means that you will get five homes in the village.

Each of the houses is worth 100,000 baht. You will get five houses, so that is 500,000 baht. That is a lot of money, Dang. And you will get one scooter and a telephone. All the furnishings inside will be paid for. If you accept this offer, you will be a very wealthy woman."

Dang resisted the urge to laugh. She had been granted permission to move back onto her land, and now the leader and his employer had gotten desperate. Dozens of families had moved into the homes the soldiers had built, and she had not heard of a single one having received a scooter, a telephone, and furnishings. What kind of woman did Petklieng think she was? Did he really think that she would abandon her people for five houses?

"Take my name off the list," Dang said proudly. "If I lose in court, I will move from this village without taking anything with me. I don't want the homes the soldiers have built."

As Petklieng turned and walked away, Dang felt victorious. But she didn't have much time to celebrate; there were more problems to solve. Before the tsunami, they'd had a well from which all the families drew their water, but now it produced nothing but salt water. Mr. Yongjaiyuth had told her to approach the soldiers in Nam Khem if she needed anything, and now she most certainly did. The soldiers had a massive water truck that they used to fill up the barrels at the camps. She asked them if they could bring some of that water to Laem Pom, enough to survive for a week or so. A couple of the soldiers came to Laem Pom to have a look at the well, but they never came back.

It was a hard blow, but in Dang's heart of hearts she had been expecting it. Powerful men ran the Far East Company, and powerful men always had tricks up their sleeves. She and her neighbors needed to find a way to get water and food. The family members at the camps brought a portion of the donations they had collected, but it wasn't enough. As she tried to find a way to keep it all together, she received a call from a female reporter in Bangkok who wanted to come to Laem Pom to learn their story. Dang, uncertain whether this was a ploy of the Far East Company or a real interview, didn't know if she should agree. Dang told the reporter that she would get back to her and then asked her husband for advice.

Tueng closed his eyes for a moment. "I think you should meet with the reporter," he said. "If you don't allow her to come here, how will we know if she is on our side? You need to meet her. You will know the moment you talk with her if she is our friend or enemy."

Dang agreed to do the interview. The reporter came the following day, and Dang told her the entire story, from start to end. The reporter was speechless. Dang could tell that she had come to do a quick story on the victims of the tsunami, but instead she had been handed something very different.

"You might not want to write about this story," Dang told her. "The owner of the Far East Company is a politician and a very powerful man. He could make problems for you."

The reporter asked to see a picture of Dang's daughter, and Dang showed her both of them. After that, the reporter agreed to be a channel through which Dang could get her story out. For the next two mornings, Dang sent one of her community members up to purchase the *Bangkok Post*, the most widely read newspaper in the country. On March 2, the article appeared. It was titled "This Land Is Our Land."

Dang couldn't read the article, because it was in English, but she hung it up on the side of a shed they had built to store food. She continued with her business, not thinking much more about it, but then, two days after the article came out, she received a 30,000-baht donation from someone who had read the article. A day after that, a construction company donated 10,000 bricks that the families could use to build their homes. Then another company donated 5,000 tiles, and another brought piles of wood. Soon she had sand and nails and hammers. They now how everything they needed to build their homes. Those who had been assigned to construction duty got to work.

Dang had envisioned building everyone a home in a matter of a month, but she now realized that this would be impossible. They just didn't have enough workers. At the rate they were going, it would take more than a year to build each of the twenty-seven families a home. Then, in the middle of March, after Dang's husband and son returned to Laem Pom to help with construction, twenty engineering students from the University of Ubon Ratchathani came marching onto their land to help them build. Apparently, their teacher had read the *Bangkok Post* interview and wanted to help. He had paid for all his students' bus tickets down to Nam Khem. When they had to go back to school a few weeks later, another group of students, from Narathiwat Province, replaced them. And when that group went away, a third team came, from Khon Kaen University. A handful of foreigners also found their way out to Laem Pom to help with construction. The frames of homes began to spring from the ground.

The volunteer workers brought more than just their knowledge of how to build a home—they brought laughter as well. For brief moments in time, when Dang found herself lost in conversation, it almost seemed as though the tsunami had never happened. It reminded her that there were still good people in this world—people whose hearts were large enough to care about the people of Laem Pom.

By the beginning of April, they had laid the foundations for more than ten homes and even erected several roofs. Dang became a hero to the people. She hadn't had a rock-solid plan—she had done everything by instinct, and, in retrospect, she realized everything could have gone terribly wrong. But they had survived, and now everyone in the community came to her with problems, and it was her responsibility to solve them. When they ran out of wood, Dang had to order more. When they ran out of money, Dang had to go out and find more. She kept a smile on her face at the meetings they held every morning, and she treated every volunteer who arrived as if they were her son or daughter. But in the evening when she crawled into her tent, the list of things she had to do faded from her mind and the pain returned. Not a single night passed without her thinking about what had been taken from her.

One night a storm passed over Laem Pom, and Dang's thoughts turned to Kwan. Her daughter had always been frightened of thunder, and Dang would have to hold her in her arms and whisper that everything would be all right. Dang crawled out of the tent in which her family slept and searched the surrounding darkness for her daughter's spirit. When she saw nothing and came back in, her son sat in one corner of the tent, giggling about something or other. Dang asked him how he could laugh while she still felt so sad. He told her that he didn't want to suffer anymore with all the things that had happened to them. Laughing helped him forget. Dang felt anger in her stomach when she lay down next to her husband, but she knew that her son was right. She needed to let go, but she just couldn't do it.

"I just miss her so much," she told Tueng.

Since she had found her daughter's body, she hadn't dreamt of her once. She figured that tonight Kwan would be frightened by the thunder and come to her, but when Dang woke in the morning, she still hadn't seen her daughter's face. The next day, she rushed through the morning meeting and then headed to Nam Khem Temple. She brought food for the monks to eat, food that would reach her daughter. With tears flowing from her eyes, she begged a monk to tell her why she couldn't dream of her little girl.

"It is a good thing," the monk said. "If you dream of the dead, it means that they are not in a good place. They are suffering. They are stuck or still need something and are calling out to you. You do not dream of your child because she is at peace."

For the first time in an eternity, Dang smiled.

For me, Thailand has always been a place of intrigue. In the midnineties, I fell in love with the culture, the people, and Muay Thai, the country's ancient art of combat. I had come this time at the end of November 2004 to compete one last time in the fighting stadiums and to write a book on their training methods. I jumped around the islands for a few weeks, and then went on a trek through the northern jungles to clear my thoughts. Emerging from the jungle two days after Christmas, I found a group of hills tribesmen huddled around a television in the market of a small village. They cried and gripped one another, and as I entered their midst, I caught my first glimpse of the unthinkable disaster that had unfolded. In the days that followed, I saw several families, so poor they could hardly put food on the table, pull money from mattresses and jars so they could send it to the relief foundations. When I returned to Chiang Mai, the largest city in the north, thousands hurried to the post office to send off large portions of their savings. Their utter commitment to help one another astounded me. The entire country was in tears.

Arriving at the island of Phuket, I asked around about how I could get involved in relief efforts, and the trail led to one woman—Sudthida "Nui" Somsakserm, a local restaurant owner who had been commuting every day from the big island to the beaches of Khao Lak. Some trips, she brought food and clothes and baby formula to the survivors. Other days, she brought bottled water for rescue workers and dry ice to preserve the bodies. The morning after we met, I helped her load box lunches into her truck and we headed out. I had studied natural disasters in college, and while living in a dozen third-world countries over the past decade, I had seen villages leveled by earthquakes and floods, but nothing could have prepared me for what I encountered as we rounded the crest of Khao Lak Mountain. Looking down upon the devastated beaches of Bang Niang and Bang Sak, I didn't know how anyone could have survived.

Nui took me to a couple of the temporary camps that had been established. My hands began to tremble as I talked with people who had lost their mothers or daughters or best friends just a few weeks before. Naively, I had brought money. They needed food. They needed clothes. They needed shelter. By the time we carried the lunches to Doctor Pornthip and the other doctors working at Yanyao Temple, where nearly 5,000 bodies were being stored, my emotions had completely run away from me. I was constantly wiping tears from my face. I wanted to know who needed the most help, and while at the temple, I heard several people mention the village of Nam Khem. It was comprised of local people, and with all the reporters and rescue workers hovering around the resorts further south, it had apparently been forgotten. I asked Nui if she had been to the village, and she told me that she had tried to head down the narrow road just a few days after the tsunami. A police officer told her not to bother, that there was nothing left down there. I asked her if we could go and try to find out what the people needed so we could bring it the following day, and she hesitantly agreed. Having grown up in the area during the tin-mining boom, she still feared the village. She could remember having seen a few bodies being hauled up to the highway in the back of a *sawngthaew* early one Saturday morning when she was eight.

When we got there, there was nearly nothing left, just rubble piled on top of rubble. Not sure where to begin, we headed toward one of the few homes still standing, and it was there that I met Ko Sa, Puek's loyal friend. He had lost thirteen fishing boats, and most of his ninety employees were missing or dead. He had opened the doors to his home and offered shelter to anyone brave enough to come back to the village. A handful of fishermen had taken Ko Sa up on his offer, and he fed them three times a day with the little money he still had. His generosity and massive heart inspired me, and I wanted to give him something in return. I offered to help rebuild some of his boats so he could get back on his feet. Ko Sa turned me down outright. He considered himself the richest man in the village, because he hadn't lost anyone in his family. He steered Nui and me toward someone who needed help a whole lot more.

A few hours later, Nui and I were sitting down talking with Puek and Lek. I noticed that their hands trembled from stress, but they tried their best to conceal it. Throughout the course of a long conversation, we learned their stories. But despite their suffering, they wanted nothing from us. They were just happy that someone had dropped by to talk. They hoped that we would come back and share some time, but there were others worse off.

When we met Wimon a few days later, he had the same selfless attitude. He needed a boat to get his family back on its feet, but he did not once ask for anything. What he did do, however, was send us off to talk with Dang, who was currently battling the Far East Company and the leader of the village for her family's survival. He figured she needed help a whole lot more. We followed his instructions, and when we sat down with Dang, we could see the grief and fear in her eyes. She too wanted our friendship, nothing more.

After hearing Dang's story, we decided to visit with the leader of Nam Khem, Sathaien Petklieng, to see why the residents of Laem Pom were being denied donations. While waiting for him to arrive, we met Wichien. He lived just around the corner from the tent where the leader conducted business, and he invited us to his home to survey the damage. There we met Nang and their son, Nueng. We ended up talking for several hours, and by the time we left, we were all good friends.

Over the course of the next month, Nui and I talked with dozens of Nam Khem families that had lost everything. We realized that it was beyond our means to help everyone, and although it was a difficult decision to make, we decided to focus mostly on the four families we had first met. Nui has an unbelievable network of friends, and within a few weeks she had collected several hundred thousand baht. We figured that the money, combined with our savings, might be enough to help one of the families get back on their feet, but certainly not all of them. Nui then aligned herself with several rotary clubs that wanted to give donations but hadn't the slightest clue how to go about getting that money to the right people. A good friend of mine, Brooke Motta, had started a foundation back in the States called Compassion in Action, and she flew over with a sizable amount of donations. Glen Cordoza, the friend whom I had first come to Thailand with, joined the mix with the money he had raised over the phone from friends and relatives back home. And then Leland Ratcliff, an old college buddy with a strong back, came over to help with the grunt labor.

We all became fixtures in Nam Khem.

By this point, Nui and I had become close friends with Puek and Lek, and they took all of us in. When in the area, we stayed with them at their temporary housing camp. Since the disaster, at least twice a week a foreigner or a government official had come to their small shack, collected their house register and their other documents, photocopied them at their expense, and then had Lek sign her name at the bottom. But nothing ever came of all those signed documents, and she began to wonder if crooks were using them to collect money in her name. She and Puek grew more worried by the day, more bored by the hour. They spent countless hours just sitting there, swatting mosquitoes. Puek began to feel his sanity slipping away again, so he asked a friend to steal him one of the coffin lids they had deposited in a huge pile behind the temple. Puek had a foreigner write on it in English, "I am a tsunami victim and professional masseuse. I give massages for 100 baht," and then he nailed it to the front of his shack.

Every time we came by, Puek and Lek greeted us with huge smiles and insisted on feeding us despite their small rations. They refused to take our donations, so eventually we started getting a couple of massages each time we turned up in order to get them to accept our money. Their daughter, Chomphu, came down from Bangkok to help support them, and she and Brooke bonded immediately. Using a portion of the money she had collected from friends, Nui contacted Chomphu's university in Bangkok and paid for two semesters so she could return to school. Nui also used the money donated by the Rotary clubs to build Puek a forty-foot longtail boat, which would be captained by Lek's brother Jui. Brooke's foundation, Compassion in Action, put in a large sum of money to help build them a new home, which they moved into at the end of June, after six months at the camp. They thanked us repeatedly, but we told them that it wasn't our doing. It was the hundreds of people in Thailand and around the world who had been so generous in the wake of this disaster. Before we parted ways, Nui received from Puek a copy of his medical reports in the hopes of finding a surgeon who could restore his vision so he could again support his family out at sea. She passed it on to several of her doctor friends, but she was informed that hospitals in Thailand weren't yet capable of performing the operation. The reports were translated into English, and all of us are currently on the hunt to find a doctor in the United States willing to perform the operation.

We didn't spend as much time with Wimon and Watcharee, but the moments we did spend with them were warm and genuine. They continued to live with Wimon's mother and their daughter at the temporary housing camp that had been built at Nam Khem Temple. Many people had heard Wimon's story through Mr. Sorayuth, and they came by frequently to offer him money. He told each of them that the money would help his family greatly, but he could not accept it. He told them that the people in Laem Pom needed it much more than he did, and then he gave them directions on how to get there. Mr. Sorayuth had also donated a staggering 8,300,000 baht to the village of Nam Khem, but it did little more than tear their community further apart. Some people thought that the families that had suffered the worst should get the most money, and other people thought that everyone in the village should receive an equal amount. Bitter feuds erupted, and Wimon couldn't stand watching the little that remained of his village getting torn apart by bickering. He made a suggestion to Mr. Sorayuth that he not give the money to the families but rather use it down the road to build a public park or something they could all benefit from. Mr. Sorayuth took his advice.

Wimon wanted to lift his family back up with his own two hands, but that would be impossible until he got a boat. At one point, he had heard that a foreign man had donated fifteen longtail boats to the village, so Wimon had instantly gone down to the leader's tent and signed his name on a list to receive one of the boats. When he didn't hear anything back, he went to ask the leader where all the boats had gone. The leader couldn't tell him, and it led Wimon to believe that the leader had actually taken the boats for himself. Wimon became even angrier when he heard that people had actually sold the longtails they'd received from generous foreigners.

Wimon grew more desperate by the day. The heavy rains started in March, and the roof of his plywood shack had sprung numerous leaks. One morning, he awoke to find his mother nearly drowning in a pool of water. He continued his hunt for a longtail, and then, one afternoon in March, he met a group of men who wanted to rent him a boat. They told him that he could keep all the fish that he caught, but he had to pay them 3,000 baht per month. Wimon took a look at the boat and saw that it was brand new. He knew then that one of the men in this group had most likely received the boat through a donation, and once again he felt his blood boil. He doubted that the person who had donated the boat had intended the recipient to rent it out at a large price to a fellow tsunami victim. Wimon needed the work, but he refused to get it unethically. He turned the offer down and resumed the hunt. By the middle of June, he still hadn't been out to sea, and his mother woke up just as wet every morning in their plywood shack. Although he didn't know it at the time, Nui had been building him a boat out of the rotary club donations. She had been given a 70,000 baht budget for the boat, but it ended up being 120,000 baht. For a while there, she wasn't sure if she would be able to have it finished, but after draining the last of her savings and receiving money from Compassion in Action, she ended up paying the boat builder the last of the money she owed him.

On June 20, we transported the boat to Nam Khem. Wimon was so touched that he burst out in tears. His mother fell to her knees. A few days later, while making my way through Nam Khem, I spotted Wimon by his boat with a can of lacquer, painting each nook and cranny with delicate care. He had lost so much, yet he took such pride in his work. In that moment, I knew that he and his family would be just fine.

Out in Laem Pom, Dang's struggles continued. Every day, she fought for water, food, and building supplies. The article written about her community had faded from the country's collective mind. Sathaien Petklieng, the leader of Nam Khem, continued to prohibit donations from reaching them. The community members flew a pirate flag high above their community for all to see, and Dang promised not to take it down until the embargo was lifted. Each of the families did what they could to start life anew, but for many the trauma of having lost their family and friends, combined with their battle with the Far East Company, became too much to bear. This was the case with an eighteen-year-old boy who had returned with Dang to Laem Pom. Unable to cope with the grief, he hung himself from a tree on May 20.

We spent a lot of time with Dang, trying to lift her spirits. Brooke, Glen, and Leland set up a tent next to Dang and spent their days helping lay cement foundations. During their stay, a thug everyone suspected to have been hired by the Far East Company came into Laem Pom to scare residents away. Glen and Leland, both having fallen in love with the people of Laem Pom, wanted to challenge the man, but Dang held them back.

To help with the cost of building supplies, Compassion in Action stepped in, and we all donated money of our own, but the help they needed was much larger than four people could provide. The day we left, Dang was all smiles, but the pain in her eyes remained just as strong as the first day we had met her. As with thousands of other residents in Nam Khem, her future would remain uncertain for some time to come.

Things had improved for Wichien and Nang. They had replaced the walls of their home, and our group surprised Wichien one day with a refrigerator and some other household supplies. Wichien's job working for the leader and Nang's job collecting trash had both come to an end, but Wichien landed another job on the other side of the isthmus, diving for sand used for ceramics. He spent a lot of his time away worrying about looters and the possibility of another wave, but he always felt better when he returned home and Nang gave him a big hug and kiss. Wichien no longer went to church every Sunday, but he continued to read the Bible. Nang waited for the day when Wichien would allow her to become a Buddhist again.

Although these four families were given a little help along the road to rebuilding their lives, hundreds of other families still struggled to get the basic necessities. Six months after the tsunami had washed over Nam Khem and claimed nearly 5,000 of its residents, the fate of the village was still uncertain. Soldiers had built hundreds of homes, but fewer than 200 families had returned. With few jobs to be found, residents feared losing the handouts that continued to trickle into the camps. They also feared another wave. At least twice a month, mass-scale rumors circulated of earthquakes in Indonesia and massive waves spotted just offshore. Few hesitated to run to the hills, and in their absence, criminals moved freely through the abandoned streets.

December 26 had come and gone for most of the world, but for the residents of Nam Khem, there will be no forgetting. When asked if they thought their village would survive, most residents gave the same answer—only time will tell.